THINKING OF
CHRIST

THINKING OF
CHRIST

Proclamation, Explanation, Meaning

EDITED BY
TATHA WILEY

continuum
NEW YORK • LONDON

For my daughter,
Rachel,
on her eighteenth birthday

2003

The Continuum International Publishing Group Inc
15 East 26th Street, New York, NY 10010

The Continuum International Publishing Group Ltd
The Tower Building, 11 York Road, London SE1 7NX

Printed in the United States of America

Library of Congress Cataloging-in-Publication Data

Thinking of Christ : proclamation, explanation, meaning / edited by Tatha Wiley.
    p. cm.
  Includes bibliographical references and index.
    ISBN 0-8264-1529-6 (alk. paper) – ISBN 0-8264-1530-X (pbk. : alk. paper)
    1. Jesus Christ–Person and offices. I. Wiley, Tatha.
  BT203 .T48 2003
  232–dc22

                              2003019943

Contents

Part Three
CHRIST AND SOCIAL TRANSFORMATION

Preface

Thinking of Christ brings one to the heart of Christian faith. A Christology is in fact a sustained and disciplined engagement with questions about the meaning and significance of Jesus Christ. This book invites the reader to probe that meaning for today.

There have always been many Christologies, and christological questions have animated the greatest minds and hearts for two millennia. At their best, Christologies reflect the burning desire of Christians to understand what they accept already in faith. At their worst, they misuse the symbol of Christ to legitimate some variation of an ideology of superiority. A pluralism of Christologies inevitably produces conflicting truth claims. No one Christology stands above all others, free of the need to be questioned and evaluated for its ability to disclose the meaning of Jesus authentically.

The pluralism of Christologies exists, too, because interpretive work is often uncertain yet unavoidable. Access to Jesus is indirect. The way is mediated by memories and interpreters — writers of narratives, collectors of sayings, formulators of creeds, composers of songs, authors of systematic reflections. The Christian tradition accorded the four gospel writers a special place among interpreters as proclaimers, but a far wider net would be cast to understand Christian origins. While the gospels are quite theologically distinct, they each use titles as one means of conveying their apprehension of Jesus and his significance. One title was *messiah*, used in the Jewish tradition to designate a king or priest as consecrated and set apart for a special role. Meaning simply, "God's anointed one," the word in its Greek form, *Christ*, in time became for Christians a means of expressing the divinity of Jesus.

Though plural, Christologies share a core of recurring questions. The modern as well as the medieval asks, "Who is Christ for us?" Yet even here the same question posed in radically different historical and cultural contexts, intellectual worldviews, and religious horizons becomes fundamentally a different question. It comes with acknowledged and unacknowledged assumptions and perspectives. Questions of Christ's significance for us, the meaning of his divinity, and his relevance for the world come up again and again, not because others failed to answer them but because contexts, worldviews, and horizons change. Formulating what belief means today will draw on new ways of thinking and different categories.

It must be admitted, however, that thinking of Christ in our cultural context is not easy. In the premodern world, being religious was the norm. Modernity reversed the norm. Classical creeds are often seen as unintelligible today. Far from providing explanations, doctrines like original sin and Christ's divinity raise even more questions. As a result, religion occupies an uneasy place in modern culture. The modern critique of religious meaning, truth, and value — its very credibility — has been relentless. Nothing is taken for granted.

The modern religious spectrum stretches from the Christian fundamentalist to the alienated and unchurched. An intellectually grounded middle often seems invisible. If religion is genuinely a value, its detractors argue, religious people would be *good*. The agnostic may find a more authentic way of living apart from the scandals of inauthentic religion. The fundamentalist claims religious certainty without need for questions. The alienated dismisses the relevance of religious meaning or questions. Further, it is taken as self-evident by many today that truth belongs, not to religion, but to science. Confidence in science extends even into the transcendent realm, and religion can be simply dismissed. A recent Nobel laureate in physics said, "One of the great achievements of science has been, if not to make it impossible for intelligent people to be religious, then at least to make it possible for them not to be religious. We should not retreat from this accomplishment."[1]

In the midst of this complex and conflictual cultural context, thinking of Christ faces many challenges. To articulate and address them, this book draws upon persons whose lifelong work as theologians, historians, biblical scholars, and ethicists has actively engaged these problems. Each contributor offers a carefully conceived chapter on one of the topics significant for the study of Christology today. The book is a collaborative effort yet allows for the distinctiveness of each contributor to emerge. I am grateful to the contributors for their willingness to participate in this project. Their generosity reflects a deep commitment to bringing their theological reflection to bear on the particular challenges we face today.

The four parts of the book, as well as individual chapters, may be used in any combination and order. Read straight through, they provide a thorough historical and systematic introduction. A glossary is included to assist readers with the specialized vocabulary of this field. Part One takes up scripture as a source for Jesus, traces the development from proclamation to creed, and treats the tradition's theories of redemption. Part Two addresses four steep challenges that require theological consideration in a contemporary Christology. Part Three turns to the creative contemporary constructions of the meaning of Jesus: from Hispanic women's perspective, from an African

American perspective, and from the perspective of ethics and spirituality. In light of Christ, we must finally ask, who and what are we to be?

In its historical, evaluative, and systematic overview, *Thinking of Christ* addresses a broad range of issues — the nature of scripture, the dynamics of doctrinal development, redemption theories, the *adversus Judaeos* tradition, religious pluralism, sexism, religious legitimation of colonialism, new Christologies, and the character of Christian spirituality and ethics. In this sense, thinking of Christ entails engagement with the full range of our most pressing cultural, political, and religious concerns. Thinking about Christ, ourselves, and theology can be engaging, worthwhile, even transforming. In fact, Christology challenges us to probe the very meaning of our lives.

Contributors

Lisa Sowle Cahill
J. Donald Monan Professor of Theology
Department of Theology
Boston College
Chestnut Hill, Massachusetts

M. Shawn Copeland
Associate Professor of Systematic Theology
Department of Theology
Boston College
Chestnut Hill, Massachusetts

Roger Haight, S.J.
Visiting Fellow
Woodstock Theological Center
Washington, D.C.

Ada María Isasi-Díaz
Professor of Christian Ethics
Drew University
Madison, New Jersey

Robert Lassalle-Klein
Associate Professor of Religious Studies
Holy Names College
Oakland, California

William P. Loewe
Associate Professor
School of Theology and Religious Studies
Catholic University of America
Washington, D.C.

John Pawlikowski, O.S.M.
Professor of Social Ethics
Director of the Catholic-Jewish Studies Program
Catholic Theological Union in Chicago
Chicago, Illinois

Rosemary Radford Ruether
Carpenter Professor of Feminist Theology
Graduate Theological Union, Berkeley
Berkeley, California

Elisabeth Schüssler Fiorenza
Krister Stendahl Professor of Scripture and Interpretation
Harvard Divinity School
Harvard University
Cambridge, Massachusetts

Rev. Gerard S. Sloyan
Professor Emeritus of Religion
Temple University
Philadelphia, Pennsylvania

Tatha Wiley
United Theological Seminary of the Twin Cities
New Brighton, Minnesota

Thinking of Christ

Tatha Wiley

Origins of Christology

The question "Who is Jesus for us?" is as pressing today as it was for the first Christians. The Christian tradition offers an answer, of course. In fact, the tradition offers lots of answers.

The New Testament alone is striking for the multiplicity of its interpretations of Jesus. The Apostle Paul's focus, for instance, is so exclusively on the significance of the risen Christ that his letters leave the Jesus of history virtually invisible. The gospel writers, on the other hand, bring Jesus of Nazareth explicitly into view. But upon closer scrutiny, it is a different Jesus that each one presents. For Mark, Jesus is the one who gives his life as a ransom for us (Mark 10:45). Matthew's Jesus meets us in the poor and hungry (Matt. 25:31–46). In Luke, Jesus is liberator of the oppressed and excluded (Luke 4:18–19). John's answer to the question "Who is Jesus?" will be decisive for the tradition yet to come: Jesus is the divine Word incarnate with us (John 1:1, 14).

The biblical accounts, though authoritative, hardly settled questions raised by the encounter with Jesus; and questioning the meaning of his life, witness, and relationship to God did not end with the New Testament writers. It continued in the lively and sometimes hostile exchanges between Christians in the early centuries of the tradition. The first creeds, formulated as professions of faith for entering catechumens, were essentially proclamations of the resurrection.[1] They carried only local authority. Like Paul's, their proclamation was more *theo*logical than *christ*ological: *God* raised this crucified man from the dead.

The later creeds of the great church councils functioned very differently from the early proclamation, and with different authority. In the fourth and fifth centuries C.E., generations of tension and conflict over the understanding of Jesus' person and status came to a head in gatherings of the "whole church" — the meaning of an "ecumenical council" — represented by its bishops. The councils were called to settle opposing views about Christ.[2] Their object was to formulate what was to be believed. The kinds of questions raised about Jesus and explanations given propelled the beginnings of a systematic or technical grasp of what was affirmed in faith.[3]

The conciliar fathers asked about the relation of the biblical metaphors to reality: Is the Son *God* in the same way that the Father is God? In reply, near-endless variations were presented: the Son is almost divine, not divine, divine at his baptism and/or resurrection, made divine, divine but subordinate.

The resulting conciliar creeds or formal statements of faith no longer functioned to test the soundness of new converts' faith. These creeds were intended to regulate the orthodoxy of those who already professed themselves Christian. Generated by theological questions, the creeds were definitive responses intended by the bishops to settle the disputes. Their content articulated a theological agreement about what could be said about Jesus. Each explicitly rejected opposing beliefs — and the opponents, too. A central component of the conciliar creed was the *anathema*, a denouncement of dissenting views and a signal that those holding such views put themselves outside the community of orthodox believers.

The crucial conciliar judgments were twofold. One regarded Jesus' divine nature, the other his human nature. The issue centered on what the metaphors Father and Son referred to in divine reality. What is the relationship between them? If the Christian proclamation, "Jesus saves," for example, is true, then to say that Jesus has a *special relation* to God is inadequate. Only God offers and gives salvation. So if Jesus *saves*, he must be *God with us* in history. The relation of Son to Father is the relation of *God to God*. The second issue regarded Jesus' human nature. If Jesus saves, he is *fully divine*. But if Jesus genuinely experienced life as a human being, as every account testified, he was also *fully human*. This further judgment affirmed two natures, human and divine.

The council fathers' use of technical terms, such as *homoousios* (meaning, of the same substance), employed at Nicea to denote the equality of the Son and with God the Father, brought discourse about Jesus to a very different plane than the gospel writers' more metaphorical speech about Jesus as ransom and liberator and shepherd and even Lord.

While the move toward systematic thought signals a development in explanatory understanding, Bernard Lonergan reminds us that "all such developments are under the sign of contradiction." That contradiction is in human beings themselves. "No less than understanding," Lonergan writes, "misunderstanding can express itself systematically."[4]

Christology and Modernity

Today we have no shortage of accumulated images, metaphors, concepts, and judgments about Jesus. Weaving our way through them is challenging enough in the historical study of Christology. Each has its own date, its own meaning, its own successes and failures as a carrier of Christian faith, its lasting power as a proclamation of Jesus and expression of his meaning, or its proffered explanation of his person and status.

While these ways of understanding, found in the New Testament, the great creeds, and theological tradition, are rich and deep, they do not necessarily function effectively today in communicating the meaning they once did. For contemporary faith to remain vibrant, we must articulate the significance of Jesus ourselves. We need to draw on terms and categories both meaningful to us and appropriate for our time.

Though pluralistic in every way, our time is rooted in a cultural context, intellectual worldview, and religious horizon shaped over the last two centuries by developments in modern empirical science, objective history, philosophies of the subject, psychiatry, sociology and other new fields of inquiry as well as by technological advances, emancipatory movements, and democratic governments. *Modernity* has served as the umbrella term for this period, and our present reality remains decisively shaped by modernity even as postmodern critique of its features and effects has emerged.

The impact of modernity on the christological enterprise has been marked, from the outside, by the modern critique of religion and, from the inside, by critical biblical scholarship. Where Christology once presumed a foundation upon which it could make confident claims about God, Christ, and humankind, the modern critique of religion has resulted in the Bible, revelation, and the church no longer being taken for granted as straightforward sources of truth.

The modern insight into ideology, derived from Karl Marx in the nineteenth century, created a new category for analysis of human knowing and living. Marx drew attention to the way in which cultural formulations of truth protect the interests of those with power. These formulations become ideologies when concepts distorted by self-interest are systematized and embedded in social patterns and institutions such as the family, law, education, and religion. Ideologies of superiority — of race, class, and gender, to name three more obvious ones — justify the privileges granted to some and denied to others. Marx saw religious doctrines as tools by which the privileged maintain the status quo. Concepts have effects. Linking salvation with eternal life, for example, pushes the resolution of present inequities off to the next world. While the ultimate destiny of human beings is rightfully included in a concept of salvation, equating salvation and heaven can serve to keep things the way they are.

Marx's insight into ideology became an influential category within Christian thought itself. Reinhold Niebuhr, one of the most prominent twentieth-century social and religious thinkers, was acutely aware of the role of power in public life and appropriated both the ideas of power and ideology into his understanding of sin.[5] Niebuhr called the ideological justification of group interests collective egotism. Competing group interests generate social conflict and are at the root of social injustice. The effect, as Larry Rasmussen writes, is that "our particular interests become identified with general interests, our piece of the truth with *the* truth, our parochial ways with God's."[6] The problem is not just short-sightedness but the fact that this identification results in "an unwillingness to value the claims of other communities as highly as our own, or consider their interests as valid as ours. We consequently act in ways which take advantage of other life."[7]

In theological terms, for Niebuhr collective egotism is social *sin*. But group interests create something distinct from and irreducible to personal sin. The notion of ideology has facilitated an apprehension of what is now a familiar concept of social, structural, or systemic sin.

The insight into ideology has altered our sense of what theological reflection does. We no longer take the task of theology to be finished by the acceptance and explanation of the theological tradition. We must also engage in a theological evaluation of the tradition. Even our most cherished religious convictions and most well-conceived theologies about Jesus the Christ may harbor sinful self-interest. They, too, may be found to protect privileges dominant groups project as divinely given.

In contemporary terms, the Bible, divine revelation, Christ, sin, and redemption must be *problematized*. What the biblical narrative says, for example, may or may not correspond with history as it happened. It may or may not disclose what is genuinely true or worthwhile. To identify the slaveholder with Christ, as we find in the letters such as Colossians 3:18 and Ephesians 6:5–6 is, from our vantage point, abhorrent. Further, to conceive of sin as the slave's disobedience of the master is a construction of sin which masks economic benefits of slave-holding for the owner and the horrific conditions under which people lived as slaves. This is an ideological conception of sin, not a genuine understanding of what estranges human beings from God.[8]

So, too, the identification of males with Christ and the command for women to be under the rule of men reflect the surrounding patriarchal culture rather than divine revelation. Women's resistance of male domination is portrayed as infidelity to Christ. But as modern insights into sexism have gradually brought into focus, it is the imperative to *obey* that is the sin, not the resistance to unjust relations of domination and subordination. Like racism, Elizabeth Johnson writes, sexism "betrays the fundamental inability of a dominant group to deal with otherness, to acknowledge equal humanity and kinship with those who are different from themselves."[9] The imperative for women to acquiesce in male rule is also an ideological construction of sin. It is the assertion of gender privilege as built into the order of creation that is the sin. Gender privilege reduces women to property. It subverts the inclusiveness of the reign or *basileia* envisioned by Jesus, the very "antithesis of patriarchy."[10] It spiritualizes redemptive equality and promotes separate gender spheres as divinely willed.

Ideology criticism has made us aware, Sandra Schneiders writes, "that the biblical text contains not only historical inaccuracies, scientific errors, mythological assumptions that are unassimilable by the modern mind, but also morally objectionable positions." The further hermeneutical question, she notes, is "how we can understand the interpretive process by which the reader identifies and repudiates the morally unacceptable subject matter of the text without repudiating the text itself and its truth claims?"[11] Culturally, we have rejected slavery and sexism as reprehensible and evil. We have exposed the injustice of rendering some human beings nonpersons. But remaining before us are biblical texts that sanctify slavery and male rule and characterize sin as disobedience of a "natural order" of domination. How are these texts *revelatory?* This question moves beyond understanding the tradition to its evaluation.

More an internal development rather than an external critique, critical biblical scholarship aimed initially to nurture and deepen faith through critical appreciation of its sources and context. Among its first practitioners were such theological giants as Erasmus of Rotterdam and Martin Luther. The dilemma was that the more the Bible was studied historically, the more foreign it appeared to Christian faith and teaching.[12] The eventual effect of critical historical studies was the further erosion of assumptions that Christology could once confidently make about scripture and revelation. Questions about the historicity of the gospels from Reimarus and others led to the conclusion by biblical scholars that the gospels are theologically motivated faith documents. They reflect historical memories, but they are not history in the modern sense. Further insights into the polemically driven character of some texts have made their use even more problematic for Christology. It is not simply that the gospel narratives do not correspond to "history as it happened" but also that the history portrayed actually distorts history, as in some of the gospel portraits of the Jews.

Illustrating the Challenge to Christology Today

The insights of modernity into history, ideology, and the complex interweaving of religious ideas with interests and oppressions in society — along with Jesus' own aversion to just such relations — call for a new understanding of Jesus and pose a steep challenge to Christology as disciplined reflection

on his significance. Taking just one facet of Christology — its relationship
to scriptural sources — let us see what these challenges might dictate.

From Jesus to Christology

Theologians today draw on the expertise of biblical scholars to establish
what can be said historically about Jesus of Nazareth and the texts that
witness to him. While the starting point for Christology is this historical
research, eventually a different set of questions and goals mark the departure
of the theologian from this initial base.

Christologies are often characterized today as *descending* or *ascending*.
Traditionally, Christologies have been descending, starting with the foundational claim that God became incarnate in Jesus. They work from the
doctrine formulated by the Councils of Nicea and Chalcedon, in 325 and
451 C.E. respectively, and they proceed "downward," as it were, from divine
reality to historical reality. What was primary was the identification of Jesus
as God, not his ministry as such.

Contemporary theologians generally raise two problems with the method
of traditional Christologies. The first problem is that descending Christologies start with what is later rather than earlier, namely, doctrines formulated
several centuries after Jesus' life. History itself was not deemed of particular
value. The historical ministry of Jesus, even the Jesus of history himself, was
not of primary significance other than as evidence of the dogmatic claim
that in *this man*, and no other, God is present. The second problem is that
they start from what is unknown (God) rather than what is known (Jesus
of Nazareth).

Contemporary Christologies are characteristically ascending rather than
descending.

Unlike its predecessors, an ascending Christology values history. It starts
from the historical events of Jesus' life, ministry, and effects on those around
him and establishes what can be known about him through exegetical and
historical studies. An ascending Christology foregrounds history to illumine
the doctrine with which traditional Christologies began. If Jesus is the Wisdom and Word of God — and that is what Christians claim — then what he
said and did and endured in the historical circumstances of his life are of
ultimate significance for us. This is the reason for putting our best efforts
forth to understand his historical life.

There is much we desire to know. What was he like as a person? What
was his message? How did he use the Jewish symbol of God's *basileia*? What
did he understand by it? How were his parables to function? What is the
significance of his table-fellowship? What is the import of his engagement
with other persons? How did he conceive of his relation to his religious
tradition? What was the object of his critique? Who killed him? Why? What

meanings did resurrection carry for Jews at this time? What did it mean for his followers to say that Jesus was divine?

There are some things that we can reliably say about Jesus. Biblical scholars have established the centrality of Jesus' use of the symbol of God's *basileia* as a means of social critique.[13] Often translated into English as *kingdom*, the term would have been understood by Jesus' audience as *empire*.[14] His use of the symbol of *basileia* to model an alternative kind of social order reflects a profound grasp of the arbitrary character of the world of privilege, power, poverty, and powerlessness. Contrary to the ideological claims of the powerful, their social order is not *natural*. An imperial and patriarchal world — a domination system — is socially constructed, not divinely willed.

Through the symbol of *basileia,* Jesus contrasted two kinds of social realities, two empires. Everyone knew the Empire of Rome. Like any domination system, it was characterized, in Walter Wink's words, by "unjust economic relations, oppressive political relations, biased race relations, patriarchal gender relations, hierarchical power relations, and the use of violence to maintain them all."[15] A domination system is sustained by an imperial economics that moves available resources upward toward elite consumption, meeting the unrestricted desires of a small minority while leaving the majority of nonelite with the means for bare subsistence, if that. The Beatitudes of Jesus, announcing God's favor on the poor and the hungry, signal the desperate conditions created by this kind of social order.[16] At the heart of the sinfulness of empire is the absence of compassion.

Jesus' ministry as a whole pointed to an alternative to the present social order. His words, relationships, and actions embodied the *basileia*. In contrast to the violence and exploitation of Rome's empire, Jesus placed equality, mutual respect, partnership, and interdependence at the heart of God's *basileia*.[17] Jesus reinforced the conditions necessary for the human good — inclusion, mutuality, acceptance, compassion.

Using Scripture in Christology

Responsible use of biblical scholarship by theologians requires making critical judgments. The whole of biblical scholarship — or the work of any one biblical scholar — is not to be accepted without question. We'll appropriate the principle of Bernard Lonergan: promote insights, root out biases. This is, however, more difficult than it sounds. Which are the insights? What are the biases? The chief feature of a bias, that it is embedded in consciousness and language and becomes "just the way things are," renders it difficult to advert to, articulate, and root out.

But for the theologian, promoting insights means understanding debates among scholars about biblical texts on their own terms. For example, how is Paul's contrast in Galatians between *faith in Christ* and *works of the law* to be used in a Christology? Most often the two terms have been understood hierarchically, with faith representing higher and works lower strands in religious life. For Christians *works of the law* carried the unspoken meaning of "trying to earn one's righteousness," and there is still deep in Christian consciousness the sense that this is particularly "Jewish." Paul is thought to have given the definitive word on the validity of the law: *no one is justified by the law*. Jesus came to deliver us from the tyranny of the law.

Early Christian theologians interpreted "works of the law" as Paul's indictment of Jewish legalism.[18] For centuries Paul's contrast was understood hierarchically as between two kinds of *religion* — a superior religion of faith and an inferior religion of works. Torah-observance was described by Christians in a pejorative fashion as "works righteousness."[19] But as John Barclay notes, the phrase actually denotes a neutral description of Torah-observance. He writes that "Paul attacks the performance of these works not because they encourage self-righteousness but because they are bound up with Jewish national identity and hence exclude Gentiles."[20]

Paul's two designations stand for two opposing conditions for Gentile membership in the covenant community of Israel. Do the Gentiles who believe in Jesus have to become Jews, as converts to Judaism were required to do? "Works of the law" stands for living as a Jew through observance of the Jewish way of Torah. Paul's opponents in Galatia, themselves Jesus-followers, apparently argued that Gentiles must "come in" and "stay in" the normal way. Paul's position was that religious conversion and the decision of Gentile women and men to join the Jesus community were enough. He thought his argument was verified by the fact that Gentile believers had received God's Spirit on the basis of their faith without taking on Torah-observance (3:2).

How these phrases are interpreted and then employed in Christology is crucial to whether one's understanding of Jesus contributes to religious exclusivism.

The Roots of Exclusivism

After his death the followers of Jesus came to focus on Jesus himself rather than on the content of his preaching. Through Christ, the evangelists announced, God's salvation is extended beyond Israel. A mystical experience of the risen Christ convinced Paul that Gentiles were now to be included in Israel's covenant of salvation but without the requirement that they live the way of life commanded for Jews by the scriptures. We know, he writes, that "a person is justified not by the works of the law but through faith in Jesus Christ" (Gal. 2:16).

In the Acts of the Apostles, Christ is portrayed as the exclusive mediator of salvation. *Belief* is the condition for salvation: "There is salvation in no one else, for there is no other name under heaven given among mortals by which we must be saved" (Acts 4:12). The acceptance of salvation takes the form of repentance and baptism, as Peter tells those who have responded to his preaching with the question, "What should we do?" "Peter said to them, 'Repent, and be baptized every one of you in the name of Jesus Christ so that your sins may be forgiven; and you will receive the gift of the Holy Spirit'" (Acts 2:37).

Early Christian theologians appropriated the New Testament proclamations of Christ's mediation of salvation. But the proclamation itself did not answer the question why Christ's forgiveness was necessary for all humankind. The idea of *original sin* — a universal sin — developed as their answer. Reading Genesis 3 in this light, theologians conceived of this universal sin as the inheritance of Adam and Eve's actual sin. This became the explanatory principle for the universality of human evil. All humankind stands in need of salvation and the forgiveness of Christ.

Once developed and accepted as part of the church's teaching, the doctrine of original sin shaped the meaning of the incarnation and redemption. Why did Christ come? To remove the sin that separates humankind from God and to restore what is required for each to attain the eternal destiny for which they were created. The roots of Christian religious exclusivism lie in this intertwining of teaching about original sin and redemption. The New Testament conception of salvation was unambiguous: "There is salvation in no one else" (Acts 4:12). Salvation required membership in the Christian assembly (Acts 2:37). By the fifth century, a theology of original sin anchored the necessity of both Christ and the church in the forgiveness needed by every human being of a sin inherited at birth.

This understanding of redemption — why Christ, why the incarnation, why the church? — is so taken for granted in Christian consciousness that it is sometimes difficult to see what is missing. What is missing is crucial. In starting from original sin, the church's theology of redemption bypassed the Jesus of history.

Jesus depicted redemption as the transformation of social and historical realities. The symbol of God's *basileia* envisions a restored creation. Its positive features — acceptance, mutuality, social and economic well-being — bring into high relief the negative features of a social order distorted by sin. A fragment from an early baptismal ritual in the Jesus movement suggests the way in which Jesus' followers both conceived of redemption and embodied Jesus' vision of God's *basileia* in their relations with one another:

> As many of you as were baptized with Christ have clothed yourself with Christ. There is no longer Jew or Greek, there is no longer slave or free, there is no longer male and female; for all of you are one in Christ Jesus (Gal. 3:27–28).[21]

The fragment points to religious, class, and gender privilege as "no longer" existing. They belong to what Paul describes as the "present evil age" (1:4). They are the *sin* now passing away. Redemption is experienced in the relations of mutuality that bind the members of the assembly together as "one in Christ Jesus." In the assembly of believers, "in Christ," believers experience redemption as acceptance and mutuality, a sign of contradiction to a civilization built on slavery, oppression of women, and conflict among peoples.

Even in the New Testament, however, this conception and lived experience of redemption is resisted. The writer of 1 Timothy describes the Christian assembly as the "household of God" (1 Tim. 3:15). In the patriarchal household, structured by relations of domination and subordination, everyone has his or her place. This designation signals a deliberate reappropriation of hierarchical relations as normative. By definition, the household excludes relations of mutuality. Already Jesus' vision of God's *basileia* as a social reality is becoming spiritualized. Freedom from subordinate status will be a heavenly reality, not an historical one. Slaves of believing masters must serve them even more (6:2). Women's redemption is linked with their acquiescence in procreative capacities, not to their independent decision of faith (2:15).

The Problem of Supersessionism

Ideologies of superiority justify privilege. We know them in many forms. Of particular relevance for Christology is the Christian assertion of privilege over Judaism and other religious traditions. In relation to Judaism, early Christian theologians made several crucial assumptions that would shape subsequent theology in tragic ways. First, they assumed that Jesus was killed by the Jews. Second, they assumed that Jesus had rejected Judaism. Third, they assumed that Jesus founded the church as the replacement of Israel in God's covenant with humankind.

The theology that developed from these assumptions was *supersessionist.*[22] In asserting the superiority of Christ, church, and Christianity and the inferiority of Torah, synagogue, and Judaism, Christians also asserted that the former superseded or replaced the latter. The Nazi genocide of Jews in World War II generated questions about the environment of hate created by Christian religious antisemitism and its contribution to the Holocaust.

The work of Krister Stendahl, E. P. Sanders, and James D. G. Dunn has been foundational. While their inquiry was exegetical, their results transformed the inherited theological interpretation of Paul.[23] Sanders described a primary purpose of his research as overcoming the depiction of Judaism as a legalistic religion.[24] Due to his thorough historical analysis, the common Christian view that Judaism was a religion of works-righteousness has been rejected by many. It is now seen as polemical caricature, not historical reality.

In their reading of Galatians, early Christian theologians missed the membership dimension of the conflict. One interference was their image that Paul converted from Judaism to Christianity, that is, from one religion to another. Historically, it is more accurate to describe Paul's conversion as from one Judaism to another, from "Pharisaic Judaism" to "Messianic Judaism." The latter began and remained for some time as a movement within the broad diversity of Jewish life. Out of this life and diversity, events of the first and early second centuries produced two distinct religions — from Messianic Judaism would come Christianity and from Pharisaic Judaism would come Rabbinic Judaism. But this development would be decades after the death of Paul.

The question in Galatians of the inclusion of Gentiles is their inclusion in *Israel*. The conflict over circumcision of male converts is an intra-Jewish conflict. Both Paul and the Jesus evangelists who oppose him are arguing a Jewish question about Gentile converts. How do they *come into* Israel? What do they have to do to *stay in?* Each side has its shorthand condition. Paul argues that the condition is "faith in Christ." The religious conversion of Gentile women and men and the gift of God's Spirit are sufficient for inclusion in Israel. The evangelists who oppose Paul presumably came equipped to argue the normativity of scripture: the way of living mandated by the Torah is a command of God, not a suggestion.

For various reasons, the Jesus movement became predominantly non-Jewish or Gentile by the end of the first century C.E. The bitterness experienced between Jew and Jew over the significance of Jesus became the bitterness of Gentile against Jew. The question "Who is *Christ?*" became one of self- and ecclesial identity, "Who are *we* in relation to the Jews?" Their answers were supersessionist:[25]

> We *replace* them in God's covenant with humanity.
> Christ *replaces* the Torah as a norm of belief and living.
> The church *replaces* the synagogue.

Supersessionist language is embedded not only in the theologies of Christ and the church, that is, in Christology and ecclesiology, but in Christian worship as well. Until removed from the Catholic liturgy by Pope John XXIII in 1959, this was the Good Friday Prayer for the Jews:

> Let us pray also for the unfaithful Jews, that our God and Lord may remove the veil from their hearts; that they also may acknowledge our Lord Jesus Christ. Almighty and everlasting God, Who drivest not even the faithless Jews away from Thy mercy, hear our prayers, which we offer for the blindness of that people, that, acknowledging the light of thy truth, which is Christ, they may be rescued from their darkness.[26]

Rooted especially in the blaming of Jews for the death of Jesus, Christian religious antisemitism invites a certain progression:

> The logical progression of anti-Jewish theology among Gentiles in the first century to the oven chambers of Auschwitz was from the Christian protest, "You have no right to live among us as Jews," to "You have no right to live among us," to "You have no right to live."[27]

There remain scholarly debates and exegetical questions about the new perspective in Pauline studies. Yet to maintain today the traditional interpretation of the contrast between faith in Christ and works of the law continues supersessionism and puts a theologian in the position of consciously promoting a religious ideology of superiority.

Supersessionist thinking remains in Christian consciousness as "the way it is" even today. The language is as real, as certain, as that of doctrine, albeit pseudodoctrine: The Jews killed Christ. Judaism is legalistic. God has rejected the Jews. The German political theologian, Johann-Baptist Metz, put the matter facing Christians simply: "The problem with a view toward Auschwitz," he writes, "is not merely a revision of the Christian theology of Judaism, but a revision of Christian theology altogether."[28]

The Task of Christology Today

Christology today therefore has a double task: it must respond anew and intelligibly to the perennial questions of Jesus' meaning and significance. But it must also deal responsibly with the exclusivist claims and other ideological distortions or effects of the christological tradition itself. Several features or criteria will distinguish a responsible contemporary Christology.

A contemporary Christology must be historically informed

An historically informed Christology appropriates into theological reflection critical biblical judgments about the nature of the gospels as sources for the Jesus of history. Drawing from the work of biblical scholars, it explores the way Jesus used the symbol of God's *basileia* to mediate a social and historical understanding of sin and redemption. It explores further the relevance of Christ's vision of God's *basileia* for today. In addition, Jesus' preaching and the symbol of *basileia* become the criteria of authenticity for a Christology. Does a Christology draw out the implications of Jesus' message and praxis? Does it resist privatizing sin and spiritualizing redemption? Does it recognize ideological interpretations of biblical texts, abandoning, for example, the long-standing interpretation of "faith in Christ" and "works of the law"?

A contemporary Christology must be religiously sensitive

If religious experience is universal, if the mediated experience of divine mystery is experience of a reality, and if religions are the social expression of this foundational experience of the divine, then isn't the multiplicity of religions a part of the created order? A Christology must engage the question of the salvific value of other religions. How are they genuine ways to God for their adherents? The universality of religious experience and the exclusivist claim that Jesus is the only way to God are difficult if not impossible to reconcile. How to explain the distinctiveness of Christ without denigrating the integrity of the other is a major task of Christology.

A contemporary Christology must be culturally responsible

The portrayal of other cultures as primitive, barbarian, savage, and inferior to Christian cultures has also functioned as a tool of devaluation of other people and as a justification for their colonization. While we are beyond the question of Christian ownership of slaves, recognition of the historic relation between religious and cultural imperialism still raises basic questions about the purpose and legitimacy of Christian mission and evangelization, as well as the function of the Christ symbol in a world order largely dominated by Christian, formerly colonial nations.

A contemporary Christology affirms gender equality

Embedded in a Christology are assumptions about who we are and how we are to relate to one another. Gender dualism divides human reality into two distinct and unequal spheres. An anthropology of two human natures, one fully human, the other less so, is a distorted conception of humanness.

The way we think about God influences the way we think about ourselves. Rosemary Radford Ruether writes that behind the argument of the necessary maleness of Christ lies a theological assumption of the maleness of God. Thus only men can represent both the divine and the human natures of Christ.[29] But if we conceived of God in terms of self-transcendence, as Bernard Lonergan does, gender dualism disappears:

> To conceive of God as originating value and the world as terminal value implies that God too is self-transcending and that the world is the fruit of God's self-transcendence. . . . God made us in God's image, for our authenticity consists in being like God, in self-transcending, in being origins of value.[30]

Recovering Jesus' understanding of redemption as the transformation of the social order distorted by privilege offers an alternative to traditional denials of the full humanity of women and to a privatized notion of justification that bypasses history to head directly to heaven.

Confronting the ideological distortions of our most deeply held religious and christological convictions can open new vistas and deepen our understanding of what God has been about in Jesus. Bernard Lonergan has argued that authentic religion will contribute to the transformation of society.[31] It generates human cooperation with God in promoting the well-being of all persons. Religious conversion promotes authenticity to the point of self-sacrificing love.[32] For Lonergan, this is the principle of redemption. Self-sacrificing love, however, is not the sacrifice of self to a natural or rightful *domination* of another — as has often been preached to subordinated groups, such as women and slaves — but the sacrifice of *self-* or *group-interests* to contribute to the good of others.

Inasmuch as the human good is promoted and evil countered, religious conversion contributes positively to the social transformation of culture. It sustains development. This means, however, that religious institutions, too, must be religiously converted. They must question whether and how the conception of their core beliefs reinforces group privilege and power or affirms the full humanness of all.

We are aware now, in a different and new way, that religious beliefs, doctrines, and values — even a Christology — are subject to the ideological distortion of knowledge and truth. The distortion of meaning contributes to unauthenticity in a tradition. The cure, Lonergan writes, is not the undoing of the *tradition,* but the undoing of the tradition's *unauthenticity.*[33] To do so requires discovering where and how the tradition has gone astray. Because Christology is the most central of theological reflections, attention to the use, misuse, and potential use of the symbol of Christ is especially acute and profoundly promising.

Who is Jesus for us? An honest and earnest search involves us in a sustained critical engagement with the Christian tradition, with a world desperate for the values Jesus espoused, and with the ultimate meaning of our own lives in Christ.

Part One

RECOVERING
THE TRADITION

— 2 —

Jesus of Nazareth in Historical Research

Elisabeth Schüssler Fiorenza

"Thinking about Jesus" in a critical scholarly fashion must be learned. This is not the case only for Christian believers but for citizens in a world that has been and still is shaped by Christian religion. Whether fundamentalist or progressive, religion always shapes individual identity and democratic society. It must therefore be critically explored to determine whether it fosters domination or makes possible emancipation and well-being.

The historical search for founding religious figures, such as Jesus, Moses, or Mohammed, is always also a search for identity. This is especially true in light of modern historical consciousness, which is not so much interested in how church dogmatics has interpreted Jesus but in what we can really say about the historical figure Jesus of Nazareth. I will therefore explore what it means to be thinking not about "Christ" as preached by the church but about Jesus of Nazareth, who lived in the first century and was called the "Christ," the messiah in Jewish terms. I will do so first by probing the difficulties of knowing how to think of and know Jesus of Nazareth as a historical figure by exploring the scholarly efforts to establish who the historical Jesus really was. In a second part I will share with you my own "thinking of Jesus," which is informed by the scholarly debates about the historical Jesus. I engage both a critical deconstructive and a reconstructive thinking to encourage you also to engage in such critical-constructive "thinking about Jesus."

Historical-Jesus Research: Problem, Result, and Bias

In the past decade a host of historical-Jesus books has appeared which range from the very scholarly to the very popular.[1] The scientific quest for the historical Jesus seeks to find the "real" historical Jesus but seems to end

up with many different and often contradicting results, despite its claims
to scientific method and disinterested objectivity. The books about Jesus
offer a "bewildering range of competing hypotheses. There is no unifying
theological agenda; no final agreement about method; certainly no common
set of results."[2]

One would think that the great disparity in the results of historical-Jesus
research would have persuaded scholars a long time ago to abandon their
quest for the historical Jesus, produced by the disciplined use of historical
methods, in favor of more fruitful endeavors. Yet this has not been the case.
Rather, the opposite seems to be true: despite the variety, the flood of Jesus
publications has dramatically increased in the past decade. Both the wide
variety of historical-Jesus studies, books, and articles and the scholarly claim
to scientific objectivity in and through the controlled use of method can be
understood if one looks at historical-Jesus research as a discursive practice
and productive site of struggle over Christian identity and the meaning of
Jesus for people today.

Why do we find ourselves in such a paradoxical situation? First of all,
we have no saying or document written down by Jesus himself. All that
we know about him is transmitted in the interpretations of his followers.
Moreover, these sources are not only hard to date, they are also multiple.
The generative discursive problem to be overcome or fruitfully transformed
by historical-Jesus research is the simple fact that the Christian canon has
not one but four gospels — that is, four quite different narratives about
Jesus — not to mention such gospels such as the Gospel of Thomas or the
Gospel of Mary that did not make it into the canon of the church. It is
this hermeneutical problem posed by the multiplicity of the gospels that has
spawned, then and now, attempts to reduce the pluriform gospels to one
uniform Gospel message.

In addition, anyone familiar with interpretation in general and the interpretation of gospel texts in particular knows that there are a multiplicity
of competing credible readings possible. The hermeneutical (that is, relating
to the theory of interpretation) and methodological discussion in biblical
studies has driven home that texts do not have a single, definite meaning
and a "final solution."[3] This is true also for the historical sources about
Jesus. Language is not a mere vehicle for the transmission of social and
historical context but itself the producer of meaning. Archival and other
sources, therefore, are not just quarries for factual information but produce
historical meaning. Such an understanding of text and language as rhetorical
and constructive challenges the absolute dichotomy between scientific and
creative writing, between fact and fiction that is typical of historical positivism. In short, the textuality of the gospels poses the rhetorical problem
that historical-Jesus research seeks to overcome.

Finally, scholars not only select and interpret archaeological artifacts and textual evidence. They also make sense of these so-called data by framing them in terms of scientific models or by rearranging them in a new narrative framework of meaning.[4] To do so, they rely on other scholars to know the ancient worlds, and they use their own experience of the world for reconstructing the historical Jesus and his world.

Is Jesus Recoverable?

Whether they reconstruct the historical Jesus as an existentialist religious thinker, a rabbinic teacher, an apocalyptic prophet, a pious Hasid, a revolutionary peasant, a wandering Cynic, a Greco-Roman magician, a healing witch-doctor, a nationalist anti-Temple Galilean revolutionary, or a wo/man-identified man, the present flood of historical-Jesus books and articles document that despite their scientific, positivistic rhetoric of facts and historical realism, scholars inescapably fashion the historical Jesus in their own image and likeness.

Such a process of self-identification is a complex one. Historical-Jesus scholars, who for the most part are still elite, educated, white males, distance Jesus as the totally other from themselves yet at the same time project either their idealized or their negative-Other image unto him. Their often-unconscious self-identification with the male hero and great individual of the Jesus story reinforces cultural masculinity for male readers, but not for wo/men readers. It is taken as a "common sense" fact that Jesus was male, and that wo/men are the other to maleness.

In the syntax of gender, wo/men readers[5] can only situate themselves in relation to Jesus the man. They can idealize him as the great Man and charismatic leader or feminize him, by projecting the "kyriarchal" cultural values[6] of true womanhood unto him. In any case, both interpretive strategies reinforce the linguistic-ideological structure of androcentrism[7] and kyriocentrism, i.e., emperor, lord, slave-master, or father. To paint Jesus not just with feminine qualities but to picture him as a wo/man goes against all "common sense" and all that is considered normal and natural, since Jesus is "obviously" or "evidently" a male. A scholarly elaboration of Jesus as wo/man would be seen as slightly crazy and definitely not as scholarship to be taken seriously.

Yet while picturing Jesus as a wo/man is jarring, a white reading public is not jarred in the same way — does not even notice it — when scholars picture the historical Jesus as a white European male with blue eyes and blond hair. Whether Jesus is portrayed as a marginal Jew, a devout Jew, a trickster Jew, or a Jewish seer, his primary identification in a modern Christian context is not as Jewish but as male. Whether Jesus is seen as a Jewish prophet or Greco-Roman cynic, his maleness is always tacitly presupposed

because of the modern sex/gender framework that is all-pervasive in Christian cultures. Just as medieval Christianity turned Jesus into a sovereign king
and noble ruler, when he clearly had not been one historically, modernity
stresses the maleness of Jesus, although our sources do not elaborate his
masculinity. A dualistic gender lens thus provides one of the unquestioned
modern frameworks of historical-Jesus research.

Successive Quests

The boom in historical-Jesus publications, I contend, is not so much about
history as about identity. This was already recognized by Albert Schweitzer
at the end of the first scientific quest for the historical Jesus. He observed
even then that scholars inevitably fashion Jesus in their own image and
likeness. However, what Schweitzer did not recognize is that scholars not
only create Jesus in their own image and likeness but also tend to project
their image onto the *other*. In a romantic vein, Jesus becomes the *same* in
the disguise of the *other* — the peasant, the revolutionary, the magician, the
ascetic, the lover, the Hasid, or the feminine man, to mention a few of such
scholarly creations — and then functions as a commodity for cultural or
religious edification.

Since the 1960s, for example, much ink has been spilled to prove that
Jesus was not a political revolutionary and had nothing whatever to do with
the Zealots, a militant political movement of his time. In the last decade a
sea change in historical-Jesus studies seems to have taken place, however.
Now Jesus is imagined as a figure concerned with the broader issues of
politics. He has become a peasant leader and social-religious reformer who
was executed by the Romans for sedition.

Thus the historical Jesus becomes an object of scholarly projection both
as the same and as the idealized or disparaged other. At best one can glimpse
his historical shadow-image or negative, but how one develops this picture
will always depend on the chemicals one uses, that is, the kind of reconstructive methods and models one adopts. The earliest portrayals of Jesus
in the canonical and extracanonical early Christian literature owe their existence to the same process of selection and reframing of traditions. Any
presentation of Jesus — scientific or otherwise — must therefore own that it
is a "reconstruction" and open up its critical methods, rhetorical interests,
and reconstructive models to critical inspection and public scrutiny.

Since the multiplicity and variety of historical-Jesus images and approaches is not a controvertible but a scientifically verifiable "fact," it is
necessary, I argue here, to look more closely at historical-Jesus research and
its social-scientific rhetoric[8] to see what values and visions it offers us for
"thinking about Jesus." Scholarship generally has come to distinguish four
periods of Jesus research and three quests for the historical Jesus. Whereas

three of the four periods have doggedly pursued the historical Jesus in various ways and with differing methods in positivist terms, the period between the first and the second quest, which began with the work of Martin Kähler in 1896[9] and ended with Ernst Käsemann's revival of historical-Jesus research in 1953,[10] was actually a declaration against liberal "life of Jesus scholarship,"[11] which had claimed to represent the "real" historical Jesus free from all dogmatic overlay. This interlude or "no-quest" period[12] lasted for about sixty years in which the quest for the historical Jesus was virtually abandoned.

This no-quest period distinguished between the historical Jesus of modern scholarship and the resurrected Christ of kerygmatic theology. Kerygmatic theology (which emphasized the importance of Christian proclamation of the early church's message or *kerygma*) insisted that it is no longer possible to distill a liberal historical Jesus freed from early Christian interpretation and apostolic tradition. The gospels are to be studied as documents of faith and theological arguments of the evangelists and the communities they address.

The third period of historical-Jesus research, or the second quest, which was dubbed the "New Quest" by James M. Robinson, owes its existence to the reaction against the kerygmatic Jesus theology of the no-quest period. The New Quest flourished in the 1950s and 1960s and insisted that it is possible to extract or distill the historical Jesus from the early Christian sources like a kernel from the husk. To that end, the New Quest articulated criteria of historical authenticity. To be regarded as authentic, words and deeds of Jesus must, first, be documented in more than one source (the criterion of multiple attestation). Second, they must not be found in the Jewish culture of the time or be explainable as stemming from the interests of the early church (the criterion of dissimilarity or exclusivity — not difference). And third, they must cohere with the material judged previously as authentic (the coherence criterion).[13] In other words: the New Quest adopted a reductionist historical method, which does not take into account that historiography must evaluate and place texts and artifacts in a coherent frame of meaning or reconstructive model to tell a story about Jesus that makes sense. There is no history that is not reconstruction.

Moreover, this reductionist method assumed that Jesus is totally separable from both Judaism and from his followers, the early church. He is the totally Other. To establish the historical singularity of Jesus and his ethics, the New Quest, like the old one, needed a negative depiction of Judaism as its foil. Jesus, it supposes, knew that his teaching undermined the fundaments of Jewish belief. The Roman imperial authority executed him allegedly because of his conflict with a ritualistic and legalistic Judaism.

Insofar as one of the most fertile grounds for Christian anti-Jewish articulations has been historical-Jesus research, assertions of the uniqueness of

Jesus (for example, by feminists who cite his atypical relations to women) merely adapt the arguments of liberal historical-Jesus scholarship, which is permeated by anti-Judaism. Some scholars in biblical wo/men's studies, who seek to avoid Christian anti-Judaism in their research on "Jesus and women," argue that it is not plausible that Jesus and his followers challenged the dominant patriarchal institutions of his time. To the contrary, they insist, he was completely in line with Jewish and Greco-Roman patriarchalism.[14] Such scholars, however, do not realize that they also fall prey to negative stereotypical assumptions about Judaism insofar as they cannot imagine that the Jesus movement, like other Jewish movements of the time, could possibly have questioned the second-class citizenship of wo/men and disenfranchised men and could have done so on Jewish theological grounds.[15]

The Third Quest

The Third Quest[16] has emerged primarily among North American scholars who have lost confidence in the criteria of authenticity of the second quest but still hold on to the criterion of "plausibility." The Third Quest is not kerygmatic but social-scientific in intent. It is characterized by its interest in social history, the integration of Jesus into Judaism, and equal attention to noncanonical sources.[17] It is split into two directions, those who advocate a noneschatological understanding of Jesus (Burton Mack, John-Dominic Crossan, Leif Vaage, et al. in the Jesus Seminar) and those who defend the eschatological, millenarian Jesus, who hoped for the restoration of Judaism (E. P. Sanders, Gerd Theissen and Annette Merz, Dale Allison, John Meier, Richard Horsley, et al.).

The Third Quest is generally dated in the early 1980s and its initiation is attributed to North American scholars. Unlike the first and second quests, the newest quest does not seek to reconstruct the historical Jesus over and against first-century Judaism but sees him as fully integrated into his time and culture. Even among the advocates of the Cynic hypothesis, the debate is not about whether Jesus was a Jew but what kind of Jew he was.

This Third Quest was prepared through studies of early Jewish writings, research of the Qumran scrolls, and archaeological discoveries. Whereas these studies have amply documented that Judaism in the first century was variegated and pluralistic, the arguments about Jesus' Jewishness seem often to presuppose a unitary patriarchal form of Judaism. Insofar as scholars do not use a sociological conflict but an integrationist model for their reconstruction, they cannot picture Jesus as part of a variegated Jewish movement centered around the *basileia,* or reign of G*d,[18] and in conflict with the hegemonic patriarchal and kyriarchal structures of the Roman empire. In short, the newest quest has not been able to articulate a reconstructive frame of reference that can conceptualize the emergent Jesus movement and its diverse articulations as participating in popular Jewish and Greco-Roman movements of cultural, political, and religious survival, resistance, and change.

Since the Third Quest justifiably rejected the second quest's reductionistic criteria of authenticity, it needed to develop new methods and criteria of evaluation. To that end, the Jesus Seminar, whose members are mostly white male and Christian,[19] has adopted forms of opinion research and voting practices to identify consensus about and to stratify the traditions about Jesus. In addition, scholars have developed the "plausibility" criterion, which judges materials by whether their content can be made plausible historically and be understood as fitting into the time and culture of Jesus.[20]

However, this criterion overlooks that what is regarded as "common sense" or "plausible" in a culture depends on its hegemonic ideological understandings of "how the world is." For instance, the assumption that wo/men were marginal or second-class citizens in all forms of first century Judaism makes it impossible to assert plausibly that they were equal members in the Jesus movement if one understands it as a Jewish movement.

Finally, I want to point to the conservative political contextualizations of the Third Quest, which emerged in the United States during the Reagan/Thatcher years and in a period during which the United States became the only superpower in the world after the demise of the Soviet Union and the failure of socialist state capitalism.[21] Moreover, the Third Quest continues to produce Jesus, the Lord or *kyrios,* as a naturalized historical fact, which asserts the importance of Western hegemonic identity formations as Christian and as elite male.[22] It does so in the face of a widespread liberal white male anxiety, which feels threatened by feminists, immigrants, Two-Thirds World persons, and everyone else who seeks to decenter academy and society in general and biblical studies in particular.

One wonders whether it is an historical accident that the Third Quest for the historical Jesus exploded not only during the resurgence of the political right and the revival of religious fundamentalism but also in a time when the wo/men's movement in the churches and the academy gained ground and developed rhetorical power. Yet, whereas the second quest stressed the difference between a "feminist" Jesus and Judaism, the Third Quest argues for his integration into the patriarchal Jewish society and religion of his time. Jesus was a devout Jewish man who did not question the dominant structures of his society but fully subscribed to them. If the dissimilarity criterion is replaced with that of plausibility within a kyriarchal frame of reference, one cannot but reconstitute Jesus' Jewishness in terms of the dominant patriarchal ethos of the first century. At this point the entrapping character of this new criterion of historical-Jesus research becomes obvious.

The refusal of the Third Quest to problematize its own methodological assumptions and ideological interests as well as its sophisticated restoration of historical positivism corresponds to political conservatism. Its emphasis on the *realia* and "facts" of history and the reliability of its methods serves to promote a kind of scientific fundamentalism. This is the case if our discourses about Jesus do not underscore methodologically that historians actively and intentionally *select* and *interpret* archaeological artifacts and textual evidence as well as *incorporate* them into a scientific model and narrative framework of meaning. The inability of such discourses plausibly to discuss the possibility of understanding the Jesus movement as an alternative Jewish movement that sought to abolish kyriarchal domination and believed in the basic equality of all the children of G*d, not only bespeaks antifeminist tendencies. It also bespeaks a lack of feminist self-affirmation on the part of wo/men scholars who subscribe to the positivist methods of the Third Quest.

Along these lines Dieter Georgi has constructed a trajectory of bourgeois historical-Jesus theology throughout Christian history, beginning with the early Christian "divine man" theology and continuing all the way to the New Quest for the historical Jesus.[23] According to Georgi, historical-Jesus research understands Jesus as the great exceptional individual, genius, and hero: "This view that Jesus had been a genius of some sort," he says, "became the dominant view in the late eighteenth, nineteenth, and twentieth centuries, not only in Germany but also in Western Europe and North America, among both Protestants and Catholics."[24] Georgi observes that the first quest's interest in Jesus, the exceptional man, is continued and reformulated in the second quest, which stressed Jesus as an active subject of history and focused on individual consciousness, intention, and decision. Jesus' unique claim to extraordinary consciousness presupposes a peerless relationship to G*d, in whose place he stood and acted. His essentially eschatological outlook and stress on G*d's sovereignty brought him, according to Georgi, into conflict not only with the Romans but also with his own people and leadership.

This emphasis in both the first and the second quest on the exemplary or unique historical figure of Jesus and his radical ethics required a negative portrayal of Judaism as its foil. Since Jesus is said to have been conscious that his preaching radically undermined the fundamental beliefs of Judaism, he is understood as having gone to Jerusalem in the full awareness that he risked death. In this interpretation Jesus' conflict with the Roman authorities is the result of his basic conflict with ritualistic or legalistic Judaism. Georgi concludes that the quest for the historical Jesus on the whole has its social location within the evolution of bourgeois consciousness, not just as an ideal but as an expression of a socioeconomic and political momentum. The contemporaneity of the New Quest with the end of the New Deal and the restoration of the bourgeoisie in the United States and Germany after World

War II and within the confines of a burgeoning market-oriented Atlantic community is not accidental.[25]

The Eurocentric Male Tendencies of the Historical-Jesus Quest

The rise of historical-Jesus research must be seen as an element in the emergence of "scientific" methods in the humanities and social sciences and their ideological function. Although Georgi does not point out the racist, Eurocentric masculine identity formation of historical-Jesus research, he concludes with the assertion that the modern quests for the historical Jesus are revived whenever a revolutionary situation abates. Historical-Jesus research therefore has always had a conservative, Eurocentric, kyriarchal (i.e., entailing domination by the lord/father/master/male) function. It shares in the scientific discourses of subordination and dehumanization that have produced modern racist, sexist, and colonialist theories. As scientific discourses, historical-Jesus discourses cannot but be affected by such theories of prejudice.

It is well known that biblical studies emerged on the scene together with other disciplines in the humanities that sought to articulate their discourses as scientific practices in analogy to the natural sciences. The feminist theorist Sandra Harding has pointed to a three-stage process in the emergence of modern science shaping and determining scholarly discourses, their presuppositions and intellectual frameworks.

The first stage, according to Harding, consisted in the breakdown of feudal labor divisions and slave relations.[26] The second stage is exemplified in the New Science Movement of the seventeenth century, which flourished in Puritan England and brought forth a new political self-consciousness with radical social goals.[27] Scientific knowledge was to serve the people and to be used for redistributing knowledge and wealth.[28] The third stage produced the notion of purely technical and value-neutral science. The progress that science represents is based entirely on scientific method. The institutionalization of science meant the separation of science's cognitive and political aims and the restriction of true science and scientists to the former.

The discipline of biblical studies is located at this third scientific stage, which constructs a sharp dualism between science and theology, or scientific discourse and ideology, to prove itself as scientific. A series of structuring dualisms[29] and dichotomies between science and politics, history and theology, knowledge and fiction, past and present, rationality and faith, male and female, white and black, Caucasian and Asian, and so on, determines the Western scientific worldview. As a scientific discourse biblical studies thus participates in the discourses of domination which were produced by science.

Science and Scientism

For it is also at this third stage of the development of academic scientific disciplines that the discourses of domination — racism, heterosexism, colonialism, class privilege, ageism — were articulated as "scientific" discourses.[30] While previously discourses of domination were developed on the grounds of Christian religion, now science took the place of religion and continued its work of hegemonic legitimization. The discourses of domination were formed as elite discourses that justified relations of ruling. Hence "soft" academic disciplines, such as history, sociology, and anthropology, in their formative stage, developed discourses of domination to prove that they also belonged to the "hard" sciences. Thereby academic social-science disciplines supported European colonialism and capitalist industrial development.

These scientific discourses were influenced by European philosophical discourses that emerged with colonialism and understood subjugated peoples as "primitives" who were considered to be more natural, sexual, untouched by civilization, and inferior because of their innate biological differences — for instance, their allegedly smaller brains. In the United States, Native Americans and African Americans were those who represented the "primitive" in sociological and anthropological scientific discourses. They were construed to be either violent or childlike or both. People who were not-white and not-male were praised as "noble savages" or feared as "bloodthirsty cannibals" on biological and cultural grounds.[31]

Most recently Shawn Kelly has published a book entitled *Racializing Jesus* that analyzes ways such racializing assumptions and scientific theories have determined German critical biblical scholarship. Although he does not analyze either British and American New Testament scholarship nor the quest for the historical Jesus, his argument still applies:

> I argue throughout the course of this book that racism is neither accidental nor peripheral to modern thought, that it permeates the perception and reasoning of many seminal modern thinkers and modern institutions. For most modern Europeans racism *was a morally and empirically justifiable way of thinking.* This was true for thinkers in most academic disciplines, including biblical scholars, for most of modern history. Repulsion in the face of overt racism is a relatively recent phenomenon.[32]

The racial dichotomy between the Occident and the Orient was articulated by philosopher G. W. F. Hegel. The static nature of its culture determines the East and its peoples who were not capable of achieving freedom, whereas the dynamic culture of the West brings forth people who are capable of achieving freedom and thus rightly rule the world. Early modern Christian scholars took over this dichotomy and understood the Greeks and Greek culture as pulsating with the spirit of freedom, whereas Judaism as an Oriental religion has articulated monotheism and religious ritualism and legalism. Christianity has taken over from Judaism monotheism but not such empty legalism and ritualism. It is seen as "pulsating with the spirit of freedom" and as the spiritual liberation of the individual. Rome transmitted to Europe not only the culture of the Greeks but also "set the stage for the Catholic perversion of the spirit of freedom."[33] Africa in turn is not seen at all as a historical force.

Even before Kelley, the Chinese-American theologian Kwok Pui-Lan pointed out that most surveys of biblical scholarship neglect to reflect on the fact that the quest for the historical Jesus flourished in nineteenth-century Europe at the height of Western colonization. She argues that there were in fact not one but two quests taking place at the same time:

> The quest for the historical Jesus was an obsession of the West. It first took place at a time when the power of Europe was at its zenith — the quest for Jesus went hand in hand with the quest for land and people to conquer. From a postcolonial perspective we must plot the quest for the *authentic* Jesus against the search for knowledge of *authentic* "natives" for the purpose of control and domination.[34]

This pernicious Eurocentrism of historical-Jesus research is confirmed by a look at Two-Thirds World biblical scholarship. Two-Thirds World scholars are not engaged in the (heroic) quests for the Jesus of history. Among others, Grant LeMarquand[35] has pointed to the ignorance in the Western academy, for instance, about African biblical scholarship. Whereas African and postcolonial biblical scholars are well aware of the issues raised by Western historical-Jesus scholarship, they frame and shape their own discourses on Jesus differently. Their major concern is to deconstruct colonialist readings of the Bible and to establish the common ground between their own cultures and the Bible. They focus on this issue not only because biblical cultures often come very close to their own but also because their own cultures were constructed by missionaries with the help of the Bible as inferior and even "satanic."

Jesus, Women, and Feminist Studies

Finally, the most extensive critical interaction with malestream historical-Jesus research has come from critical feminist studies, which have shown how the maleness of Jesus is constructed in modern scientific terms in and through the research on his relationship to wo/men. Insofar as this research still places Jesus, the heroic man, in the center of attention and does not question the andro/kyriocentric language and ideology of the original sources, it reinscribes the dominant cultural kyriocentric rhetoric as real and factual. However, many studies that employ a gender framework rather than a complex kyriarchal analytic do not see the intersection between racism, sexism, and colonialism in the research framework of the quest for the historical Jesus.

Since the first phase of "Life of Jesus" research in the nineteenth century sought to write a biography of Jesus, the great individual and heroic man, topical studies on wo/men in the life of Jesus and Christian origins have adopted an "add and stir" approach. It adds wo/men to the subject of historical Jesus and continues to make "Jesus and Women" rather than kyriarchal structures of domination the object of its research. This approach overlooks that understanding of Jesus as a powerful religious genius who transgressed all normal boundaries is itself the product of an elite masculinist Eurocentric liberal imagination. Jesus the extraordinary and heroic man becomes the paradigm of true (Western male) humanity and individuality, which can be approximated only by those who are like him.

Many popular studies on the relationship of Jesus to wo/men remain in the framework of this first phase of "life of Jesus" research when they seek to write biographies of Jesus, stress his close relationship with wo/men, or argue that he developed psychologically in his interactions with wo/men. Whereas Jesus is seen as the great (male) individual and hero who suffers conflicts and survives suffering and death, the wo/men around him, especially Mary of Magdala, are pictured in typically feminine fashion as romantically involved with him or as his loving support staff.

Yet, it must also be noted that most popularizing studies about "Jesus and women" in the gospels are not critical feminist emancipatory. Often they uncritically assume linguistic determinism (that is, that androcentric language cannot be changed), and hence cannot but "naturalize" the grammatically masculine language representation as well as the anti-Jewish tendencies of the gospels and their traditions. Such studies are especially prone to reinscribe the anti-Jewish polemic of the gospels into their own historical narrative, and they do so in terms of cultural gender stereotypes.

Scholars tend to take the grammatically androcentric language of our sources at face value and thereby reinscribe the wo/men-marginalizing and wo/men-erasing tendencies of such language. Hence, the history that they tell about biblical wo/men, and about wo/men today,[36] cannot but represent wo/men as marginal or not mention them at all. They "erase" wo/men from historical and religious consciousness not only because of the marginalizing and silencing tendencies of our androcentric sources written in grammatically masculine languages but also because of the marginalizing and silencing tendencies of hegemonic biblical scholarship, its kyriocentric frameworks of interpretation and models of historical reconstruction. As William Arnal has pointed out, the negative reactions of historical-Jesus research to the objections of feminist or postcolonial scholarship reveal that:

> What is ultimately at stake is the *desire* for objectivity: a desire to view the object of one's inquiry through the lens of things-as-they-are. The distinction between a fact and a value is itself not based on fact, but on a dichotomy between things as they are and things as one wishes them to be; the removal of so-called value from scholarship is really the removal of hope, something which is not central or necessary to the daily ideological work of the privileged.[37]

Hence some might argue that historical-Jesus research should be abandoned because it is part of the problem rather than part of the solution. In my view, however, historical-Jesus research cannot be simply abandoned but must be critically evaluated.[38] It is necessary to engage in research of the historical-Jesus traditions, if one seeks to dislodge the exclusionist tendencies inscribed in the gospel portrait of Jesus or to correct the dogmatic layers of misinterpretation.

In addition, Jesus research must be critically assessed because in Western societies it is a discourse that affects a larger public. For historical-Jesus discourses are intertwined with hegemonic cultural and societal ideologies. As master narratives of Western cultures they are always implicated in and collude with the production and maintenance of systems of knowledge that either foster exploitation and oppression or contribute to a praxis and vision of emancipation and liberation.

Hence thinking about Jesus requires that we critically explore and assess the theoretical frameworks of historical-Jesus research that make "sense" of the world and produce what counts as "reality" or "common sense." Consequently, thinking about Jesus must make visible the contesting interests and theoretical frameworks that determine historical-Jesus articulations.

An Emancipatory Re-Visioning of the Historical-Jesus: Jesus as First among Equals in the *Basileia* Movement

What then can we say of Jesus? In this second part I attempt to use the results of historical-Jesus scholarship and the insights of its critics for telling the story of Jesus in an emancipatory frame. I do so from a critical feminist emancipatory perspective to help readers "to think of Jesus of Nazareth" in a new way. To correct the liberal-historical or orthodox-theological Eurocentric malestream framework of historical-Jesus research, which focuses on Jesus the great historical leader or divine man, I have suggested in my own work that research should replace the "realist" narrative of the historical Jesus as the great charismatic individual with an understanding of history in terms of memory. The category of memory includes that of "history-making," but it is much more comprehensive and more adequate to our source texts. While the canonical and extracanonical gospels all focus on Jesus, they do so from the perspective of their own time and place. They are not interested in antiquarian documentation but in the politics of meaning-making for their own audiences, in "thinking about Jesus."

The gospel transmitters and writers were not concerned with simply writing down what Jesus said and did; rather, they attempted to comprehend what Jesus meant to his first followers and what meaning his life and ministry had for their own time and communities. Most importantly, they had to come to terms with the shocking historical knowledge that Jesus was executed by the Romans as an insurrectionist and criminal. As a result, what we can learn from the process of their transmission and redaction is that Jesus — as we can still know him — must be remembered, discussed, interpreted, critiqued, accepted, or rejected if one wants to comprehend the impulse and importance of the Jesus movement. The gospels center on the life-praxis of Jesus and the movement carrying his name, which they sought to preserve as either a "dangerous" or a "status quo" memory.[39]

This attempt requires a pragmatic rhetorical understanding of language and a radical egalitarian model of historical reconstruction, I have argued. It is able not only to tell the story of Jesus as belonging to a Jewish emancipatory movement but also to place Jewish wo/men as agents at the center of its historiography. Hence, in my book *In Memory of Her* I was concerned to reconstruct the Jesus movement as an egalitarian Jewish movement of wo/men. I argued against topical studies on "wo/men and Jesus," which frame their research in terms of the cultural model of patriarchal romance[40] between the great man Jesus and his wo/men followers. Consequently, I sought to replace this historical-Jesus research framework, which takes the study of "Jesus and wo/men" as its object, with a feminist framework that focuses on wo/men as subjects of historical-Jesus reconstruction. Imaginatively adopting the perspective of biblical wo/men rather than just looking at them as fixed objects in texts in a fixed context, yields a different world and set of possibilities. Looking as a wo/man (that is, from a wo/man's social location) and looking from a feminist perspective (that is, with a hermeneutics of suspicion rooted in a feminist social analytic) is quite different from looking at a wo/man as an objectified research object.

New Assumptions for Historical Reconstruction

Undergirding my reconstructive historical model are four basic theoretical assumptions:

First, the hermeneutical practice of anti-Judaism is contrary to a Christian feminist theology of liberation because this historical assumption does not recognize that Jesus and his first followers were Jewish wo/men. They were *not Christian* in our sense of the word. Rather, as Jewish Galilean wo/men they gathered together for common meals, theological reflection, and healing events. They did so because they had a "dream" and followed a vision of liberation for every wo/man in Israel.

Second, who Jesus was and what he did can *only* be glimpsed in the interpretations and memory of the Jesus movement understood as a first-century Jewish movement. Therefore the Jesus movement must not be separated methodologically from other messianic movements in first-century Judaism. Moreover, one must keep in mind that just as there was no unified early Christianity, neither was there a single "orthodox" Judaism yet in the first century C.E.[41] Orthodox Judaism, like orthodox Christianity, emerged only in subsequent centuries.

Third, this emancipatory movement of Galilean Jewish wo/men must be seen as a part of the variegated *basileia* (empire or commonwealth) and holiness movements that in the first century sought the "liberation" of Israel from imperial exploitation. The concrete political referent of these movements was the colonial occupation of Israel by the Romans. Hence it is no accident that in this political context these movements invoked the covenant promise of Exodus 19:6. Some of them, such as the Pharisees or Essenes, stressed the notion of "priesthood and holy nation." Others, such as the apocalyptic prophetic movements — among them the Jesus movement — stressed the political notion of the *basileia* of G*d as alternative to the Roman Empire.

Fourth, the emerging, variegated, predominantly Galilean Jesus movement understood itself as a prophetic movement of Divine Sophia-Wisdom.[42] That it named itself after Jesus, the Christ, was probably due to the conviction that had emerged after Jesus's execution that he was the Anointed one who is now the Vindicated or Resurrected One. This conviction, I have argued in *Jesus, Miriam's Child and Sophia's Prophet,* had its base in the wo/men's tradition of the "empty tomb," which centered around the proclamation "that Jesus is *going ahead* of you to Galilee," the site where the antimonarchical prophetic traditions of the Northern Kingdom were still alive. This tradition manifests the self-understanding of the Jewish Galilean *basileia* (empire/commonweal) of G*d movement as an ongoing and inclusive movement of prophets and messengers sent to Israel by Divine Wisdom. The *basileia* movement is thus best understood as a Wisdom/Sophia movement in which Jesus is *primus inter pares,* that is first among equals.

Such an egalitarian reconstructive model, I submit, is able to place the beginnings of the Galilean prophetic-Wisdom *basileia* movement within a broader universalizing historical frame of reference. This frame allows one to trace the tensions and struggles between emancipatory understandings and movements in antiquity inspired by the democratic logic of equality on the one hand and the dominant kyriarchal structures of society and religion on the other.

Ancient movements of emancipatory struggle against kyriarchal relations of exploitation do not begin with the Jesus movement. Rather, they have a long history in Greek, Roman, Asian, and Jewish cultures.[43] The emancipatory struggles of biblical wo/men must be seen within the wider context of cultural-political-religious struggles. Such an historical model of emancipatory struggle sees the historical Jesus and the movement that has kept alive his memory not over and against Judaism but over and against kyriarchal structures of domination in antiquity.

Such a reconstructive frame of reference, I submit, is able to conceptualize the emergent Jesus movement and its diverse articulations as participating in popular movements of cultural, political, and religious resistance. The resurrection of Jesus means that he is not just a memory, albeit a "dangerous" one. Rather, it means that he is the Living One who is "going ahead" as a "path finder" in the emancipatory struggles for a world of justice, liberation, and freedom from kyriarchal oppression. He is "going ahead" in wo/men's struggles to "mend the world."

Yet to speak about the Jesus movement as an inner-Jewish renewal movement, as I have done in *In Memory of Her,* still provokes several misunderstandings between Jews and Christians. This, of course, I did not intend. Rather, I had in mind such movements as Call to Action or the Wo/men's Ordination Conference in Post–Vatican II Catholicism who struggle for the renewal of Catholicism. Nevertheless, Jacob Neusner has rightly pointed out that the notion of "renewal" still carries traces of supersessionism insofar as it suggests that Christianity is a "better" form of Judaism. In other words, the notion of a reform movement still can be made to fit into the hegemonic Christian construct of the *Judeo-Christian* tradition, which posits a supersessionist continuity between Judaism and Christianity.[44] Only if one explicitly acknowledges that Judaism and Christianity are two different religions which have their roots in the Hebrew Bible and in the pluriform religious matrix of first-century Israel, can one avoid reading "renewal movement" in a supersessionist fashion. As Alan Segal has aptly put it: Early Judaism and Christianity are Rebecca's children, twin siblings of the same mother.[45]

Moreover, to speak about the Jesus movement as an inner-Jewish renewal movement of the first century can be and has been further misread as implying that the Jesus movement was the *only* reform movement at the time and that Jewish or Greek wo/men who did not join this movement suffered from a "false consciousness."[46] Furthermore, if read in a preconstructed frame of meaning that maintains the uniqueness of Jesus, the expression "renewal movement" suggests not only Christian particularity and exceptionality but also superiority. For that reason, one cannot stress enough that the Jesus movement must be understood as *one among several prophetic* movements of Jewish wo/men who struggled for the liberation of Israel. As a result, I have replaced the notion of "renewal movement" with the concept of the Jesus movement as an emancipatory movement.

Jesus and the Basileia Movement

The central symbol of this movement, the *basileia* of G*d,[47] expresses a Jewish religious-political vision that spells freedom from domination and is common to all the different movements in first-century Israel. As I have pointed out, it is difficult to translate the Greek term *basileia* adequately because it can either mean kingdom, kingly realm, domain or empire, or it can be rendered as monarchy, kingly rule, sovereignty, dominion, and reign. In any case it has not only monarchic but also masculinist overtones.

According to Dalmann, the Hebrew equivalent of *malkuth* when applied to G*d always means kingly rule and has never had the territorial sense of kingdom. Following him, most exegetes translate *basileia* with "kingly reign" and understand it as G*d's all-overpowering initiative and sovereign ruling. Moreover, most reviews of scholarship on the meaning of the expression *basileia* of G*d do not even discuss its political significance in a context where people must have thought of the Roman empire when they heard the word.

To lift the political meaning of *basileia* into consciousness, I suggest that it is best translated with words such as *empire, domain* or *commonweal.* Such renderings of the word *basileia* underscore linguistically the oppositional character of the empire or commonweal of G*d to that of the Roman empire. Since such a translation is generally not understood in an oppositional sense, however, but as ascribing to G*d imperial monarchic power, I have tended *not* to translate the Greek word *basileia* but to use it as a tensive symbol that evokes a whole range of theological meanings and at the same time seeks to foster a critical awareness of their ambiguity. The translation of the term with *kindom* that has been suggested by Ada María Isasi-Díaz also loses the political overtones of *basileia.* Such a symbolic rendering of the term seeks to bring to the fore its political impact and eschatological significance in the first century C.E. while at the same time problematizing its kyriarchal politics of meaning.

Exegetes agree that the Roman form of imperial domination signified by the term *basileia* has determined the world and experience of all Jewish movements in the first century, including that which named itself after Jesus. Jesus and his first followers, wo/men and men, sought for the emancipation and well-being of Israel as the people of G*d, a kingdom of priests and a holy nation (Exod. 19:6). They announced the *basileia* of G*d as an alternative to that of Rome.

The *basileia* of G*d is a *tensive* religious symbol[48] not only of ancestral range proclaiming G*d's power of creation and salvation. This term was also a political symbol that appealed to the oppositional imagination of people victimized by the Roman imperial system. It envisions an alternative world free of hunger, poverty, and domination. This "envisioned" world is already anticipated in the inclusive table-sharing, in the healing and liberating practices, as well as in the domination-free kinship community of the Jesus movement, which found many followers among the poor, the despised, the ill and possessed, the outcasts, prostitutes, and sinners.[49]

The story of the Jesus movement as emancipatory *basileia* of G*d movement is told in different ways in the canonical and extracanonical gospel accounts. These accounts have undergone a lengthy process of rhetorical transmission and theological editing. The gospel writers were not concerned with antiquarian historical transcription but with interpretive remembrance and rhetorical persuasion.

They did not simply want to write down what Jesus said and did. Rather, they utilized the Jesus traditions, which were shaped by Jesus's first followers, women and men, for their own rhetorical interests and molded them in light of the political-theological debates of their own day. As a result, what we can learn from the rhetorical process of gospel transmission and redaction is that Jesus as we still can know him must be re-membered, contextualized, discussed, interpreted, questioned, or rejected not only within an intertheological and interfaith context but also within a political-cultural debate.

However, one must be careful not to construe the Jesus movement as free from conflict and kyriarchal tendencies, lest in so doing one idealizes it as the very "other" and positive counterpart of Judaism understood negatively. From the very beginnings of the Jesus movement differences, divisions, and conflicts existed, as the variegated if not contradictory articulations of the extant gospels indicate. For instance, the varicolored *basileia* sayings tradition that surfaces in Mark 10:42–45 and 9:33–37 par. is an antikyriarchal rhetorical tradition that contrasts the political structures of domination with those required among the disciples.[50] Structures of domination should not be tolerated in the discipleship of equals, but those of the disciples who would-be-great and would-be-first must become slaves and servants[51] of all. While this tradition advocates nonkyriarchal relationships in the discipleship of equals, its grammatical imperative simultaneously documents that such relationships were not lived by everyone. Especially, the would-be "great" and "first" seem to have been tempted to reassert kyriarchal social and religious status positions. The argument of the Syrophoenician wo/man[52] provides another example for such debates, since this story criticizes the ethnic bias of Jesus himself.

One also must not overlook that all four gospel accounts reflect the controversies with and separation anxieties from hegemonic forms of Judaism. Consequently, they all reinscribe Christian identity as standing in conflict with Judaism. A good example of this kyriocentric process of anti-Jewish and anti-wo/man inscription can be found when one traces the transmission history of the story about the wo/man who anointed Jesus as the Christ. The Gospel of Mark places this story at the beginning of the narrative about Jesus' execution and resurrection.[53] Here Mark probably takes up a traditional story that knows of a wo/man anointing Jesus's head and thereby naming him as the Christ, the Anointed One.[54] A revelatory word of Jesus links her prophetic sign action with the proclamation of the gospel in the whole world.[55] The community that retells this story after Jesus' execution knows that Jesus is no longer in their midst. They do no longer "have" Jesus with them.

Either in the course of the transmission of this story or at the editorial stage, three kyriocentric interpretations of the wo/man's prophetic sign-action are introduced. First, the objection and debate with the male disciples introduces a kyriarchal understanding that sees "the poor" no longer as constitutive members of the community but as "the others," as people who deserve alms. The second interpretation construes the unnamed wo/man's sign-action in feminine kyriocentric terms: she does what wo/men are supposed to do, prepare the bodies of the dead for burial.[56] Finally, the third interpretation reframes the story as an ideo-story or example story that counterposes the action of the wo/man to that of Judas, the betrayer of Jesus.[57]

Insofar as the wo/man disciple remains unnamed whereas the male disciple who betrays Jesus is named Judas, the text evokes not only an androcentric response that, contrary to the word of Jesus, does not comprehend the significance of the wo/man's prophetic naming. By underscoring that the name of the betrayer is Judas, a name that linguistically reminds one of "Jew/Judaism," it elicits an anti-Jewish response that is intensified in the course of the passion narrative. Thus, we still can trace the gospels' anti-Jewish rhetorics in the reinterpretations of the anointing story, a story that was potentially a politically dangerous story. The depoliticizing rhetoric which comes here to the fore has engendered not only anti-Jewish interpretations of Jesus' suffering and execution but also has forged Christian political adaptation to Roman imperial structures that with its apologetic defense of the Roman authorities opened the door to the cooptation of the gospel in the interest of domination.

Since the process of the kyriarchal reinterpretation of the story in the gospels has produced the "preconstructed," by now, common sense, kyriocentric frame of meaning that marginalizes wo/men and vilifies Jews, it is necessary to dislodge our readings from such a preconstructed frame of reference and to reconfigure the Christian Testament discourses about

Jesus. Constructing the Jesus movement as one among many *emancipatory movements* in the first century, I have argued here and elsewhere, provides such a different historical frame of reference. It allows for a Christian self-understanding that is neither articulated over and against Judaism nor remains intertwined with theological masculinism. Such a christological rereading does not need to relinquish the quest for its historical Jewish roots nor end in Christian supremacy and exclusivism. It does not tie Christian self-identity to its previous stages of formation and their sociocultural contexts but remains obligated to the messianic *basileia* — the vision of G*d's alternative world of justice and salvation.

For Further Reflection

1. Can we know the historical Jesus? According to the author, what problems impede recovering a true picture of the historical Jesus?

2. How would you characterize each of the three successive "quests" for the historical Jesus? What is new in the Third Quest?

3. How does the search for a valid understanding of the historical figure of Jesus reflect the social functions of modern science? How do feminist studies critique this development?

4. How does the author herself reconstruct the figure of Jesus? How does her own reconstruction answer objections to previous reconstructions?

For Further Reading

Borg, Marcus J. *Jesus in Contemporary Scholarship.* Valley Forge, Pa.: Trinity Press International, 1994.

Fiorenza, Elisabeth Schüssler. *In Memory of Her: A Feminist Theological Reconstruction of Christian Origins.* New York: Crossroad, 1994.

———. *Jesus, Miriam's Child, Sophia's Prophet: Critical Issues in Feminist Christology.* New York: Continuum, 1994.

Harrisville, Roy A., and Walter Sundberg. *The Bible in Modern Culture: Theology and Historical-Critical Method from Spinoza to Käsemann.* Grand Rapids, Mich.: Eerdmans, 1995.

Theissen, Gerd, and Annette Merz. *The Historical Jesus: A Comprehensive Guide.* Minneapolis: Fortress, 1998.

— 3 —

Classical Christology

William P. Loewe

Around 111 C.E. Pliny the Younger, Roman proconsul in the province of Bithynia in Asia Minor, wrote to the Emperor Trajan to report how he was handling Christians who had been denounced to him. In the course of his letter he describes the curious customs of this troublesome group. Among them he lists their practice of gathering before dawn on a fixed day of the week to sing hymns "to Christ as to a god."[1] Within the New Testament three late texts explicitly call Jesus God. Two of these are in the Gospel of John. The Prologue to that gospel draws on the Hebrew symbol of God's Word to draw out Jesus' religious significance. Its first verse proclaims that "In the beginning was the Word, and the Word was with God, and the Word was God" (John 1:1). At the end of the same gospel the story is told of the risen Jesus' appearance to "doubting Thomas." Thomas, absent when the Lord had appeared a week earlier to the rest of the twelve, had refused to believe them, saying that unless he could see and touch Jesus' wounds, he would not believe. Then, invited by Jesus to do precisely that, he reacts with an exclamation: "My Lord and my God!" (John 20:28). Somewhat less dramatically the Letter to the Hebrews has God address the Son in the words of Psalm 45:6, "Your throne, O God, is forever and ever" (Heb. 1:8). Jesus and his first followers were Jews, and so this naming of Jesus as God can seem like a startling development. After all, the Jews were regarded as misfits within the Roman Empire for their odd and stubborn insistence that there was only one God. Jesus and his first followers no doubt followed the practice of fervently reciting the *Shema*:

> Hear, O Israel: The Lord is our God, the Lord alone. You shall love the Lord your God with all your heart, and with all your soul, and with all your might (Deut. 6:4–5).

If one recalls this devout Jewish monotheism, it must seem strange that Jesus' followers eventually came to call him God.

Yet these texts, although late in the formation of the New Testament, represent a development continuous with even the earliest christological patterns.[2] A so-called *parousia* Christology focused on the imminent return of Jesus, the coming Son of Man, who would exercise the divine prerogative of judgment. A pre-Pauline hymn preserved in Philippians 2:6–11 has God reward Jesus' obedience unto death by exalting him and conferring on him God's own name, Lord. Another pre-Pauline fragment found in Romans 1:3–4 has Jesus established as Son of God in power at the resurrection, pouring forth the spirit of holiness that texts in the Hebrew scriptures expected as God's gift in the last days. The Prologue to the Gospel of John, while it substitutes God's Word for the figure of Lady Wisdom, continues a very early pattern that found in Jesus the embodiment of God's own wisdom.

These brief allusions indicate that as the New Testament developed the Christian religious imagination was taking on a determinate shape. The hymns preserved in this literature suggest that in liturgical ritual Christians raised their hearts and minds to God and to the figure around whom they reconfigured Israel's story of God's creative and redemptive history, Jesus. They found themselves imaging Jesus, whose earthly ministry and fate they recalled, as exercising God's functions, sharing God's royal prerogatives and bearing God's name. If their Jewish heritage taught them to draw a sharp line between the transcendent God and all that God had created, they found themselves locating the man Jesus, whom God had raised from the dead, on the "wrong" side of that line. In all this the New Testament suggests that especially on the basis of their liturgical experience and through the symbolic narratives with which they sought to express and evoke Jesus' significance these early generations of Christians felt compelled to somehow broaden the notion of God to include not only the one to whom Jesus had prayed but also Jesus himself.

But if they did indeed "sing hymns to Christ as to a god," nonetheless, confessing Jesus as divine is one thing, while thinking through coherently what this involves is quite another matter. This task the New Testament bequeathed to future generations. Specifically, two questions arose. How can the Father be one, the Son another, both be divine, and yet there be only one God? And second, if the man Jesus be confessed as truly divine, how is the union of the divine and human in him to be conceived without doing violence to one or the other? The literature of the ensuing era, the patristic age, documents a centuries-long process of trial and error in which first the one, then the other of these questions was addressed. From this process emerged the classical doctrines of the Councils of Nicea (325), Chalcedon (451), and III Constantinople (681). These councils set a pattern that would dominate Christian thinking about Jesus for the next millennium and a half.

The Way to Nicea[3]

To make sense of the development of classical christological doctrine, we can begin by taking a long jump forward, from the close of the New Testament to the Council of Nicea in the fourth century. The council was summoned by the Emperor Constantine. At Nicea the bishops in attendance doctored a profession of faith, a creedal formula that was already in use, by adding several phrases and appending several curses. The phrases they added spoke of Jesus as "true God of true God, begotten not made, one in being with the Father." And they pronounced that "If anyone say that there was a time when he was not, let him be *anathema*." All this was in response to an Egyptian presbyter from Alexandria named Arius, who apparently was popularizing the opposite of those added phrases. The outcome of the council was the definition of the classical doctrine of the divinity of Christ.

To appreciate what was going on at Nicea, we want to suggest that Arius brought to a head an ambiguity that ran through previous Christian thought about Jesus. He had the merit of bringing this ambiguity out into the open, and he resolved it, though his solution was rejected. To understand Nicea's doctrine, we need to understand first of all what the ambiguity was that Arius exposed, and then why his solution was rejected.

At the close of the New Testament, a double task faced the Christian movement. One aspect of that task was cultural. Christianity had begun as a Jewish sect, but even within the period of the formation of the New Testament efforts were underway to articulate Jesus' religious significance in terms that could engage and communicate with the broader Hellenistic culture of the Roman Empire. Thus, for example, the Jewish apocalyptic mindset and Jewish titles like messiah and Son of Man soon found a complement in other patterns and other titles. The other aspect of the task facing the Christian movement was imposed, we saw, by their practice of honoring Jesus as divine. How was that practice compatible with the strong conviction of their Jewish heritage that there is but one God?

One path to a solution to the problem generated by confessing the man Jesus as divine lay in denying one term or the other of the tension. *Adoptionists*, for example, rested content to view Jesus as a human being whom God favored with an exceptionally rich outpouring of God's spirit. Such views have been labeled *psilanthropism*, from the Greek for "merely human." *Monarchians*, on the other hand, denied that the Son was really distinct from the Father. On their view God had been revealed as Father in the history of Israel, while God's revelation in the New Testament was under a different modality, namely as Son. Father and Son were but different modalities of the one God's self-revelation in history.

Oddly enough from a modern viewpoint, it was Jesus' humanity that proved problematic in *Gnosticism*, a complex religious movement that threatened to engulf Christianity in the second century. Convinced of the radical opposition of spirit to flesh, Gnostics conceived salvation as deliverance from the sordidness of the material world. Their myths pictured a heavenly redeemer sent from above to impart true knowledge, the liberating message that one's destiny lay in the realm of the spiritual and divine. The gospel accounts of Jesus' conception, birth, suffering, and death meant only that Christ "seemed" to be a human being and "appeared" to suffer and die. Hence the name *docetism,* from the Greek verb "to seem," for these views. Ignatius of Antioch and Irenaeus of Lyons wrote against them.

In addition to these various ways of relaxing the tension inherent in Christian liturgical practice another path opened up when the image of Jesus as God's *Logos* proffered by John's Prologue came to the forefront. It had the merit of bridging the Jewish and Hellenistic worlds. On the Jewish side, translated as "Word," it designated the medium through which God created and interacted with history. The Tanakh or Jewish scripture told how God created with a word of command and how God guided Israel by sending God's word to the prophets. On the Hellenistic side, translated as "reason," it represented the Stoic notion of a principle of order immanent to the universe. Its seeds, *logoi spermatikoi,* were to be found in every human mind. With this dual background the Johannine image of Jesus as God's *Logos* became a vehicle for christological development. A review of that process as it moved through three Christian thinkers, namely, Justin Martyr, Tertullian, and Origen, will lead us to Arius and the Council of Nicea.

Around the middle of the second century Justin, a wandering philosopher from the Middle East, established himself at Rome. After inquiring into several of the philosophies of the day Justin had become a Christian, but he continued to wear the distinctive garb of the philosopher, a calling that enjoyed high status in the culture of the Roman Empire. Contemplation of the eternal and unchanging was deemed the highest human pursuit.

To commend Christianity at Rome Justin presented it as the true philosophy, and in a culture that prized antiquity and despised novelty, he devised an ancient lineage for Christianity. Christianity was the true philosophy that recapitulated, corrected, and completed what was found in both the Old Testament and among Greek philosophers. Central to this proposal was the notion of Christ as the *Logos* incarnate. If the Old Testament contained a partial, intermittent revelation of God's *Logos,* and if Greek philosophy represented an imperfect human grasp of it (though Justin also argued that the philosophers had "borrowed" some of their insights from Moses), Christianity received its doctrine directly from the *Logos'* lips. It thus embraced what was good in both Judaism and Greek philosophy while superseding them. In Justin, then, the notion of Jesus as God's *Logos* provided a bridge over which Christianity could advance to engage the Hellenistic culture of Rome.

A century later we find in North Africa the figure of Tertullian, perhaps a lawyer, the first major Christian thinker to write in Latin. Important for his writings against the Gnostics, Tertullian eventually joined the rigorously ascetic Montanist sect. In addressing the question that the Christian practice of according divine worship to Christ raised, Tertullian takes a double approach. First, what defines God is power, the *monarchia,* and this power belongs properly to the Father. The Father in turn confers on the Son a share in the exercise of his power, but this no more divides or diminishes it than the imperial power is divided or diminished when the emperor appoints a governor. Thus the Father is one, the Son another, both are divine in exercising the divine *monarchia,* and yet that power remains one and undivided.

But what of the origin of the Son from the Father? For Tertullian only the Father is God from all eternity, and what makes him God is that he is made of *spiritus,* divine stuff, the divine grade of matter. When the Father decides to create, he first extrudes his *Logos,* through whom, as the Johannine Prologue says, all else is then created. Again it follows that the Father is one, the Son another, and yet both are divine because they are made of *spiritus,* yet there remains only the one batch of divine stuff. It also follows, however, that while both are divine, the Son is not so divine as the Father. He receives a share in the exercise of the divine power that belongs properly to the Father, and unlike the Father, the Son is not eternal.

Moving from the Latin West to the Greek East we encounter the figure of Origen, a contemporary of Tertullian in the middle of the third century. Origen's brilliance and originality as biblical commentator, apologist, and systematic theologian place him in the ranks of such giants of Christian thought as Augustine, Thomas Aquinas, and Martin Luther.

While Tertullian could only imagine spirit as a fine grade of matter, Origen grasps the real difference between them. Further, if God is spirit and not matter, and if both Father and Son are divine, the Son must likewise be eternal. Origen proposes a psychological analogy for the origin of the Son: the Son proceeds eternally from the Father in a nonmaterial fashion similar to the way in which an act of willing proceeds from the will.

Nonetheless Origen can also affirm that if the Son is Wisdom itself, the Father is beyond Wisdom, and that the Son does not know the Father as the Father knows himself. Thus for Origen as well as for Tertullian, while both Father and Son are divine, the Son is not so divine as the Father. For Origen the Father is divine in himself, while the Son participates in the divinity of the Father. What emerges in both Tertullian and Origen is *subordinationism,* the idea that the divinity of the Son is inferior to that of the Father.

The explanation for this trend lies in the philosophical baggage that these Christian thinkers picked up along with the Hellenistic notion of *Logos.* This explains, for instance, how Tertullian could think of the Son as divine and yet not eternal. Stoic philosophy, a form of materialism, informed his thinking in a wholly unreflective, taken for granted manner. Thus for Tertullian so long as the Son was made of *spiritus,* divine stuff, that was sufficient to ensure his divinity.

A different brand of Hellenistic philosophy functions similarly in Origen. Spontaneously thinking in terms of a contemporary version of Platonism, a metaphysical idealism, Origen locates the Father in a realm of total mystery that lies beyond rationality and intelligibility. These find their source on a level one step below the Father in the *Logos* which emanates eternally from the Father. The *Logos* in this Platonic scheme is divine, but only by participation, and hence inferior to the Father.

In both Tertullian and Origen, Hellenistic philosophical assumptions have crept unnoticed into Christian thought, and the outcome in each case is subordinationism. The ambiguity inherent in the notion of attributing an inferior degree of divinity to the Son defines the scene when Arius arrives. A presbyter of the church of Alexandria, his background lies in Origen's thought. Origen's Platonism lent itself to a view of reality as a ladder on which the top step was God, with each further step emanating from the one above and participating in it. On this view God becomes part of a larger whole, the universe, and the biblical insight into God's transcendence is lost. For the Bible, being divine is not a matter of more or less. God is God, and all else is not God but God's creation.

Against this background Arius demanded that a spade be called a spade. If the Son or *Logos* was not fully divine, then it was really not divine at all. The *Logos* was God's first creature, the blueprint according to which God created all else, a cosmological first principle. Taking on flesh in time, this cosmological first principle became incarnate in Jesus. For Arius, it seemed self-evident that Jesus was not divine because for him the divine was by definition incapable of change, while Jesus clearly moved in the realm of this changeable world and indeed showed us how to live in such a world. Yet Jesus was not really fully human either, since the *Logos* functioned in him in place of a human soul.

Arius's resolution of the ambiguity that had attended *Logos* Christologies since Justin was perfectly coherent. At the same time, however, it represented a triumph of Hellenistic thought over Christianity. A major reason for Arius's refusal to consider Jesus "true God of true God" was his very Greek repugnance at associating the divine with a world of change. On Arius's solution God was left untroubled in the realm of divine transcendence when the nondivine *Logos* took flesh. Hence, while the bishops gathered at Nicea would not have put it this way, what was at stake with Arius was the structure of Christian religious experience. One way of understanding this assertion is as follows.

First, during Jesus' lifetime, and in a different fashion after his death and resurrection, some people encountered another human being, a first-century

Jew, Jesus of Nazareth, and in response to his message and activity they
underwent *metanoia*, conversion. In encountering this human being, Jesus
of Nazareth, they also encountered the reality of the one true God, the one
to whom Jesus prayed and addressed as "Abba."

Second, on the basis of this experience those who had undergone it could
reflect on what had been happening: through Jesus of Nazareth the one
true God had been expressing, revealing, giving, and communicating God's
own self to them. In that case, third, they could proceed to affirm with
regard to Jesus himself that this human being was at the same time God's
self-communication, God's self-expression, God's self-revelation, God's own
Word. And fourthly, if God really is as God reveals God's self to be, then
this man Jesus is identical with God's eternal self-expression, God's Word.

In confessing Jesus as "true God of true God, begotten, not made, one
in being with the Father," Nicea affirmed that Jesus is divine as God's self-
expression, as the Word that proceeds from God, as Son of the one that
Jesus called Father. For Arius, on the other hand, when we encounter Jesus
we do not encounter God's own self-expression, but rather a mythic figure,
a cosmological principle clothed with flesh, one who is neither divine nor
human, and this leaves God remote, untouched, and untouchable in the infinite distance separating the realm of the transcendent from this world. What
is at stake between Arius and Nicea is the structure of Christian religious
experience whereby Jesus is Emmanuel, God-with-us.

With hindsight Nicea is counted as the first ecumenical (or whole) council
of the Christian church, but participants at the time did not realize this. In
fact, once the council was over, its formula of belief was widely rejected.
One reason for this was its use of the term "one in being" (*homoousios*) to
characterize the relation of Jesus' divinity to that of the Father. The term
was first found among the Gnostics, and some took it to mean something
like what we saw of Tertullian's position, that Jesus and the Father were
made of the same stuff, and so they rejected what looked like a claim that
God was material and divisible.

Only eventually and in the course of a great deal of political intrigue did
Athanasius, who became patriarch of Alexandria after the council, win over
Nicea's opponents. On his interpretation Nicea's *homoousios* establishes a
rule for speaking correctly about God as Father and Son. It means that
whatever you can say about the Father, you can also say about the Son and
vice versa, except what is proper to being Father or Son. Thus, if you can say
that the Father is eternal, omnipotent, etc., so also for the Son. But if you can
say that the Son is only-begotten, you cannot say this of the Father, because
being only-begotten is proper to the Son. This explanation of what it means
to say that Father and Son are "one in being" remains a rule for speaking
correctly; it does not offer an explanation, and much less a picture, of how

God can be both Father and Son. If Christian religious experience leads to this affirmation, it does not penetrate the mystery of God to explain it.

We may note that in the period of controversy and intrigue prior to the eventual acceptance of the Nicene confession[4] the older subordinationism enjoyed greater political expediency. The emperor's legitimacy could only gain if, just as on earth, there was in heaven one single ruler to which all else was subordinate. Nicea's profession of faith clashed with the imperial system inasmuch as it imaged ultimate reality not as a solitary ruler but as a communion of equals.

From Nicea to Chalcedon[5]

Nicea's acceptance was sealed at the First Council of Constantinople (381 C.E.). Ironically enough that same council issued a condemnation of one of Nicea's staunchest champions, Apollinaris of Laodicea. Even more ironically, it was precisely Apollinaris's fervent devotion to the full and complete divinity of Christ that, once certain philosophical assumptions came into play, landed him in a position that joined Arius in denying the existence of a human soul in Christ. On Apollinaris's philosophical assumptions, two wholes cannot form a single whole; two already complete beings, divinity and humanity, cannot coalesce into unity. To ensure the unity of Christ, therefore, one of his components must be regarded as incomplete and finding its completion in the other. Apollinaris theorized that, in becoming incarnate, the Word took a human body without a human soul, so that in Christ the Word substituted for the spiritual soul. Hence the incarnation can be adequately described as the union of the divine Word with living flesh.

What drove Apollinaris's reflection was a concern to ensure Christ's total sinlessness and utter conformity to the divine will. If Christ were to have a human intellect and will, he would enjoy freedom of decision, but this would put the divine plan of salvation at risk, making it dependent on Christ's human good will. Hence, to safeguard Christ's goodness and to ensure the certainty of redemption, Apollinaris argued that Christ must have been subject to transience only in his organic material being. His spiritual thinking and willing were unalterable, for they were divine. He had but a single intellect, a single will, a single consciousness, those of the divine Word. Thus Christ was a "heavenly human," insofar as he derived his flesh from Mary, but only that.

For all his good intentions, Apollinaris rendered Christ less than human by denying him a spiritual, rational soul. This in turn drained the incarnation and redemption of significance. Lacking a human soul, Christ was not like us and thus could be neither the exemplar of humankind nor the model of every virtue; his presence among us could not redeem, purify, and divinize our souls. Such was the line of criticism relentlessly pursued by the Cappadocian theologians, for whom it was axiomatic that what Christ has not assumed, he has not healed.

Condemned at I Constantinople, Apollinaris represented the extreme limit of the theological spirit that characterized a line of thinkers centered at Alexandria in Egypt. These theologians were taken by the idea that with Jesus' coming, God was at work to save the human race. Hence they stressed the oneness of the divine with the human in Jesus, using the language of the Prologue to John to speak of Jesus in terms of *Logos* and flesh. For the Alexandrians, the divine self of the *Logos* is the subject of the incarnation and remains the single subject of Christ's actions as both God and human. With their emphasis on Christ's unity, however, they found it difficult to do justice to Jesus' full humanity. For Clement of Alexandria, for instance, it was unthinkable that Jesus would have had to go to the bathroom.

In reaction to this Alexandrian tendency a different spirit developed at Antioch in Syria. Theodore of Mopsuestia was sharply critical of the Alexandrian Word/flesh schema. He insisted that at the incarnation the Word assumed not just a body but a complete human being, body and soul. Christ's human nature rendered him capable of growth in knowledge and experience. Theodore often describes Christ as "the man assumed," and while this language can give the impression of positing a duality between the Word and Christ, Theodore rejects that idea and argues that a distinction of natures does not prevent their being one individual. His chief weakness, however, lies in accounting for the unity of Christ. He often resorts to the imagery of indwelling: the Word dwelt in the humanity of Christ as in a temple, effecting a conjunction of the two natures which, though different, find unity in a single person (*prosopon*).

One hundred years after his death, the doctrine of Theodore of Mopsuestia would be condemned at the Second Council of Constantinople in 553. That condemnation stemmed from events set in motion by Theodore's pupil, Nestorius. A presbyter of Antioch, Nestorius was chosen by Emperor Theodosius II to become patriarch of the imperial see of Constantinople. Christians there had been quarreling over a fit title for Mary, mother of Jesus. Alexandrians honored her as *Theotokos,* God-bearer or Mother of God, and Antiochenes objected: Mary was mother of Jesus' humanity, and to call her Mother of God threatened the integrity of that humanity. In his sermons for Christmastide in 428 the new patriarch suggested that she be called *Christotokos,* Mother of Christ, but he also made clear the Antiochene character of his theology and ridiculed the notion that God could have a mother.

These sermons were reported to Cyril, patriarch of Alexandria, and he saw in them an opportunity to promote Alexandria's preeminence over the churches of the East by undermining Antioch's theological independence and minimizing the prestige of the new imperial capital, Constantinople. This ambition led Cyril to read Nestorius in the worst possible light. If Nestorius recognized Mary as Mother of Christ but not Mother of God then, Cyril reasoned, Nestorius was dividing Jesus into two persons, the divine Son and the human Christ, and teaching that the latter, because of his outstanding holiness, merited to have the Son dwell in him in a particularly full manner.

None of this was what Nestorius actually intended, but his infelicitous articulation of the conjunction of Christ's two natures in a single *prosopon* made him vulnerable to Cyril's reading. By *prosopon* he seemed to mean an individual considered from the point of view of his or her outward aspect or form (the term actually derives from Greek drama, where it designates a mask employed by a character). On philosophical grounds Nestorius took it for granted that for a nature to exist as a concrete reality, it required a *prosopon*. In that case the reality of the two natures in Christ demanded that each continue to exist in its own *prosopon,* while their coalescence resulted in a third "*prosopon* of the union," Christ, identical with neither the *prosopon* of the Word nor that of the humanity. Betrayed by his reliance on a Stoic analysis of the concrete existent, Nestorius lent verbal support to Cyril's charge that he split Christ and the Word in two.

Cyril launched his attack on Nestorius with a sharp exchange of letters. He also sent his analysis of Nestorius's position to Celestine, the bishop of Rome, who called a synod there that quickly decided against Nestorius. Celestine entrusted Cyril with the task of calling Nestorius to order. Among the letters Cyril sent Nestorius was one that listed twelve propositions, provocative in language and unacceptable from an Antiochene perspective, to which Nestorius was to submit. He refused, and the Emperor convened an ecumenical council at Ephesus in 431 C.E.

The proceedings of this council were highly confused and irregular. Taking advantage of the delayed arrival of the Antiochenes, Cyril had an assembly of bishops favorable to himself condemn Nestorius and canonize Cyril's second letter to the latter, in which the phrase *Theotokos* occurred, as an official commentary on the faith of Nicea. At Ephesus a canon was also passed forbidding anyone to add to the faith of Nicea. When John of Antioch and his bishops arrived, they held a council of their own and condemned Cyril. Eventually the papal legates endorsed Cyril's meeting, and thus Nestorius was condemned. After two years of mutual excommunication, Antiochenes and Alexandrians were reunited through the acceptance by both sides of a creedal formula contained in a letter of John of Antioch to Cyril and endorsed verbatim by him in a letter of his own entitled "Let the heavens rejoice." The formula spoke of the "union of two natures" in "one *prosopon*" while emphasizing the distinctness of the natures after the union. It also identified the subject in Christ as the eternal *Logos* and accorded Mary the title *Theotokos*. The end of the schism in the East involved a compromise by both parties. Cyril abandoned his ambition to impose the

Alexandrian theology on the entire East, while the Antiochenes accepted the deposition of Nestorius.

Tension between the two parties erupted again a decade and a half later. Flavian, patriarch of Constantinople, was conducting a local synod when an accusation of heresy was lodged against Eutyches, an archimandrite and favorite of the imperial household. In response Flavian reluctantly brought Eutyches to trial. In the course of the proceedings Eutyches refused to accept the creedal formula mutually accepted in 433 and stubbornly insisted on the phrase "after the union, one incarnate nature," a phrase which he had received from Cyril and which, unbeknownst to Cyril, had originated with Apollinaris. While in Cyril's usage the phrase simply meant that Christ was a single concrete individual, human and divine, Eutyches seemed to take it to mean that, though there were two natures prior to the incarnation, after the incarnation there was but one, the human being absorbed by the divine.

After his condemnation Eutyches fled to Alexandria, where Dioscorus had succeeded Cyril as patriarch. Flavian reported the proceedings of the trial to Rome, and Pope Leo responded approvingly with a letter known as the "Tome of Leo" in which he affirmed the completeness of Christ's two natures. Meanwhile, however, Dioscorus, who it turns out had engineered Eutyches' trial through his agents at Constantinople, used the condemnation of the emperor's favorite to persuade Theodosius that a new council was needed. In 449 Dioscorus presided over the "Robber Synod of Ephesus," at which, having refused to allow the papal legates to read Leo's Tome, he rehabilitated Eutyches. Flavian found himself condemned on a technicality: by insisting that Eutyches subscribe to the Formula of Reunion of 433, he was alleged to have violated the canon of the Council of Ephesus that prohibited adding to the faith of Nicea. Flavian died shortly thereafter, the result of a beating at the hands of some of Dioscorus's deacons.[6] Other major Antiochene bishops were deposed from their sees, and it seemed that Dioscorus had succeeded in making the Alexandrian dream of hegemony over the eastern part of the church a reality.

Upon the return of his legates, Leo began asking Theodosius to convene another council to undo the mischief Dioscorus had wrought. Theodosius, however, turned a deaf ear, and so the matter stood until, one day, his horse threw him and he died. His sister Pulcheria followed him on the throne. She and her husband, Marcian, began restoring the Antiochene bishops to their sees. In 451 C.E., with Leo's now reluctant consent, they convened the Fourth Ecumenical Council, first at Nicea and then closer to the capital, at Chalcedon. Sensing that the wind was turning against him, Dioscorus remained defiant; en route to Chalcedon he excommunicated Leo. At Chalcedon, however, he found himself isolated and abandoned. The bishops endorsed Leo's *Tome* enthusiastically. When the imperial couple requested a new confession of faith the council fathers at first refused, citing the canon passed at Ephesus. Under further pressure they composed a draft to which the papal legates strongly objected, causing it to be sent back to committee. The definition of faith that finally emerged marks the climax of christological development in the ancient church. After reiterating the creeds of Nicea and I Constantinople it continues:

Confession of faith

> So, following the saintly fathers, we all with one voice teach the confession of one and the same Son, our Lord Jesus Christ: the same perfect in divinity and perfect in humanity, the same truly God and truly man, of a rational soul and a body; consubstantial with the Father as regards his divinity, and the same consubstantial with us as regards his humanity; like us in all respects except for sin; begotten before the ages from the Father as regards his divinity, and in the last days the same for us and for our salvation from Mary, the virgin God-bearer, as regards his humanity; one and the same Christ, Son, Lord, only-begotten, acknowledged in two natures which undergo no confusion, no change, no division, no separation; at no point was the difference between the natures taken away through the union, but rather the property of both natures is preserved and comes together into a single person and a single subsistent being; he is not parted or divided into two persons, but is one and the same only-begotten Son, God, Word, Lord Jesus Christ, just as the prophets taught from the beginning.[7]

The first part of this text contains what the participants at the council wanted to express. Four times over they repeat the teaching of the Council of Nicea on the divinity of Christ, and each time they balance that teaching with an equally strong affirmation of his full humanity. If as Nicea taught he is "perfect in divinity," he is also "perfect in humanity." If he is "truly God," he is also "truly man," and echoing the condemnation of Apollinaris at I Constantinople, they spell this out: "of a rational soul and a body." They repeat Nicea's "consubstantial (*homoousios*) with the Father as regards his divinity" and balance it with "consubstantial with us as regards his humanity" and spell that out with "like us in all respects except for sin." Finally, if for Nicea Jesus is "begotten of the Father before the ages as regards his divinity," he is also "in the last days the same . . . from Mary, the virgin God-bearer, as regards his humanity," and this is "for us and for our salvation."

By thus balancing Nicea's affirmation of the full divinity of Christ with an equally strong affirmation of his full humanity, the formula sought to do justice to the emphases of both Alexandria and Antioch. With Alexandria it affirms that Christ is "one and the same," so that, as Cyril insisted and the Council of Ephesus also taught, Mary is rightly honored as God-bearer, while with Antioch it stresses the completeness of his humanity.

The second part of the formula introduces some terms that can be of use in thinking about what the first part affirms. Summing up the two sets of attributes, divine and human, that it has been predicating of Christ, it introduces a technical term: he exists in two natures, and these are neither changed nor confused, as Antioch insisted. What is human about Jesus remains fully human, and so also for the divine. They do not get mixed up with one another, nor does one change into the other. Jesus is not a hybrid, a third kind of being that would result from blending the divine and the human together. He is, Chalcedon affirms, at one and the same time completely human and completely divine; the two natures are not related as two parts of a greater whole.

Nor are they divided or separated, as Alexandria stressed. Reaffirming Christ's unity, Chalcedon states that these natures come together "into a single person and a single subsistent being," contrary to what Nestorius was taken to have taught. If in encountering Jesus one only encounters a human being, one has not encountered his whole reality. Fully human, the one Jesus is simultaneously completely Word and Son of God. That is, the two natures "undergo...no division, no separation."

Chalcedon thus balances the teaching of the Council of Nicea by teaching clearly that Jesus is fully and completely human. It strongly rejects any notion that Jesus is partly human and partly divine. It is the one Jesus, a fully human being, who is at the same time wholly divine as God's Word of self-expression, as Son of the Father. In this way, as did Nicea, Chalcedon affirms that the human being, Jesus, is nothing less than Emmanuel, God-with-us.

Chalcedon thus articulated the doctrine of the hypostatic union, the union of the two natures in the one person (*hypostasis*) of Christ, and this doctrine, with its terms of substance, person, and nature, would provide subsequent christological reflection with its starting point, terms, and framework for the next millennium and a half. In addition, by distinguishing person from nature, the council provided a valuable counter to all ideologies of racism or sexism that would reduce human persons to some aspect of their nature.

The council did not, however, fulfill the imperial desire for religious uniformity throughout the East. Alexandrians, unable to stomach its language of two natures, interpreted it as a victory for Nestorius and rejected it, and the eventual Monophysite schism proved permanent. In their efforts to win acceptance, Chalcedon's defenders stressed Chalcedon's compatibility with Cyril's theology, and this led to a condemnation of the writings of Theodore of Mopsuestia and two other Antiochenes at II Constantinople in 553. Meanwhile the concerns raised by Apollinaris regarding a possible conflict between the human and divine wills in Christ persisted, leading some to propose that there was in Christ but a single energy (Monenergism) and, as the Patriarch Sergius of Constantinople had it, but a single will (Monothelitism).

In 681 III Constantinople rejected this view. Drawing out the implications of Chalcedon's two natures, it affirmed in Christ the existence of two natural operations and two wills. It thus reasserted that the union of his human nature with the divine subject in no way diminishes the fullness of Christ's humanity.

The following century saw the emergence of an adoptionist position in Spain.[8] Its proponents urged that with respect to his human nature Jesus could only be regarded as God's adopted Son. A synod at Frankfurt in 794 C.E. demurred, asserting that the human nature of Christ had its foundation in the divine subject, the Second Person of the trinity. This final step concluded the formation of a body of classical patristic conciliar doctrine that proved a stable possession throughout the Middle Ages and beyond.

Classical Doctrine, Contemporary Issues

The Council of Chalcedon sought to balance Nicea's affirmation of the full divinity of Christ with an equally strong affirmation of his complete humanity. The council failed, however, to win acceptance from the church of Alexandria, and this led its defenders to respond with a concerted effort to demonstrate Chalcedon's compatibility with the thought of Alexandria's great patriarch, Cyril. This apologetic tactic in turn set in motion a path of development that stood in some tension with the council's central affirmation. A century after the council, Leontius of Jerusalem contributed a term that would become standard in the interpretation of Chalcedon. Pondering the metaphysics of the hypostatic union, he suggested that the human nature of Christ, lacking its own *hypostasis*, was *enhypostatic* in the preexistent divine Word.[9] It thus became axiomatic for the subsequent tradition that, though Christ was fully human, there was in him no human person. This axiom could function plausibly so long as the category, *person,* was construed metaphysically. The modern period, however, has witnessed the emergence of a psychological conception of person which renders the axiom problematic. In ordinary, nontechnical language it has become unintelligible to speak of Christ as someone who is fully human but not a human person.

Furthermore, the neo-Chalcedonian stress on Christ as a divine person would provide medieval theologians with the premise for a line of reasoning that, while maintaining the completeness of his human nature considered as a metaphysical principle, would seem nonetheless to undercut the concrete actuality of that nature. For example, from the principle that union with the divine person would bring Christ's human nature to full perfection, they deduced that during his earthly life Christ enjoyed both the beatific vision of God that constitutes human happiness in heaven as well as a gift of infused knowledge that shielded him from all ignorance. This left very little space in Christ for the experiential mode of acquiring knowledge that is normal for human beings. Thomas Aquinas came to acknowledge that mode of knowing in Christ only late in his career,[10] and when he did, it set him at odds with his mentor, Albert the Great, and with his contemporary, Bonaventure. Even then Thomas rejected the idea that Christ might have been instructed by others, since that would have been unbecoming his identity as head of the human race.[11] For Thomas the union of a human nature with a divine person in Christ also meant that it was impossible for Christ to fall ill,[12] while a miracle was required for Christ to die.[13] Immortality would have been the normal consequence of the hypostatic union, but Christ deliberately suspended that effect to complete his redemptive task.

These medieval theses were carried forward in the neoscholastic Christology that enjoyed official sanction in Catholic institutions from the late nineteenth century into the 1960s. For that Christology, as for its medieval antecedents, the dogma of Chalcedon enjoyed paradigmatic status, providing the framework, terms, and issues within which theologians operated. Yet a turning point occurred in 1951, the fifteen hundredth anniversary of Chalcedon, when a flurry of research brought to light the discrepancy between the dominant Christology and Chalcedon's affirmation that in his humanity, Christ is "like us in all respects except for sin." Karl Rahner noted the "cryptomonophysitism" engendered when Chalcedon's language of a divine person with an assumed humanity was repeated in the modern context.[14] While reciting the orthodox formula, people tended to imagine an Apollinarian or docetic Christ who, though human in appearance, possessed a divine consciousness that rendered him capable of reading minds, predicting the future, and exercising miraculous powers over nature. Such a figure was far from being "like us in all things except sin."

Faithfulness to Chalcedon set Christology in the last decades the task of recovering the full humanity of Christ. In a first phase of this project exegetes began to highlight those human features in the gospel portraits of Christ — ignorance, sorrow, anger, weariness, and the like — which the dogmatic textbooks had tended to suppress or explain away.[15] When, in the mid-1970s, theologians like Edward Schillebeeckx,[16] Hans Küng,[17] and Walter Kasper[18] began drawing on the results of the so-called New Quest for the historical Jesus, the wineskin of neoscholastic Christology burst and a new paradigm emerged.[19] Whereas the Christology of the manuals was basically commentary on Chalcedon, the new Christologies took as their task to render a genetic and evaluative account of the entire christological tradition to mediate the revelatory and redemptive significance of Jesus Christ into the contemporary context.

Within this new christological paradigm the doctrines of the patristic councils no longer define the entire christological enterprise. The councils are reconceived as particular moments within the ongoing tradition; and while they can claim normative status, they also require interpretation. Karl Rahner, for example, drew upon his creative retrieval of Thomas's philosophy to forge a theological anthropology that he wielded to dispel any crudely mythological understanding of the incarnation. On his view, far from representing an alien intrusion into an otherwise indifferent world, the hypostatic union effected the supreme and gracious fulfillment of the universal call to self-transcendence into the holy mystery of God that constitutes humanity as such. That fulfillment, realized in Christ, stands in history as an absolute, irrevocable promise for the rest of humankind.[20]

Similar philosophical resources enabled Bernard Lonergan to meet the difficulties attending the traditional language of a single divine person in Christ. Transposing the Chalcedonian terms into the realm of human interiority, he showed how the Chalcedonian formula and its amplification at III Constantinople call for a full, free, developing human subjectivity in Jesus coherent with the contemporary, psychologically informed understanding of what it means to be human.[21]

Another line of interpretation, initiated by Piet Schoonenberg, has proved controversial. Schoonenberg suggested that the classical understanding of Christ as both God and human give way to a view of God's uniquely full presence in him.[22] In a similar vein Roger Haight has suggested recently that the point of the doctrines of Nicea and Chalcedon resides in the confession that in the man Jesus Christians encounter God's saving presence.[23] Some find this Christology of presence helpful in reconceiving the relationship of Christianity to other world religions. Others regard it as regressive to a pre-Nicene stage of development if not an outright denial of classical doctrine.[24]

Over the past half-century the project of recovering the full humanity of Christ has contributed to the collapse of the neoscholastic paradigm within which that project began and the emergence of a new one. Often characterized as a move from a "Christology from above" to a "Christology from below," this development requires an historical reconstruction and evaluation of the process, running from the New Testament through the patristic councils, that supplied the starting point for the "Christology from above." Since a pluralism of philosophical commitments and methodological options in theology has succeeded neoscholasticism, a corresponding pluralism of evaluative historical accounts and interpretations of classical christological doctrine is to be expected in the present situation. Even as that doctrine emerged from a process of trial and error that ran through the patristic era, its interpretation today is involved in a similar process.

For Further Reflection

1. Explain Arius's role in the development of the doctrine of the divinity of Christ.

2. Why did the Council of Nicea reject Arius's teaching? What was at stake in the controversy?

3. How did the debate over calling Mary "Theotokos" bring the theological differences between Alexandria and Antioch into play?

4. Explain the significance of the confession of faith of the Council of Chalcedon in its historical context.

5. What place do the classical doctrines of the patristic councils occupy in contemporary Christology?

For Further Reading

Grillmeier, Aloys. *Christ and Christian Tradition.* Vol. 1. *From the Apostolic Age to Chalcedon (451).* Trans. J. Bowden. 2nd ed. Atlanta: John Knox Press, 1975.

Hanson, R. P. C. *The Search for the Christian Doctrine of God: The Arian Controversy 318–81.* Edinburgh: T. & T. Clark, 1988.

Lonergan, Bernard. *The Way to Nicea: The Dialectical Development of Trinitarian Theology.* Trans. C. O'Donovan. Philadelphia: Westminster Press, 1976.

Loewe, William P. *The College Student's Introduction to Christology.* Collegeville, Minn.: Liturgical Press, 1996.

Rubenstein, Richard E. *When Jesus Became God: The Epic Fight over Christ's Divinity in the Last Days of Rome.* New York: Harcourt Brace, 1999.

— 4 —

Christ and Redemption

Gerard S. Sloyan

Any attempt to explore the ways in which Jesus Christ has been viewed as "the savior of the world"[1] or the one through or in whom "redemption" (*apolýtrōsis*)[2] has been accomplished must first see how that figure of buying back or salvation/rescue (*sotería*)[3] operates in the biblical writings. The work of God with respect to the whole human race by including the gentiles is no different than the salvation of Israel frequently spoken of in the Old Testament. In early days the deliverance was political, as from Egypt, Assyria, and later Babylon in Chaldea; but increasingly it became freedom from sin and its consequences. There is no sense in which Christian faith holds Jesus Christ to have achieved such an immense benefit for humanity on his own. It is always the work of God through him in the power of the Holy Spirit, as liturgical formulas from an early date describe it.

Beyond any doubt redemption has its prototype in deliverance from Egypt. In a transferred sense it most often means being spared from death, e.g., in Psalm 103:4 and elsewhere in the Psalter, but then also freedom from sin as in Psalm 130:8, popularly known as the *De profundis*. The basic vocabulary is rooted in ancient law and custom wherein redemption (*ge'ullah*) is the buying back or exchange of family property in fulfillment of a duty to one's next of kin.[4] In the story of Ruth, Elimelech's nearest kinsman (*gō'el*) waived his right as claimant to the dead man's property and Boaz took it over. The same term is used for the next of kin who acts as expiator or avenger of a victim of homicide.[5] Another verb and noun that occur in a context of rescue or ransom, normally of prisoners taken in battle, are *pâdâ* and *padīi*.

Zechariah's poetic response to the birth of his son John contains a well-known instance of God's redemption (*lýtrōsin*)[6] or salvific (*soterías*)[7] act in prospect. If Job could say, "I know that my redeemer (*gō'eli*) lives"[8] and the Psalmist, "They remembered that God Most High was their redeemer (*gō'elâm*),"[9] the author of Hebrews felt equally secure in saying that "a death has occurred that redeems (*eis apolýtrōsin*) [those who are called] from transgressions."[10] St. Paul is widely thought to have adopted a formula already in use that said that "all have sinned . . . and are justified freely (*dōreán*) [a word added to stress the gratuity] by God's grace through the redemption that is in Christ Jesus, whom God set forth as an expiation through faith by his blood to demonstrate [God's] justness, for out of forbearance [God] has passed over sins previously committed."[11] The operative metaphor to describe God's redemptive act is *hilastçrion* ("expiation"). The NRSV renders it "a sacrifice of atonement" for readers/hearers unable to deduce the force of the image from any one word translation. This Greek noun is the Septuagint rendering of *kappōreth*, the "propitiatory" of Douai-Rheims or "mercy seat" of King James, a plaque of pure gold placed above the ark.[12] Aaron and his descendants sprinkled the blood of a young bull and a goat upon it on one day of the year, in symbolic atonement for the sins of the Israelites and their failures to observe the ritual laws.[13] The redeeming blood of Christ was seen by early believers in him to fulfill the imagery of the rite of Yom Kippur. Hebrews, cited above, says that Christ as high priest "entered once for all into the [heavenly] sanctuary, not with the blood of goats and calves but with his own blood, thus obtaining eternal redemption."[14]

The First Epistle of Peter at 1:2 speaks with ease of the sanctification of "the refugees of the diaspora" by the Spirit, coupled with the blood of Jesus Christ, and a little later of the recipients as set free from their traditional, empty way of life, not by "silver or gold but by the precious blood of Christ as of a spotless, unblemished lamb."[15] The same is found in Revelation 1:5. The metaphor, which seems to be in the realm of commercial transactions, prompted some later commentators to ask: "To whom was the ransom price paid?" But more of that later.

It was God's raising the crucified Jesus up from the dead that alone accounts for the attribution to him of the titles "the Lord," "the Christ," unique "son of God" and agent of God in the redemption of the human race. Had it not occurred, he would have been remembered for a few generations as a wonderworker and great teacher but not a martyr to Jewish peoplehood. The redeeming or restoring image emerged as primary to describe the benefit made available to all through him, although "justice" and "holiness" could occur in some phrases[16] and "reconciliation" in others,[17] solely by virtue of Jesus' resurrection from the dead. This was accomplished by an act of power on the level of spirit, "the Spirit of Holiness that proclaimed him Son of God," as St. Paul described it in an early creedal fragment.[18] The stages by which the earliest apostolic company proceeded, from taking in this amazing event to hailing him as universal redeemer, are unknown to us. Without question, however, his upraising from the dead was the primary datum of belief in the deed God accomplished in him. That he was a holy and wise itinerant teacher netted him the term *Rabbi*[19] but would not have sufficed for the faith that is recorded in him, such as was never reposed in an Elijah or a Moses. Neither would the prophetic utterance about an innocent victim who by his death would take away the sins of the many be cited as fulfilled in him as an individual rather than in a suffering people generally.[20] There had been great Jewish teachers before Jesus and many martyred for their Israelite faith, yet none for whom a claim for intimacy with God such as was made for Jesus. He alone was called by believers in him "a Son whom God appointed heir of all things, through whom he also created the worlds. He is the reflection of God's glory and the exact imprint of God's being, and he sustains all things by his powerful word."[21] Without his risen life attested to by many witnesses, none of this is conceivable.

The first we learn of the way believers looked on Jesus Christ as savior comes in Paul's earliest extant letter, which expresses the solid hope that he will come from heaven as "deliverer (*rhuómenon*) from God's wrath." This "wrath" (*orgē*) always means God's just judgment of the wicked on the last day.[22] God did not destine us for that wrath, Paul writes, but "for gaining salvation through our Lord Jesus Christ who died for us, so that whether we are awake or asleep [i.e., living or dead] we may live with him."[23]

From Paul and the Gospels to the Second Century

Paul spoke of redemption in many contexts but always to mean a hugely bettered state in this life with its consummation solidly hoped for at Christ's coming. It would come as the result of God's gift (*cháris*, grace) and consist in a return to authentic human existence, all distortion of it ("sin" personified[24] and its unhealthy offspring "transgressions"[25]) left behind. Some chroniclers of Christian history see in Paul the deviser of the doctrine of redemption from sin in Christ, but this can hardly have been the case. He provided the vocabulary derived from the Jewish scriptures that the church found useful subsequently, but a similar teaching must have characterized all the nameless apostolic evangelizers or else his writings would not have been accepted as scripture by the many churches.

The earliest comprehensive list of books regarded as authentic apostolic teaching was discovered in 1740 by the librarian of the Ambrosian Library in Milano, Lodovico Muratori.[26] Dating to ca. 180, its lines 39–68 of a total of 85 list the thirteen letters of the Pauline corpus after mentioning Mark (presumably Matthew came first in the damaged eighth-century MS.), Luke, John, and Acts. Hebrews is not named, but the epistles of Jude and two of John unspecified are, followed by a reference to the Wisdom of Solomon and then Revelation. In the books of this partial canon Jesus Christ as intermediary between God and humanity is spoken of in a variety of ways to express his redemptive role. In Mark he gives his life a ransom for the many, in the Synoptics generally and in Acts for the forgiveness of sins, while in John belief in him brings a transformation from enslavement to the bond of love called friendship. The immediate postcanonical writings like Ignatius's letters speak of "God's plan entailing passion and resurrection"[27] and "belief in Christ's blood."[28] An early letter from the church in Rome to Corinth speaks of "our salvation, Jesus Christ, the high priest of our offerings, the protector and helper of our weakness."[29] The anonymous *Epistle to Diognetus* writes that God was "long-suffering and forbearing. In his mercy he took up the burden of our sins. [God] gave up his own Son as a ransom for us.... In whom could we, lawless and impious as we were, be made just except in the Son of God alone?"[30] Justin in the context of a description of the Eucharist celebrated each Sunday in Rome says, "but as Jesus Christ our Savior, being incarnate by God's word, took flesh and blood for our salvation, so also we have been taught that the food consecrated by the word of prayer that comes from him, from which our flesh and blood are nourished *by transformation* (emphasis added) is the flesh and blood of that incarnate Jesus."[31]

The Gnostic Coptic tractate *The Apocryphon of James* admits salvation by an incarnate Christ: "The Lord...said...I say unto you, none will be saved unless they believe in my cross. For theirs is the kingdom of God who have believed in my cross."[32] Another tractate called *The Gospel of Truth* is among those same mid-third-century Greek originals found in Coptic translation in Nag Hammadi, Upper Egypt, in 1945. It says of the Word that it was not a sound only but became a body[33] and that, "coming forth from the fullness (*plērōma*), the one who is in the thought and mind of the Father is addressed as the savior. That Word describes the work he is to perform for the redemption of those who were ignorant of the Father."[34] The thought, mind and knowledge (*gnōsis*) of the truth are much more characteristic of the mode of salvation claimed by the Christianized Gnosticism of the second century than the two scant mentions of a Word in flesh cited above. The whole corpus of writings testifies to the adoption of a dualist thought world as better equipped to rescue a humanity mired in matter than the crude materiality of the Jewish scriptures and the gospels. The men and women of the latter are given speaking parts in the Gnostic tractates but only to put questions to the Master. He obligingly answers in terms of spirit only. Relatively few passages in the Nag Hammadi collection are as bizarre as those St. Irenaeus reported on in his late first-century *Refutation of the Knowledge Falsely So Called.*[35] A notable exception occurs in *The Apocryphon of John* in which the chief archon Yaltabaoth is assisted by the seventy, named "powers," who created Adam organ by organ and limb by limb, and a few dozen others with fictitious Semitic-sounding names who are "appointed over all of these."[36] The more usual types of development engaged in are like that of the three essential races of mankind created by the *Logos* who comes forth from the All: the material, the psychic and the spiritual. The last-named "will receive complete salvation in every way."[37] The material are fated for destruction, while the psychic because they are body-spirit can go either way. Those of spirit acknowledge the Son of God and savior who is "the Totality in bodily form"[38] and who will restore and redeem the spiritual. In general, human redemption in all these writings consists in regaining human perfection, which is the spiritual self. The language is frequently convoluted, as if a seriously intended imitation of Johannine style were to end in unconscious parody. Knowledge, always of a certain esoteric kind, is the key to salvation. The attempt to sound intellectual must have put a strain on any but the most earnest devotees, secure in their superiority to other, garden-variety Christians. The appeal has not died with the centuries.

> Eleleth, the great angel, spoke to me. "It is I," he said, who am understanding. I am one of the four givers of light, who stand in the presence of the great invisible spirit.... None of these rulers can prevail over the root of truth... for your [plural] abode is in incorruptibility where the virgin spirit dwells, who is superior to the authorities of chaos and to their universe.[39]

More specifically about how Gnostic redemption was thought to be achieved we read:

> The Lord [said] to [him], "James [my brother but not materially], behold, I shall reveal to you your redemption. When [you] are seized [by one of three toll collectors, a guard]... who says to you, 'Who are you or where are you from?'... You are to say to him, 'I am from the Pre-existent Father, and a son in the Pre-existent One [who]... did not have intercourse with Achamoth when she produced [the race] she brought down from the Pre-existent one. They are not alien, but they are ours.'... When he says to you, 'Where will you go?' you are to say to him, 'To the place from which I have come, there shall I return.'"[40]

This is the heart of Gnostic redemptive theology: human spirits entrapped in bodies but released by the *gnōsis* they possess to return to the All whence they had come.

A Theology of Redemption Emerges

Irenaeus of Lyon, having first challenged the absurdities of a variety of Gnostic teachings he had encountered in Rome, expounded the mystery of human redemption in terms of the flesh and blood of Christ which they denied.[41] His mode of argument was the well-remembered theory of recapitulation or renewal derived from St. Paul's two human generations, one headed by

Adam, the other by Christ.[42] The two Latin translations that we have use the verb *recapitulāre* to echo Ephesians' *anakephalaiōsásthai* (1:10) which speaks of summing up all things under the headship of Christ. Irenaeus has the virgin Mary obeying God's word and thus becoming the advocate of Eve who disobeyed it, even as her Son, the Son of Man, recapitulated in himself that primal man by whom our race went down to death.[43] The redemption of the human race consisted in the overcoming of sin and death and the ascent to life by the uniting of that race to the Spirit. The Spirit once placed in humankind is thus its head, the highest principle of the new creation. Through this Spirit we see and hear and speak. Rescue or renewal of a long vanquished human race is accomplished by the Son of Mary, the new Eve, acting in the power of God's Spirit.

The North African layman Tertullian, who wrote in his native Latin (unlike most of his contemporaries, he knew Greek) provided the first statements in that language of the way God restored a sinful, mortal race to the divine friendship. He wrote in one treatise that "God is the one to whom you make satisfaction"[44] but he did not use that term to refer to anything accomplished by the death of Christ.[45] He did, however, ask: "Who has ever redeemed the death of another by his own except the Son of God alone? . . . It was for this very purpose that he came — to die for sinners."[46] Not long after, Origen would speak frequently in his writings of the human race as in thrall to demonic powers until the ransom of the soul of Jesus was paid to him.[47] He called Jesus savior, mediator, Son of God, and Word incarnate freely in his treatise on the first principles of Christian faith. But nowhere in it does he theorize or even make a brief exposition on how Jesus acts to rescue humanity from its alienation to God.[48] Human restoration to the image of God that it had at the beginning is either assumed in throwaway lines or else dealt with in passages like the following, which may seem strange to us:

> The working of the Father . . . is found to be more glorious and splendid when each one, through participation in Christ in his character of wisdom and knowledge and sanctification, advances and comes to higher degrees of perfection; and when a person, by being sanctified through participation in the Holy Spirit, is made purer and holier, that one becomes more worthy to receive the grace of wisdom and knowledge . . . and that which exists shall be as worthy as God who caused it to exist. Thus, too, the ones who are such as God who made them wished them to be shall receive from God the power to exist forever and to endure for eternity.[49]

Obviously he is speaking about those whom Paul described as predestined, called, justified, and glorified,[50] but in language so abstract that it is not easy to grasp.

Moving ahead a century and a half, we find Gregory, bishop of Nyssa and brother to Basil, bishop of Caesarea, seeming to accept literally Origen's theory of the human race possessed by Satan until the ransom of the soul of Jesus was paid him. Gregory developed it as an offer of God that the devil accepted, only to prove unable to retain it when the humanity of Jesus that served as bait disclosed the divinity within.[51] Rufinus of Aquileia repeated the image almost to the letter, adding the detail that when the devil discovered the hook of deity on which he was caught he burst the bars of the netherworld and, dragged from the abyss, became bait for others.[52] The imagery employed by the bishop of Nyssa was by no means representative of the thought of the Cappadocian fathers or their Greek-speaking contemporary, Athanasius. Much more sophisticated was their conviction along Platonic lines that human redemption was accomplished at root by the incarnation. Seeing the human race as a unity, Athanasius wrote that once the incarnate Word became human the divinizing of his flesh was transmitted to all humanity.[53] In contest with the Arians he said: "Seeing that all were perishing as a result of Adam's transgression, [Christ's] flesh was saved and delivered before all others because it had become the body of the Word himself, and henceforth we are saved, being one body with him in virtue of it."[54]

The Development of the Doctrine in the West

Hilary of Pictavium (Poitiers), the last married bishop of the West, died in 367 when Augustine was a thirteen year-old in the Latin-speaking northern rim of Africa. He applied the term *satisfaction* to the death of Jesus as Tertullian had not done.[55] Hilary equated it with sacrifice and saw in the cross Christ's reparation to God on behalf of sinners. Augustine, who wrote voluminously on almost everything, followed St. Paul in teaching that humans (the generic *homo*, not *vir*), who had been alienated from God throughout the epoch from Adam to Christ, were reconciled by the believer's faith in God's deed in him. Jesus' freely accepted death was an act of human obedience by a man of heaven contrasted with the primordial disobedience of a man of earth. There was nothing new there, but Augustine's seeing in Adam "the pioneer of our race and of our sin," which he found in Tertullian,[56] led him to understand the Genesis account of Eden as literal history rather a paradigmatic tale of human failure to observe even one commandment at the dawn of history. Paul had indeed taken the sin of Adam to inaugurate death and sin for the whole race in the manner of Semitic solidarity thinking. He understood it, however, for the *typos* the Genesis authors intended in their eleven chapters that are a book of typologies: as a figure of human sinfulness. Augustine was no Semite in his thinking nor even a Greek acquainted with the genre *mythos*, and so he took the tale for history.

The outcome is well known. The one sin of Adam was understood to have consequences for all ages in the form of hereditary guilt transmitted to successive generations. This, not the sin itself, the bishop of Hippo termed *peccatum originale*. Part of his theory was the incapacity of humans to avoid all sin in the sex act since some exercise of passion, which is a good, was bound to escape control by reason, and hence constitute moral fault. The church of the West went with all of his theorizing except that portion. His theological influence continued so enormous that some later theologians could equate concupiscence (sexual desire) with sin and others teach with him that the human race was justly a *massa damnata*. Had God not mercifully rendered condemnation to hell inoperative for the repentant in virtue of Christ's merits, all would and should have been damned. Augustine held that God's grace alone could transform the wounded human will so as to render it capable of doing good. He wrote of the sin of Adam and its consequences that "it cannot be pardoned and blotted out except through the one Mediator between God and man, the man Jesus Christ, who alone could be born in such a way as not to need to be reborn."[57]

The Western church continued to understand the mystery of human redemption largely as expounded by Augustine, namely as a removing of the corporate burden of sin by faith in Jesus' death on the cross — although not entirely, in the view of some Reformers. Increasingly Christ's resurrection came to be viewed popularly as a separate mystery of faith from the crucifixion despite the statements of Bible and liturgy (there is none, amazingly, of a council on the question) that human redemption is effected by the death and resurrection of the Lord.[58] Eastern liturgical rites kept the two in concert successfully while at the same time the theology of the East was featuring God's redemptive act as a divinization (*théōsis*) of humanity in solidarity with Christ, the head of the body that is the church. Irenaeus was the first to write that "God made himself the man, that man might become God," and the tradition continued that the vocation of fallen humanity was deification by uncreated grace, making it a "partaker of the divine nature" (1 Pet. 1:4).[59]

Little changed in the way the redemptive mystery was explored and expounded in the West until the meditation of Anselm of Bec in *Why Did God Become Man?* This Italian-born Benedictine monk of a French monastery who died as archbishop of Canterbury (1109) wrote this treatise, as he did the previous *Monologion* and *Proslogion,* from within and for a monastic community. He was in exile at the time from his English see in Capua, Italy, as he notes in the introductory remarks. There he says that reason is the medium between faith (here) and vision (in the life of the blessed) that provides progress in understanding calculated to bring us "closer to the vision we all long for."[60] His project is to restore joy in believing to monks whose daily life of work and prayer, based on faith alone, might admit temptation

to despair. He means to provide assurance to their hope, that they may take
pleasure in the life they are living. The approach will be "by reason alone,"
"Christ having been removed." It is the *credo ut intelligam* (I believe that I
might understand) of Augustine couched in the monastic poetics of brevity,
"arguments and images alike": a quest for understanding.[61] Anselm will provide "necessary reasons" for the great truth already known by faith: that an
incarnation and a death achieved the life of the world. Why did it have to
be this way and no other? That was his question. The argument he framed
holds that God could not have acted otherwise because of two "givens": the
glory of God and the incapacity of man. Some detractors of the Anselmian
thesis have said that it reduces the pure gift of redemption to a commercial
transaction, others that it is based on the unworthy image of wounded pride
(*laesa maiestas*) like that of an eleventh-century nobleman by a rebellious
serf. Both objections are based on faulty assumptions, one that the Latin
hŏnŏr (*hŏnŏs*) means the vernacular "honor" and the other that the validity
of the argument depends on a social reality of medieval life.

Anselm knows that he can safely proceed on two presuppositions, whether
in the monastery or in the Christian, Jewish, and Muslim worlds. His whole
culture admitted the godliness of God, which meant infinite justice and infinite mercy, and that the human creature owed obedience to God in acts of
intellect and will. On this widely held twofold assumption he built a simple
argument. Human sin had deprived God of the glory due to God from acts
of creaturely obedience, causing an imbalance of justice in the cosmos. If the
imbalance were to be righted, it could be done in only one way. The offense
was quasi-infinite because it denied glory to the Infinite; hence only God
could rectify the omission. But because the offense was caused by a human,
only a human could achieve reconciliation. Case of the contradictory, hence
impossible? Not at all. Only *Deus homo,* a human who is divine, could effect
reconciliation without a compromise on the part of deity or humanity.[62] The
treatise incorporates the strongest objection to the thesis possible in the fashion of medieval dialectic. Granted that this happened, but was it necessary?
Could God not have remitted centuries of sin by simple *fiat*? No, Anselm
responded. The redemption could only have been accomplished in this way
because God, being God, is perfectly just. The only divine necessity is that
God act like God. There is no freedom to act otherwise. Humans had committed the enormity of sin against God. A human had to repent and ask God's
forgiveness in the name of all. Only God could grant that forgiveness. Both
acts of justice, divine and human, are accomplished by the one undivided
person.[63] The key to the theory of redemptive reconciliation is an adequate
concept of the divine majesty: infinite mercy and infinite justice identical with
deity. Key, too, is a conviction that a human will is at work in Christ's freely
sacrificed life and not only the divine will. Has not Anselm in his claimed
resort to reason abandoned his promise to seek a resolution *remoto Christo,*

Christ quite apart? His answer was that he had not appealed to the Jesus Christ of faith but to God active in God's way and a man active in a human way. Each acted freely according to their respective natures. Divine justice and human justice could alone accomplish the desired end. The author of *Cur Deus Homo?* was convinced he had discovered the necessary reasons for what the church knows by faith.

Later voluntarists like the Scots Franciscan John of Duns (d. 1308) were not convinced. His voice was the strongest in maintaining that in light of the divine omnipotence and divine will God could freely have foreordained redemption by any number of means. This one was chosen in freedom to show forth the divine goodness. Scotus is especially remembered for holding that the incarnation could have occurred by divine decree without respect to primordial sin, since no human action could have necessitated this supreme work of God. But the theological centuries did not go with him. Rather, Western theology followed Aquinas in his slightly modified version of Anselm in which he said, borrowing also from Peter Abelard, that

> Christ by suffering as a result of love and obedience offered to God something greater than what might be exacted in compensation for the whole offense of humanity...because of the greatness of the love as a result of which he suffered...because of the worth of the life he laid down, the life of God and a human being...and because of the greatness of the sorrow he took upon himself.... [Moreover] the head and members are as it were one mystical person; thus the satisfaction of Christ belongs to all the faithful as to his members...and the worth of Christ's flesh is to be reckoned...according to the person who assumed it, in that it was the flesh of God, from whom it gained an infinite worth.[64]

The Reformers did not depart from the Anselmian teaching in general outline despite their repudiation of the scholastics, although Martin Luther rejected the idea of satisfaction in favor of Christ reckoned a sinner by God in our place. John Calvin saw the redemption accomplished when the savior "bore in his soul the tortures of a condemned and ruined man." They were convinced that St. Paul had said what Anselm took so many words to say, only much more clearly and without the complication of "necessary reasons." Their focus was not on the deed of God by which redemption was offered to sinful humanity, which they assumed, but on the nature of the divine plan (*ordo* for the biblical *oikonomía*) to make Christ's benefits available and on what terms or conditions the individual could accept them. There was much more probing of the divine will in this period than previously, although earlier ages had done some wrestling with the problem of grace and free will that Augustine had left as his heritage.

Jaroslav Pelikan provides an enlightening summary of the writings of
Peter Damiani (d. 1072) through Anselm (d. 1109) and Abelard (d. 1142)
to Bernard of Clairvaux (d. 1153) on how, not simply the freely willed
death of Christ as in Paul but his sufferings on the cross, came to be seen
as "satisfaction" paid to divine justice.[65] He finds the origins of the idea
in medieval penitential practice. Christ's "redemption on the cross could be
seen as the one supreme act of penitential satisfaction. 'Satisfaction,' then,
was another term for 'sacrifice,' and Christ's sacrificial act of penance made
even human acts of satisfaction worthy, since of themselves they were not."[66]
Penance was the fitting way for sinners to appropriate the act by which, as
Peter Damiani put it, "our Christ has redeemed us through the cross."

The Contemporary Soteriological Scene

Contemporary Catholic and Protestant preachers and theologians alike are
at ease in that expression of the mystery of human redemption. Among the
latter would be Karl Barth, Jürgen Moltmann, and any in the Reformed
tradition; and Rudolf Bultmann, Ernst Käsemann, Eberhard Jüngel, and
Wolfhart Pannenberg in the Lutheran. In the familiar Protestant theological
style, their mode of exposition of the mystery is an exegesis and development of the pertinent biblical texts. Contemporary Orthodox theologians,
far fewer in number, do the same, supplemented by commentaries of the
Greek fathers and some writings of Greek and Russian writers of the past
century. Of the outstanding contemporary Catholic theologians, only Edward Schillebeeckx does his own exegesis while Hans Urs von Balthasar
draws on his considerable patristic knowledge and esthetic concerns, Karl
Rahner going the way of meditative speculation, often based on conciliar
teaching.

In a 1970 essay of a dozen pages entitled "The Brother for Whom Christ
Died" von Balthasar quotes Jesus' words at the Last Supper about "my
body given for you, my blood poured out for you and for all" and calls
it "his outrageous and yet simply proposed claim [that he] has died for all
and that this is confirmed by his 'resurrection from the dead.'" This, for
the Swiss diocesan priest theologian, as an "*idea* was and is a motivating
force of quite unique power...the power of a reality which encompasses
all in advance, not just those to whom it comes."[67] He goes on to speak
of the dying and rising for all in these terms: "This self-giving of Christ
is attested to us as an expression of the reconciling will of God who has
in him reconciled the world to himself (2 Cor. 5:19) who with the gift
of his most precious possession, 'his own son,' has given us *everything*
(Rom. 8:32) and hence has given witness to his unsurpassable love."[68] Von
Balthasar elsewhere speaks of the risk God has taken in entrusting us with
genuine freedom, even a freedom to deny and destroy ourselves: " 'God with

us'... [means] a coming over to our side in order to open a way for us from within our helplessness and hopelessness... without impugning our freedom in any manner.... Dying freely and obediently, God turns death, the sign of our guilt, into a monument of our love."[69]

If the Swiss is plate glass to read as given here in translation, his German former colleague in the Society of Jesus is many-faceted crystal. Rahner does not tackle soteriology head on. In his frequent discussions of Christology, however, he necessarily addresses how we are redeemed in his theological investigations of the one by whom we are redeemed. Inquiring into the universality of salvation, he says that in discussing the basic possibility of the salvation of all he cannot be raising the question of its actual realization. Yet, "contrary to the view of St. Augustine... no [one] is excluded from salvation simply because of so-called original sin... only... through serious personal sin."[70] As always he engages the problem of human freedom in the human acceptance or rejection of the divine gift held out. But then we must say, "because God wills salvation, Jesus died and rose again," not "because the crucifixion occurred, therefore God wills our salvation."[71] There is no such absurdity as God transformed from a God of anger and justice into one of mercy and love by the cross. "Rather God brings the event of the cross to pass [because] possessed from the beginning of gratuitous mercy and, despite the world's sin, [God] shares [divine selfhood] with the world, so overcoming its sin."[72] Assuming the fact of this gratuitous offer to those who hear and are open to the gospel, Rahner then asks what is to be made of an early statement in Vatican II's *Lumen Gentium* ("The Church in the Modern World") that the church is the world's salvation, therefore the basic sacrament of salvation and Jesus Christ its *primary* sacrament. He paraphrases as the explicit teaching of the church council that all humanity is open to salvation "on the basis of a strictly supernatural faith in revelation brought about by grace."[73] The theological difficulties that the document raises are made plain by the council's repeated assertions that "God alone knows how such a fact is possible in certain circumstances and under certain conditions." But if no one can know what God knows, what is the validity of the position? He answers that, since all "can only achieve salvation through Christ," those who live in a state of grace and justification who have not come in contact with the preaching of the gospel or are required by their conscience to refuse it are to be considered anonymous Christians.[74] For sincere atheists, theirs can be an implicit Christianity.[75] Certain Protestant Christians deny any such possibility, requiring explicit faith in Jesus Christ as savior. The opposite was the catechetical position shared with adults and youth alike throughout the nineteenth and twentieth centuries, however many may not have been exposed to it.

Rahner reports a conversation with the Zen scholar Keiji Nishitani (briefly a colleague of the present writer at Temple University), who knew his position on anonymous Christians: "What would you say to my treating you as an anonymous Zen Buddhist?"[76] Rahner answered that he would feel honored by such an interpretation, even though he was obliged to think him in error, if he had the same understanding of the statement regarding the other. "Nishitani replied: Then on this point we are entirely at one."

Because sin looms so large in Christian and Jewish life and thought and is that condition from which God holds out redemption, it is not surprising that the German Jesuit has an article on "Sin as Loss of Grace in Early Church Literature" in a collection based on the teachings of some second- and third-century church fathers.[77] The treatments in it of repentance symbolized in act are among his most scholarly and are to be categorized as positive theology rather than the speculative theology for which he is better known. In another essay in that collection, having first characterized the Word made flesh as "the divine self-communication [with all humankind] in God's *Pneuma* [Spirit]... (always a forgiving communication)," he goes on to say that the death and resurrection of the divine Logos taken as one, which constitutes him the Mediator of that self-communication, includes "the ultimate, radical depth of human intercommunication as well."[78] By this he means that not only Mary and the other saints but also all the baptized have a mediatorial role in the progress of God and humanity together toward "the eschatological meridian, i.e., when... the offer and the acceptance of the divine self-communication... becomes irreversible and *appears* historically... for the believer" in the incarnation. Put simply, since Jesus Christ is the "sole and absolute Mediator" in human history's progress toward its one "apogee and goal," it must be the case that mutual mediations "effected by all faithful and justified people... are not extraordinary, special functions of all believers" but are " 'elements' of *total* salvation history" depending on and actually are human intercommunications. This is clearly an exploration of the long-held doctrine of the priesthood of all believers stemming from 1 Peter 2:5, 9 in which the "spiritual sacrifices" they offer to God as priests are the mediatory intercessions they make for others. Otherwise, the phrase in 1 Peter is meaningless.

The word *atonement* had a history in English as *onement* from about 1300, a translation of *être à un,* to mean agreement between two or more parties. Wyclif used *onement* in that sense in Ezekiel 37:17 to describe the union of two sticks representing Judah and Israel, but in Romans 5:11 the *reconciliation* of God and man. The first recorded use of *atonement* occurs in Thomas More's incomplete *History of King Richard III,* of 1513 where he is speaking of discord among the nobles at the king's coronation. Tindale's Bible translation of 1534 contains the first religious use of the word. It makes its way in that spelling through Coverdale's revision to the Authorized Version of 1611, while Douai-Rheims of the previous year chose *reconciliation* for *katallagē,* NRSV's present choice. The two words have come to connote the same reality: in Anselm's theory, the satisfaction owed to God for the enormous sin of disobedience, and in the theories of penal substitution in which Christ is considered to have taken on himself the punishments deserved by a sinful humanity.

The English theologian Michael Winter says on an early page that the use of both terms by an almost universal consensus is untenable. He calls the first a "legalistic theory of quasi-compensation," a description which if it were correct rather than the righting of a cosmic imbalance *would* deserve repudiation. The second reduces the consensus to less than universality if the worldwide theology and preaching of "Christ in our place" is taken into account. Despite the cavil, this compact essay is admirable in its review of patristic and medieval theories of the New Testament mystery of atonement. It then puts forward still another in which the author sees Jesus as "competent mediator" requesting of the Father the reconciliation of the human race.

Winter considers this "a field almost totally neglected by modern writers."[79] Finding no such formal request in the scriptures like the several Abraham and Moses made to God, he relies on the occurrences of the term *mediator* in Galatians 3:19–20 and 1 Timothy 2:5, coupled with the instances where he sees Jesus exercising an intercessory role when he implicitly asks God to reconcile the people: in his baptism; in his charge to repent and believe in the Gospel; in his claim to have come to call not the just but sinners; in his prayer that all be one as the Father is in him and he is in the Father; in his blood of the covenant poured out for the many; in the crucifixion seen as an act of intercession. The idea of such intercession is attractive, even though Hebrews alone develops it in any formal way and the expression of other passages in support of it is at times weak. Winter's chapter on why Jesus' crucifixion was historically inevitable in its assumption that his teaching led to his death is the weakest of all. The strength of his argument lies in maintaining with Rahner that the crucifixion is the efficacious sign of God's self-communicating, redeeming love. This enables him to say in yet another way that it is the sacrament of Christ's intercession with his Father (132–33).

Some feminist theologians reject Jesus' crucifixion as a death endured in obedience and accepted by God as the instrument or sign of redemption because it was a violent act. One states the case in the following way: "Atonement theology...redefines...an act of state violence as...a private spiritual transaction between God the Father and God the Son. [It] then says this intimate violence saves life. This redefinition...makes intimate violence holy and salvific. Intimate violence ends sin. Behind the holy mask of intimate violence, state violence disappears."[80] Clearly this is a protest against violent acts of every sort — wars, murders, psychological cruelties, wife-batterings — couched in the charge that Christianity has made violence tolerable by proclaiming salvation through the cross. Again: "Jesus is presented as the obedient son, accepting violence because his father wills it. The salvation offered by Jesus is gained by his sacrifice of himself to abuse....He accepts violence for the sake of his love for the perpetrators of violence, whether God or sinful humanity."[81] The passage is preceded by the developed idea that Christianity's presentation of God as the benevolent, all-powerful father and human beings as sinful and helpless "inhibits intimacy and maintains inappropriate forms of dependence. Adults are asked to surrender their lives passively and obediently in exchange for salvation."

Two authors who have as their important concern the missionary outreach of the gospel identify the penal substitution model of the atonement as profoundly harmful to a Christian understanding of the mystery.[82] They acknowledge that every attempt to express the truth of redemption in Christ reflects the social structures of the era. The various statements in the New Testament about what God has done for all humanity in Christ and the Spirit are no exception. To counter the tendency to isolate the cross or the outpouring of Jesus' blood as the divinely accepted satisfaction for sins, they examine *all* the ways the scriptures speak of the redeemed or reconciled life of the baptized. John's Gospel describes the work of the "other Paraclete" Jesus would send as life and truth and way. The other New Testament books have a variety of ways to speak of the difference Jesus' death and resurrection, taken as one, continues to make.

The Meaning of Redemption, Theories Quite Apart

The liturgies of East and West, from their earliest formulation, proclaimed to all the senses that the Eucharist was a mystery in word and sacrament that made available to those who partook of it the effects of Christ's life, death, and resurrection/ascension. This prayer to the Father through the Son in the community of the Holy Spirit renews and strengthens the life once received in baptism. Setting apart any portion of God's deed in Christ as alone accomplishing redemption — even the cross — can destroy the unity of the deed. What is this redemption, so often spoken of in the pages above? It is an aspect of the mystery of human life known as creation. For the case is not that things went badly from the start requiring correction by a beneficent Creator. From the moment the human creature was conscious of the use of freedom for good or ill, the possibility existed that humanity would choose what was not best for it. To be human is to have many strengths but as part of finitude, no little weakness. That God could have "regretted that he had made man on the earth" in the poignant anthropomorphism of Genesis 6:6 is unthinkable; equally unthinkable is that God could have abandoned this uniquely free creature to a self-destructive course. There had to be grace from the start, the divine assistance needed to do the right thing when the downward pull asserted itself to do the wrong. What form it took we can only surmise, convinced that at no time was the gift of freedom impeded. But there must have been gracious assistance. The divine wisdom and love demanded it.

The fathers of the church wrestled long and hard with the question of intelligent pagans, like Celsus, of why God had delayed so many centuries to send the Son. The apologists answered that the time was exactly right in terms of world history as they knew it. Paul had answered more wisely in his letter to the Galatian churches: "When the fullness of time had come," that is, in God's good time. Jesus, in proclaiming God's reign as a reality of the future, was speaking of an age when people would live fully humanly as they ought. Meanwhile, in time present, they must live for each other and not for themselves as if that day were already here: "Thy reign come upon us, thy will be done as it is in the heavens." God's will for us is that we be true to our nature at its best, not at its worst. Redemption has to mean that state of things in which it is made possible to do the divine will easily, readily.

It could not have been that we were left entirely to our own devices for eons. The form redemption took among the people Israel for two millennia we know. How among other peoples we may glean from their holy writings, if they have them, otherwise from their tales of what the world spirit or the Great Spirit expected of them. Some were "enslaved to the elemental powers of the world," in Paul's Jewish vocabulary descriptive of pagan worship, "to things in nature that are not gods." To those in Galatia he had brought redemption from that enslavement with a knowledge of the one, true God. He did more. Like many proclaimers of the Gospel of whom we have no record, he told anyone who would listen of a man who had conformed his will to God's will perfectly, a man like us in everything but sin. This Jesus in whom God dwelt more intimately than in anyone before or since was proposed for the conformity of all lives to his life. But not only that. Faith in all that God had done in him was the first requirement, faith meaning unreserved acceptance of his birth as a Jew under the Law, his life as a teacher of God's will for Jew and gentile alike, his death on a cross in total innocence of any sin or crime, and his resurrection from the dead to be with God until the last day.

That universal apostolic teaching, which Paul and other New Testament writers spell out, meant for those who accepted it new life, the life of the final age already begun. Believers in this teaching who asked for baptism viewed it as a second birth. They knew that what God had done in them was described in a number of ways starting with John's Danielic "life of the last age (*aiōniós*)" but also redemption, reconciliation, sanctification, salvation, and justification. No term was privileged above the others. All were ways to describe the "new creation" of 2 Corinthians 5:17 and Galatians 6:15 that they knew themselves to be. All were members of a new race, children of Adam as before but newly children of God, their creaturehood marvelously improved. The life of Christ in them and theirs in him was what made the difference. What life was that? Of a man who had had every human experience including temptation to sin but had not yielded, who was born into the world like them and had left it in excruciating pain, with the normal joys and sorrows in between, a man over whom God had not let death prevail, as it will in the short run for all others. When such a man and God's work in him were proposed as the object of faith, many believed not only in him but in the difference to them meant by that life and death. They were a people redeemed — necessarily a figurative term — by the power of the Spirit he had sent from his Father.

Redemption, then, once again: what is it? It means new condition for the same unchanged humanity. The long reign of sin from Adam to Christ ended for those who would freely accept the gift of the Spirit outpoured. Daughterhood and sonship of God for whoever would claim God joyfully as Father and Jesus Christ as brother. In a word, empowerment anew to live human life in a perfectly human way. An earthly paradise? No such thing has come of God's deed in Christ because, with our nature left unaltered, freedom can be abused as well as used. But these things have marked the redeemed, whether conscious of the redemption and its cause or not: generations of a sinful race become saints; slaves of sin turned to servants of God; no longer a human wolf (*homo homini lupus*) but a shepherd to fellow humans; unjust behavior at the hands of others endured, innocent suffering not understood but accepted, and death the last enemy no longer feared. All this has been brought about by God's raising up a second Adam, Jesus, who could not sin — it had no attraction for him. He not only lived a life of perfect obedience but shared the possibility with a multitude. It was a life of love for God and humankind. His painful death was that love in symbol, his conquest of death more symbolic still.

For Further Reflection

1. How is the idea of salvation communicated in the biblical writings? What is the paradigmatic event of redemption in the Hebrew Bible?

2. In the New Testament, what event lies behind the titles given to Jesus? What are some of the ways in which the New Testament's writers interpret the significance of Jesus?

3. What are the features of a theology of redemption in the writings of the early church fathers? What do they reject as well as accept?

4. What do Augustine and Anselm contribute to a theology of redemption in the Western tradition?

5. What themes characterize contemporary theologies of redemption? In your view, what is the most significant difference between the idea of redemption as it is developed in theologies in the tradition and those developed today?

For Further Reading

Kelly, J. N. D. *Early Christian Doctrine*. London: A. & C. Black, 1958.

Brock, Rita Nakashima, and Rebecca Ann Parker. *Proverbs of Ashes: Violence, Redemptive Suffering, and the Search for What Saves Us*. Boston: Beacon Press, 2001.

Pelikan, Jaroslav J. *The Christian Tradition: A History of the Development of Doctrine*. Vol. 3 *The Growth of Medieval Theology (600–1300)*. Chicago: University of Chicago Press, 1978.

Sloyan, Gerard S. *The Crucifixion of Jesus: History, Myth, Faith*. Minneapolis: Fortress Press, 1995.

Winter, Michael. *The Atonement*. Collegeville, Minn.: Liturgical Press, 1995.

Part Two

NEW CHALLENGES

— 5 —

Jesus Christ and
Religious Pluralism

Roger Haight, S.J.

The issues connected with pluralism, like those issues connected with development during the past two centuries, are generating a great deal of
theological energy. Many different theological positions on the status of
Jesus Christ relative to other religions and religious mediations compete for
common acceptance. Many theologians have built typologies to map the terrain, so many different typologies that now one finds a pluralism of maps.
Presuppositions make a great deal of difference on this issue, and the relation of positions to each other can be schematized in a variety of ways. For
example, when a map is laid out and positions are lined up, one should note
the point of departure: does the development begin from the right or from
the left? On the one hand, a theologian may presuppose a single normative
Catholic theology on this question, and from there seek to open this position
further toward some accommodation to religious pluralism. On the other
hand, another theologian may simply accept a situation of a pluralism of
religions and of Christologies in relation to it but, rejecting relativism, seek
to establish features about Jesus that are universally relevant and normative.

I shall try to thread my way between these alternatives with my definition of pluralism and the goal and strategy of this chapter. As to pluralism, I
mean unity amid difference, or differences within a common field of shared
faith, beliefs, and commitment. In other words, I use the term *pluralism*
not to refer to sheer multiplicity, but to differences held together within
some common bond of unity. As to my goal, in this chapter I want to illustrate nonpolemically two types of thinking that are quite different and
that may be considered on the right and the left side of some mythical center on this question. Perhaps they relate to each other as late modern and
postmodern. In any case, rather than build types, I have chosen two important contemporary theologians, Karl Rahner and Edward Schillebeeckx, to

illustrate these two different theological positions, both of which I consider viable today.[1]

My strategy in representing these two theologians consists in drawing a broad, schematic outline of the position of each thinker with the intention of drawing out the contrast between them. I also want to represent their way of approaching the question as typical of two different methods and styles of theological reflection that obtain in Roman Catholic theology today, and to suggest further that they represent two distinct "generations" of theologians. Unfortunately this strategy does not allow an adequate reconstruction of their arguments. I am hoping that those familiar with either or both of these major Catholic thinkers of our time will fill in the blanks and supply the nuances. Of course one should not forget the many elements that bind them together, not least of which is a faith and commitment to Jesus Christ as savior from God. The representation of their positions will demonstrate the many things they share in common, but the point is to contrast them and thus demonstrate pluralism. I am not attempting to break new ground in this discussion but to make plain the current situation of Catholic theology and open it up for discussion. The contrasting methods, styles, and positions of Rahner and Schillebeeckx represent many of the differences among Catholic theologians today, so that charting their development and the structure of their reasoning helps to explain the situation of Catholic theology today. By drawing out the logic and contrasting these two quite different ways of approaching Jesus Christ and religious pluralism in the theologies of the two most eminent Catholic theologians of the twentieth century, I hope to demonstrate a plausible and legitimate pluralism on this question within Catholic theology.

I will proceed as follows. In a first area of contrast referred to as "life situation and context" I briefly contrast the formation of each theologian and particularly their difference in age at the time of the Second Vatican Council and how they reacted to that council. In the second part I outline two significantly different methods of theology. The third part contrasts in parallel their stances on doctrines that have a direct bearing on Christology and the evaluation of other religions. And in part four I contrast their understanding of Christ and other religions.

Life Situation and Context

I begin with a consideration of the life situation of Rahner and Schillebeeckx because their relative ages and formation periods have significant bearing on the difference in the positions they developed.

Rahner. Karl Rahner was born in 1904 and in the course of his Jesuit formation and university training was schooled in philosophy and theology during the 1930s.[2] I will say more about his method in theology further on, but one can characterize him as a theologian who mediates Christian doctrine through philosophy. Rahner accepted the turn to the subject in metaphysics, as in the Kantian-influenced philosophical work of Joseph Maréchal and the existential ontology of Martin Heidegger. One of the major problems, if not the central theological issue, that Rahner addressed in his work was extrinsicism, the pervasive supposition that God's initiative in revelation and grace comes completely unexpected from outside the human sphere.[3] Rahner's early works included a transcendental philosophical interpretation of Thomas Aquinas's theory of knowledge, a philosophy of religion, and articles that reinterpreted the scholastic theology of grace. One of Rahner's best known theological constructions, the "supernatural existential," proposes that from the very beginning, always, and everywhere human existence unfolds within the gracious and personal offer of God's self as saving grace. This grace at the time was called supernatural to plainly distinguish it from the order of creation and the suggestion that it might be owed or necessarily given. His discussions in these areas provided him with a point of view and a set of categories that remained fairly constant throughout his career. He thus possessed a broad framework within which his Christology would neatly fit.

No event influenced Roman Catholicism and its theology in the twentieth century more than the Second Vatican Council. In many ways it stands as a watershed in Catholic history and life. A definite "before" and "after" Vatican II marks Catholic theology. When the council closed in 1965, Rahner was 61. His writings up to the council provided major resources for it, and after it concluded he continued to interpret the council in an aggressive forward-looking way. One can delineate distinctive new elements in Rahner's later theology; but on the whole the structure of his thinking, which I will describe further on, did not change radically. One reason for this lies in its open transcendental character: it is able to absorb new developments into itself.

Schillebeeckx. Edward Schillebeeckx was born ten years after Rahner in 1914 and as a Dominican began his theological formation in the late 1930s, pursued his studies through World War II, and completed them with a year in Paris and continuing work on a dissertation as he began teaching in Louvain in 1947.[4] His neo-Thomism also included a turn to the subject as found in the phenomenology of Maurice Merleau-Ponty and French personalism. In 1958 he moved from a seminary situation to the University of Nijmegen. He too participated in Vatican Council II as a *peritus*, or expert theologian. In 1965, Schillebeeckx was fifty-one, in almost exact midcareer. But the historical forces that generated the council and the council itself impelled him toward a thoroughgoing transition which can almost be described as a reinvention of himself as a theologian. Over a period of several years, during the late 1960s he immersed himself in the study of secularization, the historicity of human consciousness, hermeneutics, and critical theory, all of which contributed to the construction of a new set of presuppositions and a distinctly new method of theology relative to the first phase of his writing. In many ways Schillebeeckx mirrors in his own person the change that was occurring within a large segment of Catholic theology itself.

Let me draw the contrast between these two theologians in this first topic. Without having the space or resources to develop the point here, I believe that the ten-year difference in age of these two theologians made a significant difference in their future work after the Second Vatican Council. Other factors also played a part. But the fact is that while Rahner did not substantially alter the structure of his theological method, Schillebeeckx did. Rahner remained consistently modern in his universally relevant transcendental method. He is quintessentially modern in addressing the problem of extrinsicism and, in overcoming it, providing an understanding of divine grace as a divine appeal within the human itself that can be understood by all. Schillebeeckx too began as a modern but was so deeply affected by the problems of the absence of God, negativity and suffering, social oppression, pluralism, and historical relativism that they elicited the creation of what was for him a distinctly new method in theology. In many respects Schillebeeckx internalized many of the concerns which would later be called "postmodern."

Method in Theology

Nothing carries more weight as a prerequisite for understanding a theology than the method of the theologian. Given this crucial importance, let me try to capture the contrast in the methods of these two theologians in concise and terse formulas that add up to no more than caricatures, but very different ones. Here more than ever I am offering broad interpretations of these theologians which stand in great need of added nuance. But the point lies in underlining the difference between the two theologians and bears no polemical intent.

Rahner. Rahner's transcendental method in theology can be characterized as a correlation between an analysis of the self-transcending structure of the human person and the doctrines given by the Christian tradition. Rahner generates the meaning of these doctrines by an analysis of their saving significance as that is actually or implicitly experienced in the human subject. In this way Rahner's method combines dialectically a dynamism "from below," provided by a transcendental existential anthropology and epistemology, and what comes "from above," as given by revelation and supplied through the tradition.

Rahner's method in theology presupposes the unity of the human race, a universal human structure, and the participation of each person in this formal a priori structure of nature and existence. Rahner also posits the theological premise drawn from scripture that God communicates God's self as Spirit or light or love or grace to all humankind, every single person, for his or her salvation. This forges an existential unity of nature and grace, while preserving their distinction, and provides the platform for Rahner's use of phenomenological analysis of the human subject to discover and draw out the existential meaning of the doctrines and thus overcome extrinsicism. For example, God's initiative in grace does not stand over against the human but fulfills it by drawing the human spirit in knowledge and freedom out of and beyond the self toward transcendent fulfillment. Also, Rahner finds that Jesus of Nazareth is the Christ not because the divine Word stands over against the human but because Jesus is constituted as "hypostatic union," the unity of Jesus of Nazareth and the divine Word as one subject. This union represents the fulfillment of the human as such, the archetypal unity of the divine with the human, and the human fulfilled. Methodologically, therefore, the Christian message does not announce something alien to the human but is transcendent ratification of what was created for this end in the first place.[5]

Schillebeeckx. I turn now to the method of theology that Schillebeeckx employed after 1970.[6] It may be characterized as an historical method of critical correlation by which the data of Christian doctrines are mediated through a concern for the social historical conditions of human existence. Schillebeeckx does not completely dismiss transcendental analysis, as is shown in his characterization of basic human trust and negative experiences of contrast.[7] But he distinctly moves through these formal analyses to fix on the concrete negativities of human suffering and the frustration of human existence in various historical forms. This historical consciousness drove him to take up history and exegesis to reconstruct Jesus' ministry and the origins of Christology. Thus he too combines elements that come "from below" and "from above," but the consistent framework within which they mingle lies in historical existence. For example, he refers to formal anthropological constants, but he derives these empirically from historical description rather than from an appeal to the a priori conditions of personal existence.[8] Also Schillebeeckx begins Christology with Jesus of Nazareth, who, he concludes in the first moment of his Christology, is the parable of God in the way his ministry unfolded. Then, with an historical imagination in place, he traces the biblical testimony to resurrection and Christology.

The contrast between these two theologians on method roughly mirrors the contrast between early and late Schillebeeckx, and it can be sharply drawn. The framework of Rahner's theological thinking is universal or total; it encompasses all human existence, although he became increasingly concerned with historical applications. Schillebeeckx's later theology is confessionally based in Christian faith, focuses on human suffering in history,

but it reaches out toward universally relevant significance. Rahner breaks
out of the trap of extrinsicism, but remains concerned with making sense of
Chalcedon, hypostatic union, the appearance of the Christ in an evolution-
ary world. By contrast, Schillebeeckx, against the backdrop of historical
existence, its contingency, suffering, and seemingly ultimate annihilation,
mounts an apology for Christian faith by telling the story of Jesus and interpreting his resurrection as grounds for hope in the future. Rahner tends
more to accept doctrines as a given and then goes to work reinterpreting
them; Schillebeeckx tends to do a critical historical archaeology of their
genesis. Rahner's transcendental method is smooth and stresses the continuity of human existence and Christian doctrine; Schillebeeckx's historical
method attends more to negativity, inequality, and the jagged character of
human development. These two methods are not contradictory; one might
even make an argument for their complementarity. But in themselves they
are significantly different, and they lead in different directions.

Premises to Their Christological Positions

I move now to what I call premises to the positions of each theologian
on Christ and other religions. These premises consist in various theological
stances on doctrines which directly influence an appreciation of Jesus Christ
and the status of other religions. To accentuate the differences here I will
line up the doctrinal themes and contrast Rahner and Schillebeeckx on each
one. I have, in fact, drawn these themes mainly from Rahner where they
are related systematically, and I make the contrast by drawing Schillebeeckx
into the framework of Rahner's thought.

Trinity. *Trinity* is the name of a doctrine about God and not a name
for God, and Rahner carefully crafted a theology of the immanent trinity.
Other trinitarian theologians frequently quote his use of the Barthian axiom
that the economic trinity is the immanent trinity, an axiom which forbids
disjunction between the two dimensions of this mystery. In the economy
of salvation the Son and the Spirit are like the two arms of God in the
one personal self-communication to and embrace of humankind: the Son or
Logos having become flesh in Jesus of Nazareth, and the Spirit being the
self-communication of God to all humankind in grace. The distinction of
"persons" within the Godhead is real, just as the distinction of God's self-
communication in Jesus, which can only be the incarnation of the Son, is
really different from the general communication of God as Spirit. The former
self-communication of God as Son involves hypostatic union, the latter self-
communication of God as Spirit is not hypostatic union but a presence of
God to human beings by what Rahner calls quasi-formal causality. This
represents God's real personal presence which, unlike a created form, does
not constitute a being or quality as such but is a divine self-communication

or offering.[9] Rahner postulates that there is no real distinction between God communicating God's self in this threefold pattern of creation, incarnation, and sanctifying self-gift as Spirit and the essential character of God's own reality.

Interestingly, Schillebeeckx has no developed theology of the trinity. Schillebeeckx confesses belief in the reality of the immanent trinity but provides no indication whether his failure to develop a theology of the trinity is just something he never took up or a matter of principle. In other words, whereas one can say that Rahner's theology of the trinity is both a premise and a context as well as a conclusion to his Christology, one cannot say whether a doctrine of the trinity is operative in Schillebeeckx's later Christology at all, nor whether this is systematically deliberate or not. But it is "of a piece" with his Christology from below, which begins with a consideration of Jesus of Nazareth.

Nature and grace. I return to the issue of the relationship between nature and grace because it provides a fundamental framework for understanding the economy of God's dealing with human beings and their response, and because of the contrast between the language of Rahner and Schillebeeckx on this topic. Rahner's major contribution to Catholic theology in this crucial area consisted in overcoming an extrinsicist understanding of a supernatural intervention of God, while at the same time preserving the transcendent and utterly gracious character of God's salvation. He did this with a simultaneous distinction between the natural and supernatural orders of creation and redemption and an affirmation of their intimate unity. Finite creation is created for salvation. Creation or nature or more simply human beings, while possessing a certain autonomy, have always existed within the actual offer of God's supernatural love and self-gift, so that in fact nature and grace are inseparable orders and existentials. Rahner supported this vision of reality with a metaphysical distinction of a twofold "relation" of God to humankind by efficient causality of creation and the quasi-formal causality of self-presence or gift of divine self. This distinction preserved both God's freedom and human freedom for a real dialogical relationship. But the contribution of Rahner lay equally in the inseparable and intrinsic unity of these two orders.

The contrast with Schillebeeckx at this point remains subtle, undeveloped, but in many ways crucial. In his later theology Schillebeeckx does not discuss the issue of nature and supernatural grace in the terms laid out by neoscholasticism. By contrast he does discuss the theology of creation and the creator in terms that include within creation itself the saving love and intention of the creator. In other words, Schillebeeckx collapses the discussion of nature and grace into the theology of creation itself. But this does not amount to a reduction of God's grace or self-communication to necessity; he employs the terms of personalism and proposes a personal creator who creates out of love. Freedom, gratuity, and love are built into the creative act itself and do not have to be distinguished from it.

The prominence of Schillebeeckx's doctrine of creation allows him to make moves that avoid certain problems that in the past had encumbered Catholic theology. First, he bypasses completely the possible dualisms that the natural/supernatural distinction tends to foster. We saw that Rahner too overcame this problem with a more complex construction of the supernatural existential. Schillebeeckx encompasses Rahner's view in his notion of creation. Thus, second, Schillebeeckx conceptually simplifies the relationship between God as creator-savior and humankind. The creator God is savior; God as savior is creator. The very idea that these are two different kinds of actions of God is eliminated before it becomes a problem that has to be solved. Third, Schillebeeckx's turn to the doctrine of creation encourages a theocentric point of view for understanding the person and role of Jesus Christ.[10] I will draw this out further on.

Universal offer of salvation. The idea that God offers salvation to all human beings is actually a major premise that Rahner supports with considerations of the Old and New Testaments.[11] Its importance appears negatively when contrasted with traditions maintaining a restricted order of salvation, and positively in the pressure it puts on explaining the role of Jesus Christ. Schillebeeckx shares this conviction.

The salvation mediated by Jesus. This point and the next draw near to the heart of the matter, and one can begin to see method and premises coming together in a distinct systematic vision in both thinkers. The issue here concerns the broad lines of each theologian's theory of redemption. Rahner conceives of Jesus as the event in history that fulfills or brings to completion the history of God's self-communication for human salvation. It is not that grace or God's offer of saving love had been absent from the world prior to Jesus Christ. But the decisive, definitive, final, and as it were total self-communication to humankind occurred in the hypostatic union of the Son or divine Logos with human nature in Jesus of Nazareth and Jesus' human response. All of God's being-present to and with human beings finds its completion and fulfillment and archetypal goal in Jesus Christ whom God intended from the beginning. Jesus really is the center and keystone of Rahner's overarching and total vision of creation and the dialogue between God and human beings in history. For Rahner, the reality of the relationship between God and human beings was altered in the event of Jesus Christ. What began as promise and was offered provisionally in the course of history up to Jesus became definitively and publicly ratified or sealed in the Jesus event.

Schillebeeckx's redemption theory appears modest relative to the breathtaking cosmic vision of Rahner; he brings a reader down to earth. In fact, Schillebeeckx does not want to make a distinction between a theory of how

Jesus saves and the actual salvation that he mediates in history. But forcing what he does say of how Jesus saves into these categories, it appears that Jesus saves by revealing and actualizing God at work for human salvation in history. The creator God has always been saving from the very beginning, so that what occurs in Jesus is a revelation of what has always been going on. He also proposes a traditional exemplarism through which Jesus provides the God-given model of who God is and what it means to be human. In other words, salvation went on before Jesus and goes on outside his historical influence; historically Jesus saves where he saves, where people actually come under his influence. Compared with Rahner, these theological conclusions also constitute serious religious claims, but they stay closer to the ground.

Jesus the universal cause of salvation. Focusing even more pointedly on the role and place of Jesus Christ in the salvation that God offers to humankind, one should not forget three positions that Rahner defends and that are all of a piece. The first is the traditional claim that all grace is the grace of Christ. No grace or salvation comes from God that is not christic or mediated by Christ. The main logic for Rahner's understanding of this comes from its being integral to the whole vision that includes a trinitarian God. The creator is the triune God, who creates through the Son and in view of the incarnation. But, second, Rahner also holds that the facticity of the historical life of Jesus plays a role in the salvation of all, including especially the active surrender of Jesus on the cross. Jesus' historical acting out of the divine self-communication and his total positive response to it constitute the unity between God and human existence that is the very goal toward which all saving grace was oriented as toward its fulfillment or climax. And, third, since such a divine movement can have only one goal or climax, there can be only one incarnation of the Logos. The incarnation of the Son in Jesus could happen only once, and it is thus the absolute fulfillment of God's saving will toward which all other experiences of grace in history are oriented as to their climactic realization.

In contrast to Rahner's large and encompassing vision, Schillebeeckx begins with Jesus. His method leaves him dealing with Jesus as part of human history, which is also a history of salvation. His historical focus in a Christology from below leads him to consider Jesus, first, as the savior of Christians, and then to examine his universal relevance, without moving to the more abstract or general level of metaphysical characterization. I am not aware of Schillebeeckx denying that all grace is the grace of Christ or that the Logos could only become incarnate once. But his overall Christology and view of other world religions do not fit with such claims.

In sum, this survey of certain key doctrinal areas enables one to see how logically the methods adopted by each thinker and the way they construe certain basic issues surrounding Christology proper, inevitably lead them in

different directions. I referred earlier to Rahner's theology having a component that begins "from below" in an analysis of transcendental human
existence. But it also derives from the acceptance of authoritative doctrines
that constitute the pervasive context of his thinking. Trinity, the cosmic
framework in which he understands what occurred in the event of Jesus,
and the universal causal role that Jesus plays in salvation add up to a relatively tight metaphysical vision of all reality and the human phenomenon
in it. By comparison, Schillebeeckx's thinking stays closer to historical data,
from its starting point in Jesus to its claims regarding the impact of Jesus'
saving action. Jesus mediates salvation, but the question of whether Jesus
causes the salvation of all is almost precluded by the historical boundaries
that contain Schillebeeckx's imagination. I now want to draw the conclusions of these two diverging ways of theological reflection on the case study
in point, the relation between Jesus Christ and the mediations of salvation
in other world religions.

Christ and Other Religions

We arrive at the fourth and last point of this discussion of comparative constructive theology. How does each theologian understand Jesus Christ in his
relation to other religions, and the status of other religions relative to him?
I shall not deal with the christological problem in the terms of Chalcedon,
although both theologians have something to say on that. I restrict my remarks to more general issues by summarizing Rahner's view of Christ and
the other religions in three points and considering Schillebeeckx in contrast
with these.

Rahner.[12] The first feature defining Rahner's position on the relation of
Christ to all other religions and media of God's salvation resides in his
christocentric vision of the whole of reality. It is not simply that Rahner's
faith finds its mediating focus in Jesus Christ; such is true of all Christians
because it defines what a Christian is. It is rather that Rahner's objective con-
ceptualization of the cosmos itself is trinitarian in a way that places Christ
at the center. Christ provides the lens from which everything is understood
because, in the metaphysical scheme of things, Christ is the keystone of overarching reality. Metaphysically Christ the Son is the beginning of reality as
the medium and goal of God creating, the middle or center of human history by his incarnation, and end of human history as representing its final
or eschatological goal in resurrection.

Second, within this grand metaphysical vision, other religions are truly
valid and willed by God, but their liceity or continued being willed by God
is conditional upon the nonexistence or nonpromulgation of the revelation
of Jesus Christ. Relative to a full acceptance of religious pluralism this view
may seem narrow, but Rahner proposed it first against Christian exclusivism,

and in that context it is genuinely expansive; the religions play a real saving role in the lives of their constituents. Moreover, the condition that Rahner postulates for the liceity of other religions, namely, the lack of an objective promulgation of Christianity, could be broadly interpreted within Rahner's framework in terms of a real existential availability, that is, that Christianity be a concretely viable option, which for most non-Christians it is not. Therefore, relative to the availability of salvation and the possible mediation of salvific grace in other religions, Rahner's position is open to a fairly broad interpretation. But it remains the case that the religions themselves are interpreted intrinsically within an objective christological framework.

Third, therefore, the world's religions do not enjoy theological autonomy. When located within Rahner's conception of the role of Christ and the place of the Christian phylum in human history, the grace mediated by other religions is really the grace of Christ. Jesus Christ is thus actually constitutive of the salvation which, on an historical level, may concretely be mediated by any given non-Christian religion. One can say that Jesus Christ is the cause of the salvation that occurs in the lives of people who live their religious lives within other religions.[13] Jesus of Nazareth is the incarnation of God in an absolutely unique way that is qualitatively different than the presence and effectiveness of God in other religious mediators. Such an incarnation could happen only once, and its occurrence makes Christianity God's own religion, so to speak, in an absolute way. Absoluteness here means that everything else is related to it, and it entails the logic that the religions are in themselves lacking and bear within themselves an orientation toward being completed by Christianity. All religions are related to Christianity as to their fulfillment. Thus Rahner recognizes a de facto pluralism of religions, but not pluralism in principle. Religious pluralism is something that is anomalous and in principle should be overcome.

Schillebeeckx.[14] Lining up the parallel but contrasting positions on Schillebeeckx's part, we can begin with his overall vision of reality as being theocentric. Schillebeeckx reappropriates the doctrine of creation, and he sets up the two doctrines of creation and eschatology to form the framework for a theology of history.[15] Consistent with this, his Christology from below begins with the historical person of Jesus and not with trinity nor the metaphysics of nature and grace. Thus Christ is not portrayed as the center of Schillebeeckx's cosmology. That position belongs to God, creator of heaven and earth, and the goal of the movement of history. Schillebeeckx's large vision of reality is theocentric. I should not, however, give the impression that Schillebeeckx has counter assertions to each of the elements of Rahner's christocentrism; he does not emphasize that his vision is theocentric, for in other ways, as with all Christians, his faith in God and appropriation of God is mediated by Jesus of Nazareth and thus christocentric. It is important to keep this distinction already alluded to in mind: Christian faith in God is by definition christocentric because it is faith in God mediated by Jesus. But this does not necessarily translate into a christocentric vision of reality. For example, Jews and Christians relate to the same God and share elements of a common body of scriptures and revelation, but Jews are not christocentric in their world view and many Christians are not as well.

Second, all religions are finite, none are absolute; even Christianity is mediated historically through the finite creature Jesus of Nazareth. Schillebeeckx works with the traditional principle that God is transcendent infinity, so that God's absoluteness cannot be contained without remainder in any finite piece of created reality nor the whole of it. Uniqueness does not mean absoluteness despite the fact that uniqueness and absoluteness tend to be confused. Thinking within the context of historicity, Schillebeeckx understands that all religions share a measure of particularity, individuality, and autonomy. When they are taken together in a theocentric framework, on Christian principles of the universality of grace and God's saving will, one must think that there is more revelation in many religions including Christianity than there could be in only one.[16] The uniqueness of religions refers to their historical individuality and particularity, a logic that also applies to the uniqueness of Jesus Christ. More practically, and referring to a growing general consciousness, Schillebeeckx makes a point of saying that in today's world one cannot affirm the superiority of one religion over another. Many factors converge to call the a priori superiority of one religion over another into question. Globalization, a sense of the radical character of historicity and pluralism, a sense of how religion defines a culture and a people, and life together on the planet, all make the doctrine of the superiority of one religion over others the equivalent of a declaration of war.[17] One has to take account of the intrinsic ethical implications of doctrinal views.

Third, other religions according to Schillebeeckx are valid or legitimate in principle. I take the phrase "in principle" to mean that the fact of religious pluralism is a good. This view derives from an historical consciousness that recognizes the limited character of every religion relative to ultimate reality itself. All religions are particular, autonomous, unique; and religions other than Christianity do not take their value from their anonymously mediating what has been effected by Jesus Christ and what is on that basis contained in Christianity. The fundamental issue that Christian theology should address in this matter relates primarily to its own self-understanding, that is, of Jesus Christ, in such a way that it protects the autonomy of the other religions rather than absorbing them into itself. In Schillebeeckx's theology this is achieved by interpreting Jesus Christ not as constitutive of the salvation that is mediated by other religions but as the mediator of specifically Christian salvation and more generally as revelatory of the character of salvation as such. On the one hand, Christian revelation and salvation are universally relevant because the God revealed in Jesus is the creating and redeeming God of all. On the other hand, that same God is present to the world religions independently of Jesus.[18] Religious pluralism in principle, in Schillebeeckx's view of human history, does not have a negative valence. He is quite explicit on the point that it cannot and should not be overcome. "From all this I learn that (even in the Christian self-understanding) the multiplicity of religions is not an evil which needs to be removed, but rather a wealth which is to be welcomed and enjoyed by all."[19]

Summing up this contrast between Rahner's and Schillebeeckx's appraisal of Christ and the religions one could say that Rahner's is a totalizing view of Christianity. His christocentrism relates all other religions to Christianity as their fulfillment. Schillebeeckx too has a totalized view of reality but the worldview does not revolve exclusively around Jesus Christ. His is a Christian vision of God as creator of heaven and earth, and a theology of history leading to eschatological fulfillment. Jesus is universally relevant in revealing that eschatological fulfillment in the kingdom of God but other religions are autonomous; they too contain revelation and do not necessarily relate to him as their fulfillment.

Conclusion

As a conclusion to this exercise in comparative theology I wish to submit the proposal that, as different as these two positions are from each other, they are both acceptable or valid, at least at this time. Let me first draw out how different these two Christologies are and then take up the question of how they can live together in a pluralistic situation within one church.

The differences between Rahner and Schillebeeckx on the question of Christ and other religions are quite dramatic, and this can be illustrated by reviewing their contrasting stances on foundational conceptions. First, although Rahner proceeds methodologically from below in some respects that were mentioned earlier, his theology on this issue is really controlled by an imagination that also works "from above," specifically by his reliance on the doctrine of the immanent trinity. By contrast, Schillebeeckx argues consistently from below and within a framework of history and historical consciousness. But his method is far from reductionistic, and he is not lacking in metaphysical and transcendental principles. Second, Rahner proposes a christocentric vision in which Jesus Christ is the absolute bringer of God's salvation. The descending incarnation of the Logos that occurred in Jesus can happen only once. By contrast Schillebeeckx works within a theocentric framework in which Jesus is the bringer of God's absolute salvation; he nowhere limits the decisive saving presence of God in history to a single event. Third, Rahner accepts religious pluralism in fact, but not in principle. The religions actually mediate God's salvation, but in his metahistory, with the

coming of Christ, they no longer should exist but should find their fulfillment in Jesus Christ. Schillebeeckx, by contrast, accepts religious pluralism
in principle. His historical consciousness recognizes that the pluralism and
fragmentation of history suggest that the same God's saving presence can
be mediated differently and independently in different religions. These are
two significantly different christological conceptions of the person of Jesus
Christ in relation to other religions.

Without passing judgment on these theological stances of Rahner and
Schillebeeckx, I can address the place where each will appear vulnerable to
critiques from the other side. First, relative to Rahner: the weakness of his
position when viewed from the pluralist quarter concerns its intelligibility.
The pressure appears in his dogmatic insistence that Jesus is the absolute
savior while all other religions are relative and inferior to Christianity. This
looks like simple dogmatism and Christian imperialism or self-assertion in
a de facto pluralistic world. In response, I believe that Rahner still expresses
the faith of the majority of Christians on this point. Also, one can remain
within his position and at the same time soften the absoluteness of Christ
by raising up other religions toward a more autonomous status.[20]

Second, relative to Schillebeeckx: when people view his pluralist position
from the perspective of theologies that have controlled the field since the
period of the christological councils, they will likely question its fidelity
to scripture and tradition; the tradition seems to affirm the absoluteness
of Jesus Christ that Schillebeeckx questions. In response, it is crucial to
recognize that his granting autonomous validity to other religions in no way
undermines the high Christology established at Nicea and Chalcedon. This
fallacy is actually quite common: theologians enter the list on the basis of
an adversarial framework, as though what God does in one place competes
with what God does in another. But affirming that God acts in other religions
independently of Jesus in no way minimizes what God has done in Christ.
Therefore, while Schillebeeckx expresses the faith of a minority of Christians
today, they are a significant minority and on the increase both in Africa and
Asia where there is greater familiarity and appreciation of other religions,
and in the West as formerly Christian nations increasingly become religiously
pluralistic.

Finally, what can be said about the validity and viability of both of these
positions? Can they coexist in one church? I am not sure whether one could
find a knock-down proof of the viability of both of these positions, but I
can suggest two arguments that explain why it may be possible to consider
them as being able to coexist in one church.

The first argument rests on the distinction between theology and Christian
faith. What holds the Christian community together is not a common theology but a common faith. Both of these theological positions are grounded
in a common Christian faith, which they try to render intelligible in the

circumstances of the world today. That faith is faith in God as God has been revealed in the ministry and person of Jesus of Nazareth, understood to be the Christ. Jesus in Christian faith is sacrament or symbol of God, making God present and revealed for our salvation, and thus the object of worship. Both positions are based in this faith and bring it to expression in an uncompromising way.

The second argument appeals to the discipline of theology and its criteria: both theological positions possess a coherent, comprehensive, and integral character. By their *coherence* I mean that each theologian operates with a distinct method of theology and a broad range of intelligible and traditional premises, and each generates systematically a holistic view of things. By *comprehensive* I mean that each thinker has a broad sweeping view of reality in which his particular theological position on this matter is a part. Their positions on this issue are not erratic but are consistent with broader plausible interpretations of Christianity that in turn support their particular thesis. And by *integral* I mean that each has conformed to the general formal rules of theological method for generating a valid conclusion: their theological conclusions are faithful to scripture, intelligible in our world today, and generative of Christian life. One can also add another dimension to these qualities in both of these theologies: they are recognized as such by others. Each position has a constituency that more or less resonates with each construct.

In conclusion, then, a consideration of the two significantly different Christologies of Karl Rahner and Edward Schillebeeckx seems to show that a real pluralism of such theologies of religion is possible and even desirable within a single Christian church.

For Further Reflection

1. How would you characterize the difference between the theological methods of Karl Rahner and Edward Schillebeeckx?

2. What is the most significant or telling difference between Rahner and Schillebeeckx among the elements presented as the premises of their positions?

3. Relative to other religions, Karl Rahner's Christology is often called "inclusivist" and Edward Schillebeeckx's Christology is often called "pluralist." What would each of these terms mean in relation to these thinkers?

4. Which of the two positions relative to Christ and other world religions is more adequate for understanding Jesus Christ in our time?

For Further Readings

Dych, William V. *Karl Rahner.* Collegeville, Minn.: Liturgical Press, 1992.

Haight, Roger, S.J. *Jesus: Symbol of God.* Maryknoll, N.Y.: Orbis Books, 1999.

Kennedy, Philip. *Schillebeeckx.* Collegeville, Minn.: Liturgical Press, 1993.

Knitter, Paul. *Introducing Theologies of Religion.* Maryknoll, N.Y.: Orbis Books, 2002.

Rahner, Karl. *Foundations of Christian Faith: An Introduction to the Idea of Christianity.* New York: Crossroad, 1994.

Schillebeeckx, Edward. *Church: The Human Story of God.* New York: Crossroad, 1990.

Schreiter, Robert, and Mary Catherine Hilkert, eds. *The Praxis of the Reign of God.* New York: Fordham University Press, 2002.

— 6 —

The Christ Event and
the Jewish People

John T. Pawlikowski, O.S.M.

The formal process of rethinking theologically the meaning of Christ, Christian identity, and the Jewish people is generally regarded as having begun with the historic meeting of Jews and Christians (Catholics, Protestants and Greek Orthodox) at Seeligsberg, Switzerland, in 1947. The Christians who participated in that consultation, the memory of the Nazi Holocaust still fresh in their minds, produced a declaration that set Christian thinking regarding the Jewish people on a totally new course. Several prominent European Christian scholars began to speak out, including Karl Barth, who defined the "Christian-Jewish relationship" as the fundamental "ecumenical" problem confronting the churches. Other prominent Christian scholars joined the chorus led by Barth. They included Jean Daniélou, the future Cardinal Augustin Bea, James Parkes, and Hans Urs von Balthasar.

While not in complete agreement on every point, their voices were clearly in accord on one central issue: Jews must now be regarded as continuing in a covenantal relationship with God, however Christian theology might eventually interpret the meaning of the Christ event. The notion of continued Jewish covenantal *inclusion* undercut the theology of Jewish covenantal *exclusion* that had dominated Christian thinking since the era of the church fathers. A number of these early pioneers found it challenging to combine their new theological perspective on Jews and Judaism with their continued commitment to "newness" in the Christ event. A number fell into a "mystery theology," rooted in the writings of St. Paul, where the proper reconciliation of these two theological affirmations went beyond human understanding. It was something known only to God.

Christological Polemic against the Jews

This post–World War II theological development, motivated in part by the reality of the Holocaust, began to turn the churches from the centuries-old *adversus Judaeos* tradition (that is, Christian polemic against Jews) and its claims of Jewish rejection for the supposed murder of the messiah. Rosemary Radford Ruether has demonstrated in her now-classic volume *Faith and Fratricide* that anti-Judaism lay at the heart of this tradition which began in the writings of the major church fathers.[1] Anti-Judaism in effect became what Ruether terms "the left hand of Christology" in such patristic writers as Tertullian, Origen, Irenaeus, and Eusebius.

In many of his writings, but especially in those directed against Marcion, Tertullian presented Jesus as the messiah who ought to have been recognized by the Jewish People but was not. As a result of their "blindness," Tertullian argued, Jews were subjected on an ongoing basis to divine wrath. For him, Jesus' severity toward Jews was completely in line with the antagonism toward Jews expressed by God the Father. As David Efroymson has put it,

> What seems significant here is not the negative picture of the Jews of Jesus' time, which was, of course, already firmly embedded in the tradition. It is rather the heavy emphasis on the appropriateness of the opposition between Jesus and Jews, or between God and Jews.... Not only was there an emphatic heightening of an anti-Jewishness ascribed to Jesus; there was the additional element, apparently now crucial against Marcion, of a God who for sometime had "opposed" Israel and had wanted to rid himself of the "old" covenant in the interest of something new and better.[2]

Tertullian's theology thus regarded Jews as "tolerated" by God as covenantal partners until a better group of people could be found. In the divine perspective the initial covenant with Moses was a burden that God bore for some centuries until Christ could appear on the scene. With Christ's coming, God was finally liberated, as it were, from the severe limitations of the covenant with the Jewish people.

Origen's approach was marked by a particular emphasis on what he called the "spiritual sense" of the scriptures. Reading the biblical texts in this way, he insists in *On the First Principles,* is the solution to the problem of the "hard-hearted and ignorant members of the circumcision" (i.e., the Jews) who "refused to believe in our Savior" because they could not get beyond the literal sense of the text.[3]

Irenaeus explained Jewish law as necessary for a time because of human sinfulness. But the coming of Jesus and the destruction of Jerusalem signaled that the time of the Jews and their law was now over. According to Irenaeus,

Jesus attacked the Jewish claim to be able to know the Father without accepting the Son. He relied on the parables of the wicked servants (Matt. 21: 33–44) and the wedding feast (Mark 22:1–14) to "prove" that God had destined the gentiles to replace unresponsive Jews in the kingdom.

Finally, Eusebius, in his early fourth-century *Ecclesiastical History*, confines the role of the Jews to that of witness to divine justice. That was especially true in the first century, when Jews were being punished at the hands of the Romans while Christianity was flourishing and growing.

The above descriptions of the patristic attitude toward Jews and Judaism are but a sampling of the texts that could be referenced. Augustine, John Chrysostom, Lactantius, John Damascene and several others added their voices to this theological attack on the Jewish people. Rosemary Ruether is quite correct in arguing that the *adversus Judaeos* literature of the church fathers did not have as its goal converting the Jews or simply attacking them for their supposed failures in covenantal faithfulness. Rather, this literature responded to what Ruether calls an "intrinsic need of Christian self-affirmation." The goal of this theological literature was primarily "to affirm the identity of the Church, which could only be done by invalidating the identity of the Jews."[4] She goes on to add that this theology might have remained on a theoretical level if Christianity had remained a minority religion. But when it became the state religion of the Roman empire, this theology became meshed with political power to the legal and physical detriment of the Jewish community.

Over the centuries, this original patristic *adversus Judaeos* tradition has continued to exercise a sometimes direct and sometimes more subtle influence on Christian theological formulation of the meaning of Jesus' public ministry, death, and resurrection. It has given rise to a decided emphasis on Christ over God and Spirit, leading at times to what Dorothee Soelle has described as a "cryptoracist" tendency in christological doctrine.

This deep-seated tradition of anti-Judaic Christology has continued to find expression even in recent attempts at theological reformulation. Liberation theologians, for example, have not been free of its shadow. Gustavo Gutiérrez has written that since "the infidelities of the Jewish people made the Old Covenant invalid, the Promise was incarnated both in the proclamation of a New Covenant, which was awaited and sustained by the 'remnant,' as well in the promises which prepared and accompanied its advent."[5] And Clark Williamson, in a detailed study of Jon Sobrino's *Christology at the Crossroads,* makes use of the basic anti-Judaic framework for Christology set forth in the writings of Tertullian, to show that each aspect of Tertullian's anti-Judaic model is replicated in Sobrino's approach to Christology. Each theme, according to Williamson, can be documented in his text.[6]

The christological perspective of Leonardo Boff in his volume, *Jesus Christ Liberator,* parallels that of Sobrino in many respects relative to the theological understanding of Judaism.[7] While Boff acknowledges some positive aspects of the Hebrew scriptures that he says brought God into history, and while he admires the eternal optimism of the Jewish apocalyptic vision, his interpretation of Jesus' liberating power rests almost entirely on a rejection of the Judaism of Jesus' day. Like Sobrino, he totally ignores the liberating dimension of the Exodus covenantal tradition. For Boff, the ministry of Jesus inaugurated a new image of God and a new approach to God. Here Boff walks the same path as Sobrino. "God is no longer the old God of the Torah," he insists, but rather "a God of infinite Goodness, even to the ungrateful and the wicked. He draws near in grace, going far beyond anything prescribed or ordained by the law."[8]

Interpretations of Christ with a decidedly anti-Judaic bent have also been part of feminist theologies over the past several decades, as Barbara Bowe has noted.[9] The very legitimate critique of patriarchy and its negative impact on the role of women in the churches often was presented in ways that showed Jesus in a favorable light in comparison with the prevailing Jewish mentality of his day. According to Jewish feminist scholar Judith Plaskow, this resulted in feminism becoming "another weapon in the Christian anti-Judaic arsenal."[10] Plaskow adds: "The impulse to vindicate Christianity by laying its patriarchal elements at the feet of Judaism seems to have emerged along with Christian feminist interpretation."[11]

Feminist theological anti-Judaism has taken on a variety of forms. Katharina von Kellenbach has summarized these forms in a succinct manner. She identifies three general tendencies: (1) a dualistic pairing of the negative (Jewish) and positive (Christian) through the rubric of biblically based language (e.g., "letter and spirit," works versus faith, particularism versus universalism); (2) the persistent scapegoat of Jews who are blamed for the death of Jesus; and (3) the identification of Judaism exclusively with the "Old Testament" and hence only with Christian prehistory. Von Kellenbach argues that each of these tendencies supports a pernicious form of traditional Christian supersessionist theology in a feminist key.[12]

Another major point of linkage between Christology and antisemitism arises from the interpretation of Jesus' approach to the law, particularly as presented by Paul in his epistles. Protestant Christianity has shown a marked tendency to build a great deal of its christological understanding around the belief that Jesus brought to the fore a new sense of freedom that obliterated any further need for the Jewish Torah tradition. Because Torah observance was at the heart of Second Temple Judaism in the time of Jesus, total rejection of this tradition was tantamount to rejection of the Jewish tradition as such. Hence this "freedom" Christology, so commonplace in Protestantism, undercut any continuing validity for Judaism. Christian exegetes and theologians, such as Jon Sobrino, have especially targeted the Pharisees and have described Jesus as strenuously opposed to supposed "Pharisaic legalisms" in the name of a new Christian freedom of the spirit, ignoring the considerable new scholarship on the Pharisaic movement[13] and ignoring the 1985 Vatican *Notes* on Christian-Jewish relations, where Pharisees are described as the Jewish group that was closest to Jesus in outlook and practice.

The christological tradition of the churches never advocated outright extermination of the Jewish people in the manner of Nazism, although individual Christian preachers did sometimes suggest such a fate. Rather, this tradition argued that Judaism was to continue until Christ's return in glory but as a religious shell that has lost all status and was bereft of spiritual vitality. It was to survive as a "pariah" to highlight the superiority of the church, which had accepted Jesus as Lord and redeemer. The desperate plight of the Jewish people was also intended to serve as a warning to anyone in the Christian community who might be tempted to stray away from belief in Christ.

We have already seen Rosemary Reuther's argument that the church was not content to keep its notion of Jewish displacement confined to the theological realm.[14] While the institutional church has opposed any notion of a "final solution" (the final fate of the Jews was entirely in divine hands and would be decided as part of the final eschatological drama), it did attempt to translate this theology into concrete forms of "social misery." As Ruether puts it, "the legislation of Christian emperors and Church councils on the status of the Jew in Christian society reflects the effort to mirror this theological theory in social practice." While there were some exceptions to this approach to the Jewish place in Christian society in such places as Spain and Poland,[15] they were usually initiated by Christian lay leaders and often opposed by the local hierarchy and clergy. On the whole, such efforts to marginalize the Jewish community socially remained commonplace in Western society, in some places until the twentieth century. And even the Nazi legislation against the Jews, though it was ultimately rooted in a new form of biological racism, owed much to ancient and medieval legislation promulgated against them. While the Nazi approach to the Jewish question set it apart from earlier forms of antisemitism in Christian societies, it would be wrong to posit any complete disconnect between Nazi antisemitism and the much more explicitly theologically based antisemitism that existed in Christianity for centuries.

These two central theological trends in Christianity, that is, viewing the church as displacing the Jewish people in the basic covenantal relationship with God and understanding the Gospel as a total replacement for the Jewish Torah, have stood at the heart of christological statements in Christianity over the centuries. They have profoundly affected liturgical expression within the churches. As a result, any definitive cleansing of antisemitism from the Christian heritage will necessarily involve some reshaping of basic christological language in Christianity's faith proclamation.

New Impulses

The post–World War II erosion of Christian supersessionist theology in reference to Jews and Judaism has been generated in large measure by a new focus on Paul's reflections on the Christian-Jewish relationship in Romans 9–11. This was the scriptural basis for the Second Vatican Council's about-face on the theological understanding of the Jewish-Christian relationship; and it has been pivotal for many parallel statements from Protestant ecumenical and denominational statements, such as the recent statement from the Leuenberg Church Fellowship of Reformation Churches in Europe.[16]

The first generation of postwar Christian theologians saw, in Paul's insistence in Romans 9–12 that God remains faithful to the original chosen people, a justification for their efforts at christological restatement. They at least insisted that, however Christians might interpret the "newness" in Christ, it cannot be in a manner that obliterates Jewish membership in the covenant. Some of these scholars, after considerable reflection, wound up arguing that we cannot go further than Paul himself did on the christological question when he insisted that reconciliation between an assertion of "newness" in Christ and the affirmation of the continued participation of the Jewish people in the covenant remains a "mystery" understandable only to God. Associated with this line of thinking were theologians such as Kurt Hruby, Jacques Maritain, Jean Daniélou, and Augustin Cardinal Bea, who played a central role in securing Vatican II's approval of the statement on the church and the Jewish people and organized the initial implementation of this document immediately after the council.

These initial efforts at moving from a Christology focused on notions of Jewish covenantal displacement toward a perspective more accepting of an ongoing post-Easter Jewish covenantal presence continued to remain uncompromising on the centrality of Christ and the fulfillment resulting from the incarnation and the resurrection. No real attempt was made to erase the apparent contradiction between the affirmation of Jewish covenantal continuity and fulfillment in Christ. Following Paul's lead in Romans 9–11, these theologians insisted that the church needs to make these twin proclamations a part of its fundamental faith statement, even though ultimate reconciliation lies beyond human comprehension. In their view God remains sovereign of both Jews and Christians, and therein is to be found the basis for the reconciliation of these two seemingly contradictory assertions. As we shall see later in this chapter, this tension has not yet been totally overcome in more recent theological attempts at stating the theology of the Christian-Jewish relationship from the side of the church.

The process of eradicating the *adversus Judaeos* tradition from Christian theology gained new impetus at Vatican II, as has already been indicated. After a dramatic meeting between French Jewish historian Jules Isaac and

Pope John XXIII prior to the opening of the council, the Pope decided that the conciliar agenda would include a statement on Christianity's relationship to Judaism and the Jewish people. Chapter four of the conciliar Declaration on the Church's Relationship with Non-Christians was the end result of this process. Though this was an internal Catholic document, its impact extended far beyond the parameters of the Catholic church. Chapter four of *Nostra Aetate,* which revolutionized the church's understanding of its relationship with Jews and Judaism by insisting that Jews could not be blamed collectively for the death of Christ, by stressing the positive influence of the Jewish tradition on Jesus and his disciples, and by affirming continued Jewish covenantal inclusion after the Christ event, sparked parallel reexaminations within many mainline Protestant denominations.[17]

Confronting the supersessionist tradition within Catholic theology regarding the Jews at Vatican II proved a challenging task. There were times when it appeared that the document might not make it through the conciliar process. This is not surprising since Gregory Baum has referred to chapter four of *Nostra Aetate* as arguably the most profound change in the ordinary magisterium of the church to occur at Vatican II.[18]

The actual composition of the Vatican declaration proved quite revealing, as Eugene Fisher has noted. For it showed the poverty of the Christian tradition relative to any positive understanding of the relationship with the Jewish people. Every other conciliar document from Vatican II abounds with references to the tradition of the church — church fathers, papal statements, declarations by previous church councils. Not so with chapter four of *Nostra Aetate.* There were simply few, if any, positive dimensions of church tradition upon which the bishops at the council could draw to support their statement on the church and the Jewish people. So the bishops at Vatican II were forced to go back to the beginning, to where Paul had left off in his reflections on the Christian-Jewish relationship in light of the Christ event in Romans 9–11. In so doing, they established this biblical text as the prevailing one for the church's thinking about this relationship over the passage in Hebrews where the original covenant with Israel appears to be severed with the coming of Christ (Heb. 8:13).

In light of this conciliar action, where the church's teaching authority was utilized to decide between two apparently contradictory biblical texts, theologians such as Cardinal Avery Dulles who seem to want to restore the text from Hebrews as a major resource for the theology of Christian-Jewish relations today are very much off target.[19] Such a restoration of the Hebrews text is clearly contrary to the fundamental stance taken by the church at Vatican II. Constructing a new theology of the church and the Jewish people freed from its classical supersessionist and displacement motif represents an epochal undertaking since it touches upon the very nerve center of Christian faith, that is, its christological understanding. Supersessionist theology, as it emerged in the writings of the major church fathers, has stood at the core of Christian belief over the centuries. Because of this the pace of theological reformulation regarding the Jewish-Christian relationship must inevitably be slow and carefully done for, as Johannes Metz has strongly emphasized, reformulating the theological understanding of the church's linkage with the Jewish people carries significance for the whole of Christian theology. Metz puts it this way: "It is not a matter of revision of Christian theology with regard to Judaism, but a matter of the revision of Christian theology itself."[20]

The Role of Biblical Scholarship

The process of revising Christianity's theological approach to Judaism has been enhanced by the work of biblical scholars and theologians. We are witnessing a genuine revolution in New Testament and early Christian scholarship, as well as parallel scholarship on the Judaism, or what some would prefer to call "Judaisms," of the period. Within Christian biblical scholarship we are seeing a rapid end to the dominance of the early *Religionsgeschictlicheschule* which emphasized the almost totally Hellenistic background of Pauline Christianity, as well as its later, somewhat modified, manifestations in the writings of Rudolf Bultmann and some of his disciples, such as Ernst Käsemann and Helmut Koester. These exegetical approaches to the New Testament seriously eroded Jesus' concrete ties to, and dependence upon, biblical and Second Temple Judaism. This in turn tended to produce an excessively universalistic interpretation of Jesus' message that harbored the seeds of theological anti-Judaism and reinforced the traditional supersessionist interpretation of the Christian-Jewish relationship.

There have been a number of leading biblical scholars, some with a continuing transcontinental influence, who have contributed to the de-Judaization of Christian faith and to an interpretation of Jesus and Christology stripped of all ties to the Jewish tradition. One of the most prominent was Gerhard Kittel, the original editor of the widely used *Theological Dictionary of the New Testament*.[21] Kittel viewed postbiblical Jews as largely a community in dispersion. "Authentic Judaism," he wrote, "abides by the symbol of the stranger wandering restless and homeless on the face of the earth."[22] And the prominent exegete Martin Noth, whose *History of Israel* became a standard reference for students and professors alike, described Israel as a strictly "religious community" that died a slow, agonizing death in the first century C.E. For Noth, Jewish history reached its culmination in the arrival of Jesus. His words are concise and to the point in this regard:

> Jesus himself no longer formed part of the history of Israel. In him the history of Israel had come, rather, to its real end. What did belong to the history of Israel was the process of his rejection and condemnation

by the Jerusalem religious community...the history of Israel moved quickly to its end.[23]

The implication of Noth's perspective is that the Jewish people and its tradition have no part to play in the understanding of Jesus' ministry and of the church's theological interpretation of that ministry. As we shall see subsequently, church leaders and theologians such as Pope John Paul II stand in a quite opposite place in this regard. But the Noth thesis was quite prominent within the churches prior to the Second Vatican Council's declaration and the parallel changes in Protestant theological depictions of Christian-Jewish relations.

A third example is Rudolf Bultmann, who exercised a decisive influence over Christian biblical interpretation for decades. Unlike Kittel, who was removed from his teaching post at Tübingen in 1945 because of his explicit pro-Nazi sympathies, Bultmann's exegesis did not carry over into politics. But, theologically speaking, his understanding of the Christ event also left Jews and Judaism bereft of meaning after the coming of Jesus. Again, Jews and Judaism have nothing positive to contribute to the meaning Christians attach to Jesus' public ministry and to Christology. In his *Theology of the New Testament*[24] Bultmann held a view similar to that of Martin Noth. For Bultmann, a Jewish people cannot be said to exist with the onset of Christianity. For him, Jewish law, ritual, and piety removed God to a distant realm. In contrast, the continued presence of Jesus in prayer and worship enabled each individual Christian to come ever closer to God. Again, Bultmann's perspective is totally contrary to the position of most biblical scholars and church documents today which portray Jesus and his disciples as profoundly influenced in their fundamental religious outlook by the Judaism of their time. Bultmann's understanding of Judaism in Jesus' day was rooted in a seriously inadequate use of source materials in terms of Second Temple Judaism and Jesus' relationship to its teachings and spirit.

This deep-seated tradition of separating Jesus from Judaism has continued to manifest itself in more recent biblical scholarship. Scholars such as Norman Perrin and John Dominic Crossan have often interpreted Jesus' parables in a way that make them anti-Judaic in tone. This is where the work on the parables by a scholar such as Clemens Thoma, in which there is clear evidence of a positive correlation between Jesus' parables and those found in the Judaism of the same period, represents such an important counterforce to this continuing Bultmannian legacy.[25]

There is little question that the dominant exegetical approaches during most of the twentieth century sustained the classical displacement theology of Judaism. It is only in the latter part of the twentieth century and into the present one that we have witnessed the beginnings of a dramatic shift away from the predominant understanding of the New Testament regarding the significance of Jesus and his ministry advanced by the likes of Kittel, Noth, and Bultmann. Led by such scholars as James Charlesworth, W. D. Davies, E. P. Sanders, Douglas Hare, Daniel Harrington, Clemens Thoma, and Robin Scroggs, the list of those repudiating what Arthur J. Droge has termed the "Bultmannian captivity" of New Testament scholarship continues to grow. This new exegesis is gradually forcing theologians to rethink significantly the Christian-Jewish relationship, especially as it affects Christology, redirecting it away from the long-dominant supersessionist approach toward an emphasis on a continuing interrelationship rooted in the affirmation of continued Jewish covenantal inclusion after the Christ event. One example is a need to rethink certain christological interpretations that rest heavily on the so-called *Abba* experience of God as totally unique to Jesus as contemporary biblical scholarship has uncovered a heightened sense of divine intimacy within Second Temple Judaism. This scholarship has undercut the claim of Jesus' absolute uniqueness in this regard and raised serious questions about any Christology that builds on Jesus' so-called *Abba* experience.[26]

We have seen, both in official church statements and among New Testament scholars, a growing appreciation of Jesus' rootage in the progressive Judaism of his day. James Charlesworth and Cardinal Carlo Martini, S.J., the retired Archbishop of Milan, are two prime examples of such new interpretation. Martini has written that "Without a sincere feeling for the Jewish world, and a direct experience of it, one cannot fully understand Christianity. Jesus is fully Jewish, the apostles are Jewish, and one cannot doubt their attachment to the traditions of their forefathers."[27] And the 1985 Vatican *Notes* on preaching and teaching about Jews and Judaism declare that "Jesus was and always remained a Jew.... Jesus is fully a man of his time, and his environment — the Jewish Palestinian one of the first century, the anxieties and hope of which he shared."[28] In other words, both recent biblical scholarship as well as official church teaching are saying that any portrayal of Jesus that separates him from the Judaism of his time in the manner of Bultmann or Noth represents a truncated and distorted presentation of his message and mission. Certainly it is legitimate to present the image of Jesus through various cultural symbols and images. But Jesus the Jew is not one among manifold ways of presenting Jesus. It is the base for authentically understanding his fundamental message. Without maintenance of this base, efforts to translate the meaning of Jesus' message into a variety of cultures, a quite legitimate and necessary effort, will likely eviscerate important dimensions of his message.

One of the best summaries of where we are today in terms of Jesus' relationship to the Judaism of his time and the implications it has for understanding the significance of the Christ Event has come from New Testament scholar Robin Scroggs. His view was endorsed by the late Cardinal Joseph

Bernardin of Chicago, a leader in promoting Jewish-Christian reconciliation, in his own writings.[29]

Scroggs emphasizes the following points: (1) The movement begun by Jesus and continued after his death in Palestine can best be described as a reform movement within Judaism. There is little evidence during this period that Christians had a separate identity from Jews. (2) The Pauline missionary movement, as Paul understood it, was a Jewish mission that focused on the gentiles as the proper object of God's call to his people. (3) Prior to the end of the Jewish war with the Romans in 70 C.E., there is no such reality as Christianity. Followers of Jesus did not have a self-understanding of themselves as a religion over against Judaism. A distinctive Christian identity only began to emerge after the Jewish-Roman war. (4) The later portions of the New Testament all show some signs of a movement toward separation, but they also generally retain some contact with their original Jewish matrix.[30]

While not every New Testament scholar may subscribe to each and every point made by Scroggs, a consensus is growing that the picture he lays out is basically accurate. Such a picture significantly challenges how we have classically stated the meaning of the Christ event. Clearly many people in the very early days of the church did not understand the significance of the Jesus movement as inaugurating a new, totally separate, religious community that would stand over against Judaism. It does not appear that Jesus conveyed to his disciples and followers any sense that he was creating a totally new and distinct religious entity called the church. This "separate" identity only developed well after his death. And we now know through the research of scholars such as Robert Wilken, Wayne Meeks, Alan Segal, and Anthony Saldarini that this development was of several centuries duration in a number of areas of the Christian world.[31] Evidence now exists for regular Christian participation in Jewish worship, particularly in the East, during the second and third centuries and, in a few places, until the fourth century.

The challenge now facing the church in light of this new understanding of its origins is to ask whether the creation of a totally separate identity was actually in the mind of Jesus himself. This is something that Martini has addressed. He has introduced the idea of "schism" into the discussion of the basic theological relationship between Jews and Christians. He applies this term to the original separation of the church and synagogue. In so doing he has interjected two important notions into the conversation. For schism is a reality that ideally should not have occurred and that should be seen as a temporary situation rather than a permanent rupture. A term that previously had been used exclusively in connection with intra-Christian divisions, it implies a certain contemporary mandate to heal this rupture. There is legitimate room for debate as to the appropriateness of the term *schism* proposed by Martini. But behind it one finds a strong conviction on his part that Christian-Jewish relations and in particular Jesus as the Christ cannot be properly understood without a restoration of Jesus' deep ties to Judaism.[32]

Clearly the church will not return to an understanding of itself as one among many Jewish sects. But, in light of recent biblical scholarship, it may have to rethink its christological understanding in a way that will enhance its appreciation of its ongoing Jewish roots.

Christ and Covenant

As biblical scholars and theologians have begun to probe the implications of this new vision of Jesus as profoundly intertwined with the Jewish community, two initial approaches have come to the fore in terms of understanding his significance for the Christian community's relationship with the People Israel. While within each approach different nuances appear as we move from scholar to scholar, we can generally characterize the two trends as "single covenant" and "double covenant" perspectives, with a few scholars such as Rosemary Ruether and Paul Knitter arguing for multiple covenants.

The "single covenant" perspective holds that Jews and Christians basically belong to one covenantal tradition that began at Sinai, a covenantal tradition that was not ruptured through the Christ event. The coming of Christ rather represented the decisive moment when the gentiles were able to enter fully into the special relationship with God that Jews already enjoyed and in which they continue. Some holding this viewpoint maintain that the decisive features of the Christ event do have application to all people, including Jews, but not in a way that breaks pre-existing Jewish covenantal ties. Others have argued that the Christian appropriation and reinterpretation of the original covenantal tradition, in and through Jesus, applies primarily to non-Jews. Jews represent a special case in the history of salvation from the Christian perspective. One major Protestant theologian who argued the single covenant theory with considerable force was the late Paul van Buren, although he appeared to be moving back toward a more conventional understanding of Christology along the lines of his mentor Karl Barth near the end of his life.[33]

The "double covenant" theory, which I have personally favored over the years, begins at the same point as its single covenant counterpart, namely, with a strong affirmation of the continuing bonds between Jews and Christians. But then it prefers to underline the distinctiveness of the two traditions and communities, particularly in terms of their experiences after the final separation of the church and synagogue. Christians associated with this perspective insist on maintaining the view that through the ministry, teachings, and person of Jesus a vision of God emerged that was distinctively new in terms of its central features. Even though there may well have been important groundwork laid for this emergence in Second Temple or Middle Judaism, what came to be understood regarding the divine-human relationship as a result of Jesus has to be regarded as a quantum leap.

An important example of the double covenant approach is to be found in the writings of German theologian Franz Mussner.[34] Mussner underscores Jesus' deep, positive links to the Jewish tradition of his day. He likewise rejects any interpretation of the Christ event over against Judaism in terms of Jesus' fulfillment of biblical messianic prophecies. Rather, the uniqueness of the Christ event arises from the complete identity of the work of Jesus, as well as his words and actions, with the work of God. As a result of the revelatory vision in Christ, the New Testament is able to speak about God with an anthropomorphic boldness not found to the same extent within the Jewish biblical or postbiblical tradition.

In answer to the question of what the disciples finally experienced through their close association with Jesus, Mussner speaks of "a unity of action extending to the point of congruence of Jesus with God, an unheard-of existential imitation of God by Jesus."[35] But this imitation, Mussner insists, is quite in keeping with Jewish thinking, a contention that many Jewish scholars would no doubt challenge, though Elliot Wolfson has argued that the rabbinic corpus does reveal some evidence of a modified incarnational theology.[36] For Mussner, the uniqueness of Jesus is to be found in the depth of his imitation of God. So the most distinctive feature of Christianity for Mussner when contrasted with Judaism is the notion of incarnation rather than the fulfillment of messianic prophecies. And even this Christian particularity, he insists, represents an outgrowth of a sensibility profoundly Jewish at its core.

In recent years, considerable dissatisfaction has emerged regarding the viability of the single/double covenant options. Neither now appears to capture adequately the complexity of the Christian-Jewish relationship, particularly as it affects christological formulation within the churches. Two scholarly developments have had a special role in contributing to the unease with these two early options for rethinking the theological relationship between Jews and Christians, and ultimately for rethinking Christology, which in many ways has been framed in the context of the connection between the church and the Jewish people.

The first development concerns our understanding of the nature of the Jewish community in the first century of the common era. Scholars such as Jacob Neusner, Hayini Perelmuter, and Efraim Shmueli have emphasized that the Judaism of the first century was far from monolithic.[37] In fact this era was marked by considerable creativity and change within Judaism, contrary to the image propagated by Christians. New Jewish groups were emerging that challenged the viewpoints of traditional Judaism. What Ellis Rivkin has termed "the Pharisaic revolution," a revolution that clearly seeded the perspectives of Jesus and early Christianity, was challenging established Jewish perspectives in many areas. Neusner and Shmueli prefer to speak of "Judaisms" rather than "Judaism." Christian interpretations of the meaning of Christ are often based on a far more uniform understanding of Judaism at the time of Jesus and present the Christian-Jewish relationship in linear terms. This applies especially to christological perspectives that see the church as the replacement of Judaism as well as to those which argue that Christ represents the point of entry for gentiles into the ongoing Jewish covenant. Such Christologies have difficulty answering the questions, to which of the Judaisms is Christianity linked and which might it complete? Most advocates of a single covenant theory have not really grappled with this new, complex picture of the Jewish tradition.

The other dimension of recent scholarship has to do with the view of how and when the separation of church and synagogue took place. Most Christians were weaned on the idea that the church was basically established as a distinct religious entity by the time Jesus died on Calvary. And the establishment of the church, the new Israel, was integral to his divine mission as Lord and savior. On the Jewish side, the prevailing position was that, while Jesus obviously retained ties with the Jewish community, it was Paul, through his mission to the gentiles, that really brought about the total separation between Christianity and Judaism. Both perspectives now appear quite simplistic. Even if we factor in the supposed decisions made on the Christian side at the so-called Council of Jerusalem (spoken of in the book of Acts) and on the Jewish side at the Synod of Jabneh (which supposedly placed Christians outside the parameters of the Jewish community), we now know that neither the council nor the synod gave final closure to the issue of whether Christians are merely followers of the way of the Jew Jesus or a distinctively new religious community whose christological understanding has permanently ruptured any original ties to Judaism.

As we have seen, important Christian and Jewish scholars are now arguing that the actual separation between the church and the synagogue, while well advanced by the end of the first century of the common era, was not in fact completed for several centuries after that, as ties continued between certain Jewish and Christian communities, particularly in the East.[38] Evidence of such is apparent in the second, third and in a few places even the fourth century. And these ties were not just on the level of intellectual religious self-identity; they also affected popular practice. John Chrysostom, for example, launched a harsh critique of Judaism partly out of frustration that some Christians in his area were continuing to participate in synagogue services on a regular basis. What sort of role these Christian synagogue attendees played is unknown and likely will remain so unless someone discovers a new cache of documents in a cave. It obviously would be terribly illuminating to have such information. But short of this, we can say that on the Christian side people believed that their acceptance of Jesus did not undercut the importance of participating in Jewish ritual. On the Jewish side there certainly had to be some recognition that the Christians authentically "belonged" to the community since no evidence exists that they had to fight their way into the synagogue for Shabbat services over the opposition of the local Jewish community.

This new research is central to christological understanding today. Christological approaches rooted in the belief that the Christ event brought about the fulfillment of Judaism and the inauguration, in Jesus' own lifetime, of a new religious community to replace the "old Israel" no longer meet the test of historical accuracy. Clearly a significant number of Christians did not understand their acceptance of Christ as involving their transfer from a Jewish community to an entirely new religious body with no continuing links with the Jewish people. So Christology needs serious rethinking in this area, as the recent statement from the Christian Scholars Group on Christian-Jewish Relations, *A Sacred Obligation,* makes clear: "Affirming God's enduring covenant with the Jewish people has consequences for Christian understandings of salvation."[39]

Rethink the Christ Event

Because Christology stands at the very nerve center of Christian faith, reevaluation of christological affirmations cannot be undertaken superficially. There is a trend found in some sectors of Christianity, especially among those most open to general interreligious understanding, that the Christ event is one of several authentic revelations with no particular universal aspect. Such a starting point is not acceptable to myself nor to many people who have called for a significant rethinking of the church's theology of the Jewish people, such as Cardinal Walter Kasper or the biblical scholars and theologians associated with *A Sacred Obligation.* We must maintain from the Christian side some understanding that the Christ event carries universal salvific implications.

As I have expressed in my major writings on this topic, for me incarnational Christology holds the best possibility for preserving such universalistic dimensions of the Christ event while opening up authentic theological space for Judaism (as the late Cardinal Joseph Bernardin of Chicago termed it).[40] Kasper, to whose views we shall return shortly, has insisted that in any reconsideration of our understanding of Christology as a result of new biblical scholarship and official church statement some understanding of Christ's salvific mission as universal in nature must be retained. I support Kasper in this affirmation.

An important contribution to the church's ongoing reinterpretation of the meaning of the Christ event, in light of its new insights into the Christian-Jewish relationship, appears in the document issued by the Pontifical Biblical Commission, which carries an introduction by Cardinal Joseph Ratzinger, who bears ultimate responsibility for the commission as prefect of the Vatican's office on doctrine. Released without much public notice in 2001, this new document opens up several new possibilities in terms of expressing the significance of Christ while leaving theological space for Judaism.[41]

The Pontifical Biblical Commission document, despite some significant limitations in the way it portrays postbiblical Judaism, makes an important contribution to the development of a new constructive christological understanding in the context of Jewish covenantal inclusion. Picking up on *Nostra Aetate's* assertion that Jews remain in the ongoing covenant after the Christ event, the document includes two statements that are particularly relevant for any discussion of Christology. The first is that Jewish messianic hopes are not in vain. This represents an understanding that Jews can attain salvation through their own messianic understanding. Kasper has made this point on several occasions in recent years, as he has argued that Jews do not need to be targeted for evangelization and can achieve salvation through their obedience to the Torah.[42] In an address at Boston College, Kasper put the matter in the following way:

> This does not mean that Jews in order to be saved have to become Christians; if they follow their own conscience and believe in God's promises as they understand them in their religious tradition they are in line with God's plan, which for us comes to its historical completion in Jesus Christ.[43]

This same perspective has been underlined in two recent study documents, the first coming out of an ongoing dialogue between the U.S. Bishops' Committee on Ecumenical and Interreligious Affairs and the National Council of Synagogues entitled *Reflections on Covenant and Mission*[44] and the other *A Sacred Obligation* from the ecumenical Christian Scholars Group on Christian-Jewish Relations, referred to earlier. The latter asserts that "Christians should not target Jews for conversion."[45] Certainly these new assertions do not resolve all outstanding theological problems, for, as Kasper has insisted, salvation in Christ continues to have universal implications. And important theologians, such as Dulles, have criticized this approach.[46] But these documents have definitely interjected a new discussion within Christian theology on the salvific dimensions of the Christ event with regard to the Jewish people.

The second affirmation within the Pontifical Biblical Commission document with special significance for Christology is that when the Jewish messiah appears he will have some of the same traits as Christ. Though this statement is rather oblique in its formulation, its importance for Christology lies in the opening it presents for authentic messianic understanding within Judaism that it not totally tied to Christianity's use of the Christ symbol. It likewise retains some sense of a profound link between the two messianic visions, reaffirming the theological bonding between Jews and Christians that Pope John Paul II has made so central in his many writings on the subject.[47] Again, such an affirmation leaves many theological questions unanswered. But it clearly opens the door to constructive reflection on the way the church understands the role of Jews and Judaism in the process of salvation.

The Pontifical Biblical Commission document is a study rooted in biblical exegesis, not a work of systematic theology, which lies outside of the commission's mandate. Hence it did not amplify the theological kernel it has provided us. That remains a task for contemporary theologians in the church. But the affirmation opens the door for the possibility of exploring whether one can speak about the universal significance of the Christ event in a way that allows for its articulation through religious symbols not directly connected with Christology, such as Jewish religious symbols. This may in fact prove the most fruitful way of developing a Christology that remains open to religious pluralism, particularly with respect to Jews who are acknowledged to have authentic revelation from the Christian theological perspective.

Some may say that the above approach is nothing more than the "anonymous Christian" notion put forth by the late German theologian Karl Rahner at the time of the Second Vatican Council. I do not believe this to be the case. It is suggesting, in my view, an understanding that the process of human salvation revealed in the Christ event goes beyond its articulation within the church through the use of symbols associated with the Christ event. Hence Jews, and perhaps some other religious people, do not have to apprehend it directly through christological symbolism. It suggests that while the salvific reality behind the Christ symbolism is indeed universal, the specific symbolism associated with this salvific reality within the churches may be more limited in scope than the actual reality. This, in my judgment, goes considerably beyond what Rahner proposed, where the Christ event remained the dominant religious symbolism. This proposal certainly remains in the realm of a hypothesis. And clearly it is a hypothesis that primarily aims at helping Christians come to a new self-understanding in light of recent biblical scholarship and magisterial pronouncements regarding the Christian-Jewish relationship. This approach would follow the direction suggested by Luke Timothy Johnson.[48] It would be a way of helping Christians think about *themselves* with reference to Jews, rather than focusing on a theology of Judaism and the Jewish people from the church's perspective. While, unlike Johnson, I believe both avenues of reflection need to be pursued, he is correct in claiming that a certain priority should be given to Christian *self-understanding*. It is also true to say, and Christians need to realize this, that Jews and other religious communities may not feel any necessity for theological confirmation of their faith perspective from the churches.

For the sake of completeness, I should mention one other possibility now under discussion. It is the perspective offered by Ratzinger in several of his recent publications. Ratzinger would maintain that Jews are a special case in terms of salvation. It would seem that he would exempt them from the framework presented in *Dominus Iesus,* the controversial Vatican statement on Catholicism's relationship with other churches and other religions.[49] According to Ratzinger, the Jewish community would move to final salvation through obedience to their revealed covenantal tradition. But at the end time, Christ's second coming would confirm their ultimate salvation. It is not clear whether Ratzinger would demand explicit recognition of Christ as the messiah from Jews as a requirement for their salvific confirmation. In my judgment this "delayed" messianism of the Christ event in terms of the Jewish people is not as fruitful a starting point for rethinking christological understanding today as is the direction found in the Pontifical Biblical Commission document. It would be interesting to know whether Ratzinger would wish to adapt his position in light of the recent Pontifical Biblical Commission document for which he wrote a supportive introduction.

In rethinking Christology in light of the Christian-Jewish dialogue, we will also need to include the relations that have emerged regarding God's relationship to humanity after the experience of the Holocaust. Both Christian and Jewish scholars have addressed this issue.[50] Obviously, any alteration of our understanding with respect to God will necessarily affect Christianity's understanding of the Christ event. We may have to move much more in the direction of a narrative Christology and to an emphasis on Jesus' ministry as a prime example of what Vytautas Kavolis has termed the "humanization of morality."[51]

In such a christological vision, the saving power of Christ is manifested in the lives of those who stand up for victims in the midst of social oppression. The rescuers during the Holocaust period are one important example of such witness. Writing in this vein, James Moore argues that any "redemptive" emphasis in Christology must always "be tied to the historical reality of any point in time, dismissing all efforts to thoroughly spiritualize the notion of redemption."[52]

We are thus at a very early stage in the process of rethinking Christology in light of recent developments in scholarly understanding. As Christians, we may never come to a point where our christological affirmations will lead us to a theology of religious pluralism that squares totally with the basic faith affirmations of Judaism or other world religions. But in our globalized world, in which interreligious understanding is not merely confined to the realm of theological ideas but directly impacts people's life together in the human community, we can ill afford to shrink from this task.

For Further Reflection

1. Can we continue to call Jesus "the messiah"? If so, does our understanding have to be modified in any way?

2. Is there a way in which Christian belief in the universal significance of Christ can be reconciled with the need to provide authentic theological space for Judaism?

3. What are the most significant changes in recent biblical studies regarding Jesus' links with the Judaism of his time? How does this new understanding from biblical scholarship affect our understanding of Christology?

4. Does an emphasis on "incarnation" in Christology, rather than an emphasis on Jesus as the fulfillment of messianic prophecies, provide a better basis for a Christology that allows for a continued affirmation of Jewish covenantal identity?

5. How might we imagine the Christian-Jewish relationship today?

For Further Reading

Boys, Mary C. *Has God Only One Blessing? Judaism as a Source of Christian Self-Understanding.* New York: Paulist Press, 2000.

Charlesworth, James H., ed. *Jesus' Jewishness: Exploring the Place of Jesus in Early Judaism.* Philadelphia: American Interfaith Institute, and New York: Crossroad, 1991.

Pawlikowski, John T. *Jesus and the Theology of Israel.* Wilmington, Del.: Michael Glazier, 1989.

Ruether, Rosemary Radford. *Faith and Fratricide: The Theological Roots of Anti-Semitism.* New York: Seabury, 1974.

Soulen, R. Kendall. *The God of Israel and Christian Theology.* Minneapolis: Fortress, 1996.

Willebrands, Johannes Cardinal. *Church and Jewish People: New Considerations.* New York: Paulist, 1992.

Christology and Patriarchy

Rosemary Radford Ruether

In recent Vatican and Roman Catholic Episcopal statements, Christology is used as the keystone of the argument against women's ordination. It is said that women, by their very nature, cannot "image" Christ. Therefore they cannot be priests, since priests "represent" Christ.[1] This argument has been echoed in other "high church" statements — Anglican, Lutheran and Eastern Orthodox. What is the meaning of this use of Christology against women's full participation in the Christian church? If women cannot represent Christ, in what sense can it be said that Christ represents women? Does this not mean that Christ does not redeem women but reinforces women's bondage in a patriarchal social system? If this is the case, shouldn't women who seek liberation from patriarchy reject Christianity?

It has traditionally been claimed that Christ is the redeemer and representative of all humanity. He is the one who overcomes that bondage to sin that is the universal human condition. Thus it would seem that the symbols that the Christian church uses to express Christology should manifest a like universality and inclusivity. These symbols should embrace the authentic humanness and fulfilled hopes of all persons. How is it possible that more than one-half of humanity, more than half of the Christian churches themselves, find themselves inferiorized and excluded by Christology?

In this chapter I wish to examine the development of the christological symbols and how they have been shaped by an androcentric ideology that becomes explicit when they are used to exclude women from representation of Christ. I will then ask whether Christology can be liberated from this androcentric bias and become genuinely inclusive of women.

Christ and the Image of God

Early Christianity used the word *Logos* to define that presence of God made incarnate in Jesus the Christ. This term drew on a long tradition of religious philosophy. In Greek and Hellenistic Jewish philosophy, the divine Logos was the means by which the transcendent God came forth in the beginning to shape the visible cosmos. The Logos was simultaneously the immanence of God and the ground of the visible cosmos. In Hellenistic Jewish terms, the Logos, or Sophia (Wisdom), was God's self-manifestation, by which God created the world, providentially guided it, was revealed to it and through whom the world was reconciled to God.

The Logos was particularly identified with the rational principle in each human soul. By linking the term *Christ* (anointed or messiah), through whom God redeemed the world, to the Logos, as the creational principle, early Christianity prevented a split between redemption and creation that was threatened by Gnosticism. Christians affirmed that the God revealed in Jesus Christ was the same God who created the world in the beginning. Christ was the authentic ground of creation, manifest in fulfilled form, over against the alienation of creation from its true being. This concept of the Logos as the divine identity of Christ would seem to be inclusive of women, pointing all humans, male and female, to the foundation of their true humanness.[2]

But this Hellenistic philosophical tradition was also shaped in a patriarchal culture that gave the terms *Logos* and *Christ* an androcentric bias. Since divinity, sovereign power, rationality and normative humanity were all assumed by this culture to be male, all the theological reference points for defining Christ were defined androcentrically. Normative humanity, the image of God in "man," and the divine Logos were interlocking androcentric concepts in the theological definition of Christ, reinforcing the assumption that God is male and that the human Christ must be a male to reveal the male God.

Christianity has never said that God was literally male, but it has assumed that God represents preeminently the qualities of rationality and sovereign power. Since it is men that were assumed to be rational, and women less so or not at all, and men who exercised public power, normally denied to women, the male metaphor was seen as appropriate for God, while female metaphors for God came to be regarded as inappropriate and indeed "pagan." The Logos who reveals the "Father," therefore, was presumed to be properly imaged as male, even though the Jewish Wisdom tradition had used the female metaphor, Sophia, for this same idea. The maleness of the historical Jesus undoubtedly reinforced this preference for male-identified metaphors, such as Logos and Son of God, over the female metaphor of Sophia.

Within trinitarian theology, to term the Logos or second person of the trinity as the Son is odd and misleading, since it suggests a subordinate and derivative status of the Logos, as the male child is begotten by and under the power of his Father. This Son-Father metaphor is used to represent the immanence of God as "under" and derivative from divine transcendence.

Taken literally, these metaphors reinforce the maleness of God, in both aspects, and set up a patriarchal relationship between the two "persons" of God. These notions of the maleness of God also affect the interpretation of the concept of the human as image of God or *imago dei*. Genesis 1:27–28 says, "So God created humankind (Adam) in his image, in the image of God he created them; male and female he (they) created them" (NRSV). This formula, with its plural, collective term for God, leaves open the possibility that the human thus created is to be understood generically, and that Genesis 27b teaches that the image of God is possessed by both male and female. This would mean that woman shares in the stewardship over creation referred to in Genesis 1:26.[3]

However, most of the patristic and medieval tradition rejected the possibility that women were equally theomorphic.[4] In most interpretations the concept of *imago dei* was distinguished from gender difference. One way to interpret this distinction was to make the *imago dei* asexually spiritual, and so neither male nor female. Gender difference would then refer to bodily characteristics, which humans share with animals but not with God. Following Philo, some church fathers saw gender as appearing only in the fallen state of "man." Gregory of Nyssa read the text in this way.[5]

St. Augustine drew a different conclusion. For him it is the male who possesses the image of God normatively. Women also possess the image of God as a gender-neutral spiritual capacity, but women as women (*femina*) are not the image of God. They are the image of the bodily creation that the human male is given to rule over.[6] Such an interpretation of the image of God reflects the patriarchal legal and social order in which the *paterfamilias* or male head of family is the corporate head and representative of the whole *familia* — women, children, slaves, animals and land — under his control. He alone possesses personhood juridically in the public order.

Augustine and the other church fathers never denied that women have redeemable souls. But, nevertheless, they believed that women in their specific femaleness, psychic and bodily, are the opposite of the divine. They image bodily, creaturely reality. The idea of woman as body takes for granted the androcentric perspective of the male as the one who "looks at" at woman, controlling and defining her as bodily object. In this framework the male is "mind" or subject, and woman is body or object. Woman's own experience of herself as subject is not taken into account in this definition.

This androcentric view of woman as object allowed the church fathers to ignore the contradiction between woman's possession of a redeemable soul and her lacking the status of *imago dei* in her own right. This concept of women as lacking full personhood, as image of God only derivatively, was reinforced by the later scholastic appropriation of Aristotelian biology in the medieval period. This false biology asserted that the male alone provides the seed or "form" of the offspring, while the female contributes only the material substratum, which is formed.[7]

If this process is fully carried out, and the male seed fully forms the female matter, another male will be born. Females therefore, in Aristotle's terms, are the result of a defect in gestation in which the maternal matter fails to be fully formed by the male seed. In this construct of male to female as form to matter (which denies the existence of the female ovum), the female is defined as a defective human, lacking in full humanity, inferior in bodily strength, adequate rationality, and moral self-control. These defects preclude both autonomy and rule over others for females, and they demand that the woman be subject to the male. The female, then, is defined by medieval theologians, such as Thomas Aquinas, who appropriates this Aristotelian view, as a non-normative human who lacks the fullness of human nature. The male is the "perfect" or complete expression of the human species. Aquinas concludes from this anthropology that the maleness of the historical Jesus was an ontological necessity, not a historical accident. For Jesus as the Christ to represent humanity as a whole, he must be male, because only the male possesses the fullness of human nature. The female cannot represent the human, either for herself or generically.[8]

This interlocking set of ideas about the maleness of God, the Logos of God, the *imago dei* and Christ threaten to undermine the basic Christian belief that women are included in the redemption of "man" won by Christ. The church fathers assumed she was included, while being humanly non-normative and non-theomorphic, because they assumed a patriarchal ideology in which women are included "under" an ontological maleness theologically, just as they were included "under" and juridically represented by the male head of the family in patriarchal society and law.

Gender-Inclusive Symbols for Christology?

Today women have won the rights of citizens or civil persons in the political-juridical order. Higher education, opened to women, has disproved the notion of women's inferior intelligence. Aristotelian biology has been shown to be false. Indeed the actual gestation of the child proceeds in the opposite way, with the female ovum and uterus shaping a female generic fetus, from which a differentiation process must take place to make a male.[9] All the androcentric assumptions on which the christological symbols were based have been thrown into question.

Today a Christology that elevates Jesus' human maleness to ontologically necessary significance makes the Christ symbol noninclusive of women. To reaffirm the basic Christian belief that women are included in redemption "in Christ," all the symbolic underpinnings of Christology must be reinterpreted. Is this possible? What might this mean? To reassess the relationship of Christology and gender, we might start by examining the more gender-inclusive possibilities of the basic symbols of God and the image of God, Christ, and the Logos of God, on which Christology was built. We should also ask about Jesus' own teaching and praxis.

God. Jewish tradition thinks of God as beyond gender. God is thought of as like both a ruler and a parent. This divine ruler-parent sometimes exercises power in wrathful and judgmental ways, but, at other times, can be thought of as merciful, forgiving, compassionate and even as patient and long-suffering. In terms of gender stereotypes, God is androgynous. Sometimes female metaphors are explicitly used for these "maternal" aspects of God.[10] However, since the male pronoun is used for God, this might suggest that God is an androgynous male.

But Judaism also rejects literalism about verbal or visual images used for God. God is beyond all such creaturely images, and to take any image literally is idolatry. In order to combine these two insights: God's "androgynous" nature and yet transcendence of all anthropomorphic literalism, we must become clearer about the metaphorical character of such gender images. In God's self, God is neither male nor female (or humanly gendered at all). But our metaphors for God must include both male and female. It is not enough to simply add together patriarchal masculine and feminine gender stereotypes, or even to give a male God a "feminine" side, for this still leaves women without full humanity.

We must use gender symbols in a way that affirms that God both transcends and yet includes the fullness of the humanity of both men and women. Women must gain their "male side" in relation to God, as men, historically, were allowed to gain their "female side" through the androgynous "motherly father." Only then can we say that both men and women possess the image of God, in mutuality and yet also as full persons in their own right, and not simply by including women under a male "head," or as complimentary parts of a whole found only as the heterosexual couple.

Wisdom and Logos. Another way the Hebrew tradition brought androgyny into God was to picture the immanence of God in female metaphors. The most notable of these is the Wisdom metaphor. Wisdom caring for the cosmos is pictured as like a woman caring for her household.[11] This Wisdom idea is of particular significance for Christians, because, theologically, Wisdom plays the same roles as the Logos (and was the original version of this idea). She is the presence of God as means of creation, revelation, and redemption. Jesus' divinity is sometimes identified as the Wisdom of God.[12]

Recognition of the Wisdom version of this concept deliteralizes metaphors for the second person of the trinity, revealed in Christ, as Son of God. The idea that the immanence of God is like a son, or male offspring, in relation to a genitor, or father, cannot be taken literally. God as Logos-Sophia is neither male nor female and can be imaged in both male and female metaphors. We must also ask whether the parent-child metaphor, for imaging the relation of divine transcendence and immanence, needs to be discarded as more misleading than revealing.

But surely, one might say, the Jewish notion of messiah was always and only a male! The messiah idea originated as a title for the kings of Israel and, later, as the ideal and future king of Israel.[13] Although rulers, representing divine sovereignty, were generally thought of as male, female rulers were not unknown in the ancient Middle East. Jesus' own preferred title for the Coming One (whom he probably did not identify with himself) was *ben Adam*, usually translated *Son of Man*. This term, drawn from the Book of Daniel and other apocalyptic literature, sees the messiah as the collective expression of Israel, itself the representative of corporate humanity.

In Jewish liturgy *ben Adam* refers to females as well as males, despite its androcentric form. Since generic humanity cannot today be seen as normatively male, a more accurate translation of this term would be *the Human One*. This is the way the *Inclusive Language Lectionary*, prepared by the National Council of Churches of Christ of the U.S.A., chose to translate this term for liturgical reading of scripture.[14]

Jesus' Ministry and Women. From an examination of the symbols used for Christ, we turn to the praxis of the historical Jesus, as interpreted in the gospels. Here we see the figure of an iconoclastic prophet of God who stands in judgment on social and religious systems that exclude subordinated and marginalized people from divine favor. Jesus' mission is seen as one of bringing "good news to the poor," hope to despised people whom the priestly and clerical classes regarded as unworthy of redemption. Jesus' prophetic praxis confronts these male leaders for their pretences of special privilege with God and their exclusion of the unlearned and the "unclean."

Over against these male leaders, it is often women among the despised groups who are able to hear God's prophetic word and be converted, while the male elites close their hearts against it. Because women were at the bottom of those systems of privilege decried in the gospel stories, they become the representatives of the "last who shall be first in the kingdom of God." Luke, in the Magnificat, makes Jesus' mother, Mary, potentially despised as one whose child is not her husband's, the exemplar of the messianic community. She is the servant of God who will be lifted up, as the mighty of the world are put down from their thrones.[15]

All four gospels tell the Jesus story as a drama of mounting conflict in which the messianic prophet is rejected, first by his family and hometown folk, then by the religious leaders, then by the crowd of his popular followers, and then by his own male disciples. It is the core group of his female followers who remain faithful at the cross and are first at the tomb, first witnesses of the resurrection, commissioned by the Risen Lord to take the good news back to the male disciples huddled in the upper room.[16]

Scholars have rejected this "empty tomb" story as secondary and unhistorical.[17] But they have failed to ask the question of why all four gospels tell the story in this way. Is it not to make dramatically clear that despised women, last in the present social and religious order, are the faithful remnant who are first in the redeemed order?

Luke also includes women in his account of Pentecost. Luke uses the text of the prophet Joel to buttress his story of the restoration of the prophetic Spirit to the messianic community, in which the Spirit is given to the "men servants and the maid servants," and "your sons and your daughters shall prophesy."[18] This inclusion of women reflects the fact that women were included in the prophetic office in Hebrew scripture, as well as in early Christianity.[19] The late second-century church order, the *Didache,* shows that there were still Christians in that period who saw the prophet as the normative church leader.[20]

Emergence of Two Constrasting Christologies

Despite these didactic patterns of early Christianity, which saw the messianic community as overturning established hierarchies and including women as the first believers, first witnesses, and prophetic spokespersons of the Risen Lord, it is not clear how much impact such patterns had on early Christian social practice. We get only glimpses of some ministry of women that seems quickly suppressed by an insurgent patriarchal concept of the church.[21] Why did this happen?

I suggest that one clue to this repression of women lies in the ambivalent understanding of the church as messianic community. One group of early Christians understood this apocalyptically, as an impending end of this present world, terminating its mortality and need for reproductive renewal. For them, women have been liberated from traditional gender roles by Christ, since both male and female Christians belonged to a transcendent, heavenly order where marriage and reproduction will be no longer necessary.[22]

The insurgent patriarchal Christianity of the deutero-Pauline tradition (that is, the later letters in the New Testament attributed to Paul but composed after his death) repressed both the apocalypticism and the incipient egalitarianism of this eschatological interpretation of the church. These churchmen were the authors of the church's historical survival and institutionalization. But they also reaffirmed the patriarchal, slave-holding social order as still normative for Christian society. The new freedom of women to travel as itinerant preachers, freed by Christ from marriage, was repressed in favor of a Christianity that declared that women were second in creation, first in sin, are to be silent in church and saved by childbearing.[23]

The conflict between egalitarian, eschatological Christianity and patriarchal, historical Christianity continued in the second and third centuries in the Gnostic and Montanist struggles.[24] It was resolved in the late fourth to sixth centuries in a new synthesis of the two. In this new synthesis the eschatological ideal of chastity was shorn of its egalitarianism and began to incorporate the patriarchal, clerical leadership class.[25] Marriage, as the lifestyle of most Christians, was reaffirmed, but as a second-class, lay stratum of the church.[26]

From the fourth to the ninth century, celibate women were gradually deprived of the remnants of pastoral ministry and segregated into convents, under male episcopal control.[27] The patriarchal, hierarchical church leadership could then be incorporated into the Roman empire as new agents of its rule. This fourth-century synthesis of patriarchal, imperial church organization, together with a clericalized monastic counterculture, is passed on as normative Christianity for the next thousand years. Yet a resistance to it from both celibate women and married clerics continued through the Middle Ages.[28]

The Reformation represents a revolt against clerical celibacy. It restored the married clergy, but went on to abolish monasteries for men or women.[29] This meant that it rooted itself all the more exclusively in the patriarchal type of Christianity. The patriarchal family is now stressed as the nucleus of the church, modeled by the married pastor and his obedient wife and children. The household codes become the norm for Christian society with a new force.[30]

Yet the eschatological counterculture did not disappear with the suppression of monasticism. Rather it returned in its more radical form, in mystical and millennialist sects who again see the church as a messianic community living in the last days of world history. They anticipate the coming kingdom by withdrawing from the evil structures of the worldly society and its church. Some of these sects rediscover the early Christian idea that the redeemed have transcended the patriarchal order of history. Freed from gender roles, men and women "saints" become equal in a new redemptive society. Women again are mandated to preach and prophesy "in the Spirit." Some also rediscover Gnostic ideas of divine androgyny.[31]

We have here two different lines of Christianity, which lend themselves to different Christologies. Patriarchal Christianity moves toward the integration of the Lordship of Christ with the Lordship of Caesar. Christ as divine Logos is the apex of a hierarchical social-political order baptized as Christendom. As delegate of the heavenly Father, Christ rules over the cosmos and is, in turn, the source of the ecclesiastical and political hierarchies of church and state.[32] On the familial and personal level, Christ mandates the headship of husband over wife, and the rule of reason over the body.

Women as wives, as laity, and as subjects of monarchs, under the rule of their husbands, represent the bodily realm that is to be ruled over by the male christological principle in each system of dominance and subjugation.

In the mystical and millennialist Christologies, by contrast, Christ is the transcendent ground of being for the redeemed, who have departed from this fallen world and its corrupt social systems and are both awaiting and anticipating a redeemed order beyond this world. For some of these sects, Christ is asexual and spiritually androgynous. He encompasses both men and women on a level transcendent to the separation into genders and re-productive roles that happened through the Fall, restoring the redeemed to their prelapsarian or pre-fall unity.

The redeemed participate in the eschatological new life in Christ by putting aside sexual activity and reproduction. Thereby they recover the sinless and spiritually androgynous mode of being before the fall into sin and death, which necessitated gender, sex, and reproduction. Since sex, re-production, and family relations are no longer necessary, gender hierarchy can also be abolished. Women, as spiritual peers of men, can participate equally in church leadership.[33]

These two Christologies appear as opposites. But they are both based on a common presupposition, that is, that patriarchy is the order of creation. They assume that patriarchy can only be left behind by leaving behind the created order. The equality of men and women "in Christ" could be seen as a historical, and not just an eschatological, possibility, only when this fusion of patriarchy and creation was uncoupled. To change this pattern, creation itself must be defined as egalitarian in its authentic nature. This original egalitarianism must be seen, not as a heavenly state before embodiment, but as our "original nature" as embodied, historical persons. Only then can patriarchy be placed under judgment as an unjust distortion of our human capacities and social ordering of relationships. Equality between men and women can then be envisioned as a social reform within history that restores our original nature, rather than something possible only by an ahistorical departure from history and embodied existence.

The basis of this egalitarian anthropology was laid in Europe and America in the late eighteenth and nineteenth centuries. The feudal churches, which reflected the old class hierarchies, were repudiated as representatives of a moribund and unjust society. The redemptive future was severed from its institutionalization in the churches and secularized in reform and revolution-ary social movements. These revolutionary liberal and socialist movements rooted themselves in a revised myth of original nature as one of equality of all humans in their "essential" nature. The feudal hierarchy of separate "estates" was rejected for one of equal political "rights."

However, the first stage of such liberal, democratic revolutions only dis-mantled the hierarchy of aristocracy over the third estate or the bourgeois. It left intact the patriarchal dominance of the male head of family over women, children, propertyless servants, and slaves.[34] The "self-evident" truth that "all men [humans] are created equal and endowed with inalienable rights" would only be gradually applied to these subjugated groups — to propertyless men (universal manhood suffrage); to slaves (abolitionism), and to women (feminism). Socialism would try to extend egalitarianism to economic rights, creating a conflict between political visions of liberty and economic visions of justice that is still unresolved at the beginning of the twenty-first century.

Yet, by the mid-twentieth century, both liberals and socialists had come to take egalitarian anthropology for granted, at least in theory. The notion that women are fully human and should have equal rights is officially accepted in both views, however much it may be contradicted in practice. Even the pope and the Catholic bishops now feel compelled to affirm that women are fully human, are not inferior or defective in human capacities, and are equal sharers in the "image of God." But they still cling to a Christology based on a patriarchal anthropology, attempting to use this to exclude women from equality of leadership in the church, while abandoning the more basic exclusion of women from political rights in secular society.[35]

This contradiction between egalitarian anthropology, for secular society, and patriarchical Christology, for the church hierarchy, reflects a new church-world split. Patriarchy, no longer defensible for secular society, is sacralized as a special sacred order for the church. The result is that Christology loses its basic integration with creation. Christ does not restore and redeem creation but stands now for a sacred patriarchal order of the church, unconnected with creation. This new creation-redemption split reverses the dilemma of classical Christianity. There creation was assumed to be patriarchal, while redemption in Christ overcame female inferiority, at least spiritually.

Christ after Patriarchy

To recover the integration of Christ and creation essential to a coherent theology, Christology must be recast by integrating it with an egalitarian anthropology. Once we have discarded patriarchal anthropology, with its false biological underpinnings, which regarded women as less complete expressions of human nature than men, one must also affirm women as equally theomorphic, that is, capable of imaging the divine. If women share equally in the image of God, then they also share equally in the care of creation. This cannot be limited to a dependent, domestic sphere.

If women are equally theomorphic, then God must be imaged as female as well as male, as the ground of that fullness of personhood present in both women and men. This means that the maleness of the historical Jesus

has nothing to do with manifesting a divine "Son" of a divine "Father."
Both the gender and the parent-child character of these symbols must be
deliteralized. God transcendent is the depth of being that we encounter in
redemptive experiences, but as one and the same God.

In Jesus we encounter, paradigmatically, the Logos-Sophia of that one
God who is both mother and father, liberator, lover, and friend. But what is
the significance of the maleness of the historical Jesus, if it is not ontologically necessary that a male manifest God? Doesn't the very fact that Jesus is
a male continue the assumption that women receive redemption from men
but cannot represent God as redemptive actors?

Christian feminists cannot resolve this problem by suggesting that, because Jesus was nonpatriarchal in his sensitivity to women and in his
vulnerability in suffering, that somehow this makes him "feminine" and
thus inclusive of women. All that does is to make Jesus a model for an androgynous male, presumably the holistic capacities that every male should
develop. But this does nothing to affirm a like holistic humanity for women.
Rather, I believe Christians must affirm the particularity of Jesus, not only
in gender but also in ethnicity and culture, and the limitations of any single
individual to be universally paradigmatic.

What we find in classical Christology is a dissolution of all other aspects
of Jesus' historical particularity, his Jewishness, his first-century cultural setting, while elevating his gender to universal ontological significance. Instead,
I believe we should encounter Jesus, not only as male, but in all his particularity as a first-century Galilean Jew. We then must ask how we can see him
as paradigmatic of universal human redemption in a way that can apply to
females as well as males, to people of all ethnicities and cultures.

This investigation must take us through several stages of revisionist
thought about Christology. First, we must see that what is paradigmatic
about Jesus is not his biological ontology but rather his person as lived
message and practice. Jesus becomes paradigmatic by embodying a certain
message. That message is good news to the poor, the confrontation with
systems of religion and society that incarnate oppressive privilege, and affirmation of the despised as loved and liberated by God. Jesus did not just
speak this message; he risked his life to embody this presence of God and
was crucified by those in power who rejected this message.

Second, we must cease to isolate the work of Christ from the ongoing
Christian community. This Jesus we find as a historical figure exemplifies a
way of life that is still critical in a world where false and oppressive privilege
still reign, often sacralized by religion. As Christians we are followers of
this Way. While Jesus is the foundational representative of this Way of the
cross and liberation, he is not its exclusive possibility. Each Christian must
also take up this same way and, in so doing, become "other Christs" to
one another. The church becomes redemptive community, not by passively

receiving a redemption "won" by Christ alone, but rather by collectively embodying this path of liberation in a way that transforms people and social systems.

If we are clear that the redemption signified by Christ is both carried on and communicated through redemptive community, this means that Christ can take on the face of every person and group and their diverse liberation struggles. We must be able to encounter Christ as Black, as Asian, as Aboriginal, as woman of all classes and races. This also means that the coming Christ, the future of a still-incomplete redemption, is not the historical Jesus returned, but rather the fullness of all this human diversity gathered together in redemptive community. This is the "Human One" who is to come, who bears the face of all suffering creatures longing for liberation.

Finally, this way of Christ need not and should not be seen as excluding other ways. The creating, inspiriting and liberating presence of God is present to all humans in all times and places. It has been expressed in many religious cultures, some of which parallel the Christ-way, and some of which complement it with other spiritualities — spiritualities of contemplation, for example, or of renewal of nature. The challenge of Christology today may be, not to try to extend the Christ symbol to every possible spirituality and culture, but rather to accept its limits. Then we can allow other ways and peoples to flourish in dialogues that can reveal God's many words to us.

For Further Reflection

1. How did the emergence of christological ideas in the early church relate to maleness or to how women were imaged?

2. What does the author mean by *androcentric* theology and *patriarchal* culture? Why are they problematic?

3. What insights does the author find in biblical images of God and Christ?

4. How would you characterize the two contrasting historical Christologies — patriarchal and egalitarian — and their relation to patriarchal culture?

5. In the end, does the author identify a women-affirming understanding of Jesus the Christ?

For Further Reading

Børresen, Kari E. *The Image of God: Gender Models in Judaeo-Christian Tradition.* Minneapolis: Fortress, 1995.

Irwin, Joyce I. *Womanhood in Radical Protestantism, 1525–1675.* New York: Edwin Mellen, 1979.

Johnson, Elizabeth A. *Consider Jesus: Waves of Renewal in Christology.* New York: Crossroad, 1990.

Kvam, Kristen E., Linda A. Schearing, and Valarie H. Ziegler, eds. *Eve and Adam: Jewish, Christian, and Muslim Readings on Genesis and Gender.* Bloomington: Indiana University Press, 1999.

Ruether, Rosemary Radford. *Sexism and God-Talk: Toward a Feminist Theology.* Boston: Beacon, 1983.

———. *Women and Redemption: A Theological History.* Minneapolis: Fortress, 1998.

— 8 —

A Postcolonial Christ

Robert Lassalle-Klein

Twenty-five years ago the noted German theologian Karl Rahner wrote, "Vatican II derives its importance from the fact that it proclaimed . . . a transition from the western Church to the world-Church."[1] Largely forgotten, however, is Rahner's sobering prediction that the transition from the Christianity of Europe to an actual world religion would involve a break as painful as the transition inaugurated by the apostle Paul in the first century C.E. from Judaeo-Christianity to a Christianity of the Gentiles.

Rahner's assessment seems prescient at the dawn of the third millennium, as Christians and representatives of other religions from around the globe offer startling new insights on the meaning of Jesus. Like Peter and Paul before us, however, Christians, church leaders, and scholars have been surprised and scandalized by the conflict, pain, institutional resistance, and confusion that beset our struggles to come to terms with the faith of Christians in Latin America, Africa, Asia, and Oceana. Reflecting this trend, Euro-American Christology has barely registered, much less accepted, the importance of two of the most promising breakthroughs from beyond its borders. These breakthroughs draw our attention to the ongoing drama of faith, crucifixion, and resurrection unfolding on the globalized borders of the world's last remaining superpower. And they represent the hundredfold harvest flowering from the worldwide commitment to global justice and intercultural dialogue sown by Catholic social teaching at the close of history's most violent century.

This chapter introduces the *mestizo Jesus* discovered on the Mexico-Texas border by Virgilio Elizondo and the symbol of the *crucified peoples* created in El Salvador by Ignacio Ellacuría (and partially inspired by Archbishop Oscar Romero). The latter forms the centerpiece of Jon Sobrino's recently published two-volume Christology. These images capture the popular Catholicism of millions of Christians crushed at different moments under the relentless wheels of the American century. Yet they are suffused by luminescent faith, hope, and communal solidarity, and they have helped desperate communities survive in the face of overwhelming odds.

Part of the enabling power of these images of the *mestizo Jesus* and the crucified peoples offered by Elizondo and Ellacuría lies in the fact that they work as theodicies. Theodicies are religious explanations that give meaning to experiences of suffering or evil that threaten the peoples' fundamental assumptions about the societies in which they live. Few if any first world Christologies have incorporated these images. But I would argue that they provide valuable resources for Christology grounded in the needs of a global church.

Virgilio Elizondo and the *Mestizo Jesus*

The cradle of global Christianity has moved, as Cuban-American theologian Roberto Goizueta notes, from "the great cathedrals of Paris and Cologne," to "the poor neighborhoods of Lima, Manila, and San Antonio."[2] It is in these neighborhoods that Virgilio Elizondo has lived, labored, and encountered Jesus Christ and where he created an approach to theology that reveals "for us all the 'mestizo' face of... Christ — and... the church." In Goizueta's view, Elizondo's *mestizo Jesus* has unrealized potential as a template of future Christologies for a global church.

The core of Elizondo's theology emerges from the symbolic "sacred triad"[3] that he sees shaping Southwest Mexican-American popular Catholicism. The three elements of this triad include what Elizondo has called *mestizaje,* the *mestizo Jesus,* and Our Lady of Guadalupe. Our Lady is understood as Mary, the mother of Jesus. Jesus and Mary are core manifestations of Latino/a popular religion. By "popular religion" is meant the everyday beliefs and religious practices of common people.[4] Scholars of U.S. Latino/a religion understand *mestizaje* as involving some form of racial or cultural intermingling. Elizondo's dual focus on racial and cultural mixing and popular religion created a pattern that has framed the subsequent development of Hispanic/Latino theology in the United States.

In my teaching, I have discovered another aspect of the enduring power of Elizondo's work. Elizondo's retrieval of Latino popular Catholicism in particular highlights and challenges the destabilizing and crippling history of racism, conquest, and oppression suffered by Latinos since the arrival of Columbus in the Americas. It is a valuable resource for a theodicy, though it has rarely been explicitly addressed as such by U.S. Latino/a theologians.[5] In fact, its extraordinary power as a theodicy for racism makes the *mestizo Jesus* an image of Jesus Christ relevant to the sufferings, hopes, and aspirations of Christians across the globe.

Popular Catholicism

Elizondo's methodological emphasis on popular religion has become profoundly influential among scholars of U.S. Hispanic/Latino religious experience.

Orlando Espín, a leading expert on Latino/a popular religion, explains that popular Catholicism "refers to Catholicism as practiced, believed, etc., by the common people."[6] Espín highlights the singular importance of this form of everyday Latino religiosity for students of U.S. Latino religion and culture. He writes, "It can be argued that, first of all, popular Catholicism is the manner in and through which most U.S. Latinos are Catholic: and secondly, that this popular Catholicism is the key matrix of all Hispanic cultures."[7] And he concludes, "If this is the case, and I believe it is, then . . . the study of this religion is crucial for an adequate understanding of all Hispanics." These voices help us to appreciate the implications for all Latino/as of Elizondo's claim that the *mestizo Jesus* lies at the core of Mexican American popular Catholicism.

Mestizaje

Our first task, however, is the explanation of *mestizaje* and its role in creating a Mexican American theodicy. Many scholars regard *mestizaje* as a defining aspect of Latino culture and popular Christianity in the United States. Elizondo's work presents his reinterpretation of this traditional Mexican concept and applies it to Mexican Americans in the United States.

Elizondo's approach is framed by the historical claim that, "Contemporary Mexican-Americans can trace their origins to two great invasions and conquests: the Spanish and the Anglo-American."[8] Both conquests are responsible, Elizondo writes, for ushering in an era of colonization, oppression, and exploitation. With no small irony, given his focus on popular Catholicism, Elizondo dates the first invasion to "Good Friday, April 22, 1519, the day Hernando Cortez arrived in Mexico."[9] He describes the tragic brutality of murder, rape, racism, and the ferocious destruction and degradation of Mesoamerican religion and culture that followed the Spanish conquest of the Aztec empire in 1521. From this inauspicious beginning, asserts Elizondo, the Spanish-Catholic conquest of Mexico brought about what he calls "the first mestizaje."[10]

Elizondo's second *mestizaje* begins with the white Anglo-Saxon Protestant invasion of Catholic and Latino Northern Mexico. It is driven by the expansionist ideology of Manifest Destiny and gains momentum with the unilateral declaration of war against Mexico by President James Polk in 1846. With the end of the Mexican-American War in 1848, Mexico was forced to cede the northern half of its territory to the United States in the Treaty of Guadalupe-Hidalgo. The Mexican population inhabiting what is now California, Arizona, and New Mexico and large sections of Colorado, Nevada, and Utah woke up one day to find that their northern border with the United States had suddenly moved south. Millions of Mexican families became foreigners in their native land, faced with an uncertain new future as "Mexican-Americans."

Living at the crossroads of two cultures, they were members of both, Elizondo says, but fully accepted by neither. He speaks frankly of the suffering caused by the evils of racism and American imperialism in this two-fold mestizaje lived by Mexican Americans in the Southwest United States. He asserts that, "Since 1848 there has been a nearly unbroken history of direct and indirect, spontaneous and institutionalized violence throughout the West and Southwest. Leading institutions, both public and private, secular and religious, have adopted prejudicial attitudes and practices in regard to the Mexican-American population."[11] Citing well-documented patterns of racial discrimination in schools, churches, law-enforcement agencies, the workplace, and social agencies, Elizondo argues that racism is not all in the past. One has only to look at the strong correlation in the 2000 U.S. Census of Hispanic origin or African American race and negative social indicators (e.g., low income) to verify his claim.

Theodicy

But Elizondo's perspective is by no means completely negative on this two-stage history of invasion and conquest, the double *mestizaje* of Mexican Americans. On the one hand, their *mestizaje* has emerged from the catastrophic confrontations of two civilizations, and the evils of racism, suffering, and death. On the other, however, each *mestizaje* has produced "a new ethnos, a new people." As Elizondo states, "the Spanish-Indian confrontation gave birth to the Mexican people," and "the Anglo-American-Mexican confrontation gave birth to the Mexican American people."[12] He then compares what the second *mestizaje* has produced to "the birth of Europe, thirty-five thousand years ago," and "the birth of Mexico, less than five hundred years ago." Indeed, Elizondo asserts, an "event of at least equal magnitude has already begun to take place in the Southwest of the United States of America — an area larger than Western Europe and populated by...million[s.]"

And this is Elizondo's key point. The "painful birth of the mestizo [Mexican-American] people,"[13] is an event of tremendous hope and grace. Elizondo uses the word *mestizaje* as a kind of shorthand for this convoluted process of life, death, rebirth.[14] For Elizondo, the concept of *mestizaje* symbolizes the simultaneously tragic and resilient history of Mexican Americans. It functions as the first leg of a theodicy that brings a degree of meaning and coherence from the evils of racism and conquest and the suffering they produced for generations of Mexican Americans.

Further contextualizing the term, Goizueta says that while the term "traditionally referred . . . to the mixture of European and Native American races and cultures, . . . among U.S. Hispanic theologians . . . 'mestizaje' is now generally used as a broader, umbrella term that encompasses any type of racial-cultural mixture."[15] This is most certainly true. I would add, however, that U.S. Hispanic theologians have adopted not only the terminology of *mestizaje*[16] but also the theodicy it represents. I believe this goes a long way toward explaining why *mestizaje* is such a universal concept (by whatever name) in U.S. Hispanic/Latino/a theology. Elizondo's reinterpretation of the term *mestizaje* captures something essential about the hope and optimism of not only Mexican Americans but the vast majority of U.S. Latino/as, as they struggle for a better life, overcoming the evils suffered, past and present.

The Mestizo Jesus

Elizondo's work eventually led to his discovery of the *mestizo Jesus* and the liberating role this image plays in Mexican-American popular Catholicism. Elizondo's autobiographical recollections illustrate both the meaning and interrelationship of *mestizaje* and the *mestizo Jesus,* as well as their liberating power as a theodicy for U.S. Latino/as.

Elizondo's original insight into "the reality and function of mestizaje . . . during the summer of 1968"[17] eventually led him to the *mestizo Jesus.* Elizondo recalls that, while flying over Mexico City with Professor Jacques Audinet from Paris, the latter described "how he had been captivated by the monument to 'La Raza' . . . and especially by an inscription on the site of the final battles between Cortes and the Indian nations: 'Neither a defeat nor a victory, but the painful birth of the 'mestizo' people that is Mexico today.' " Elizondo states that, "From a realization of the uniqueness of the Mexican 'mestizo,' as proclaimed in that inscription at the Plaza de las Tres Culturas in Mexico City, I moved to a discovery of the new 'mestizaje' of the Southwest that was pulling Anglos and Mexican-Americans alike into the formation of a new humanity."

A year later in 1969, Elizondo recalls, Mexican American priests gathered from around the country for the first time in San Antonio and "started to realize that a civil rights crusade was needed within the church itself."[18] The group "decided to establish a center where we could bring people together with our own native scholars and pastoral workers, as well as others who wanted to be a part of our struggle, to reflect on our reality, construct our own theological interpretation of our faith journey, and design pastoral practices that would bring about Vatican II renewal in the context of our culture and heritage." Within a year, Elizondo had helped to cofound and become the first director of the Mexican American Cultural Center (MACC).

For six years, MACC and its collaborators began turning out research, books, pastoral materials, and a new generation of Latino leaders. However, as Elizondo often noted, there was not a single native-born Hispanic theologian in the United States. He recalls that Jacques Audinet and others challenged him personally with how he could demand of others what he had not done himself. Elizondo accepted Audinet's invitation to the Institut Catholique in Paris. There he was to develop the research carried out by the MACC team into a doctoral thesis. He soon found himself mired in an interpretive impasse that derailed his best attempts to formulate theologically what MACC was doing. Elizondo recalls, "As I was working on my doctoral dissertation on *mestizaje* in Paris, I kept struggling to find a connection between what appeared to be two theses that did not connect: the socio-historical process of the twofold *mestizaje* of Mexican-Americans and the socio-historical identity and mission of Jesus." Still, "some unidentified inner drive kept pushing me to discover a connection between Jesus and our own situation. Intuitively I felt it was there."[19]

Elizondo's lifelong experience with Mexican American popular Catholicism taught him to ask: "What does *mestizaje* really have to do with Jesus?" and "What does Jesus really have to do with the double *mestizaje* that defines the history of Mexican-Americans?" He intuitively identified the pieces of the puzzle but could not formulate theologically how *mestizaje* and Jesus fit together. At times, he says, he thought he should develop one or the other of the two emerging theses and keep the other one as a subject of personal interest. Finally, however, the all-important element started to come into focus. Things started to fall into place when it struck Elizondo that the key to Mexican American popular Catholicism was "the closest friend and companion of our people: El Nazareno, Jesus of Nazareth in Galilee."[20] Next, he began to see the similarities between the geographical region of Jesus' homeland and that of south Texas. His study of archaeological research revealed that Galilee was "a borderland, the great border region between the Greeks and the Jews of Judea. People of all nationalities came along the caravan routes on their way to and from Egypt.... The Jews were forced to mix with their gentile neighbors." This was "a land of great mixture and of ongoing *mestizaje* — similar to our own Southwest of the United States."[21]

From here, Elizondo moved to the hypothesis that, "By growing up in Galilee...culturally and linguistically speaking, Jesus was a 'mestizo.'"[22] Elizondo captures the liberating power of this insight by contrasting it to the negative value historically assigned to this aspect of the identity of Jesus. Thus, he says, "The apparent non-importance and rejection of Galilee are the very bases of its all-important role in the historical eruption of God's saving plan for humanity." His point is that, "The human scandal of God's way does not begin with the cross, but with the historico-cultural incarnation of his Son in Galilee."[23] Accordingly, he argues, "It is in the Galilean identity of Jesus that the ultimate meaning of the cultural identity of an oppressed people is to be sought."[24]

Elizondo formulates this meaning in what he calls "the Galilee principle — namely, what human beings reject, God chooses as his very own."[25] This statement draws our attention to why and how the *mestizo Jesus* functions as a theodicy. Elizondo believes that the *mestizo Jesus* "speaks directly to the deepest level of our [Mexican-American] human suffering and to our most fervent aspirations."[26] The key, says Elizondo, is that "he liberates us by giving a totally new signification to our identity and a challenging mission to our movements. In him, curse is transformed into blessing and rejection becomes election for a sacred mission."

Given our interest in Christology, and the emergence of the world church, it is worth noting that Elizondo wonders, "Why had I never thought about this before?" He answers, tellingly, "The Christologies I knew, written from the dominant cultures, had made no special mention of Galilee."[27] While the sociohistorical context of the historical Jesus has become a standard topic in Christology, I know of no Christology that deals with the *mestizo* aspect of the identity of Jesus. Writing from the Mexican American border, however, Elizondo states, "For me, the Galilean identity of Jesus became the most important interpretive key for my thesis, as it would continue to be in all my subsequent work." Attributing the power of this insight to the genius of the popular Catholicism of Aztec[28] and Mexican American Christians, he says, "I consider the Jesus-Galilean-Mestizo theme one of the great innovations in Christology, a sort of Christology of the new world."[29]

I believe Elizondo's insights have the potential to make a major contribution in the years ahead.

It is curious that Euro-American Christology has barely registered, much less incorporated, the importance of Elizondo's discovery of the *mestizo Jesus*. For globalization of Euro-American economic interests, seemingly endless wars, and massive migration in the last century have made us into a world of *mestizo* races and cultures. And, ironically, Christianity is most vital among the races and tribes crushed by European colonialism and the American century, now reborn as *mestizo* peoples. It is difficult to avoid the conclusion that the lack of interest in the *mestizo Jesus* may reflect Euro-American discomfort with the generally subversive character of the Christian theodicy about Jesus. It is well known that the apostle Paul encountered similar difficulties in Greece and Rome. More to the point, however, is Goizueta's insight that, through the eyes of Virgilio Elizondo, "the mestizo victim is revealed as the sacrament of God's reign, the witness to a truly global ecclesia."[30] This analogy to Jesus as the sacrament of God speaks to the role of the *mestizo Jesus* as a powerful contemporary Christian theodicy. I believe it is precisely this aspect that makes the *mestizo Jesus* one of the most significant breakthroughs in the development of new approaches to Christology better suited to the needs of a global church.

The *Crucified Peoples*
as a Christological Category

> The situation in Latin America is that we are not doing theology "after"
> Auschwitz, but "during" Auschwitz, and this is what has moved me
> to write ... on the crucified God and ... on the crucified people.
> — Jon Sobrino, *Jesus the Liberator*

Jon Sobrino, S.J., uses the fruitful symbol of the *crucified people* to frame
his recently completed two-volume Christology. Sobrino unifies the books
by his insight that the crucified people functions for many Salvadorans as
the root metaphor of a truly christological theodicy. His basic assertion is
that this popular spirituality draws an analogy between the faith, hope, and
communal solidarity of the suffering church of El Salvador, on the one hand,
and the life, death, and resurrection of Jesus, on the other. Important questions can be raised about the accuracy and the legitimacy of this analogy.
But I argue that Sobrino's approach is philosophically coherent and a legitimate development of similar arguments presented by Ignacio Ellacuría, S.J.,
Karl Rahner, S.J., and some leading biblical scholars.

Ignacio Ellacuría introduced *the crucified peoples* as a christological
image in 1978, built on a famous homily by Archbishop Oscar Romero[31] It
has found resonance with Christians interested in an "option for the poor"
in Africa, Asia, Latin America, Europe and the United States.[32] His essay,
"The Crucified People: An Essay in Historical Soteriology,"[33] reexamines
the figure of the suffering servant from Second Isaiah used as a template by
the primitive Christian community to interpret Jesus' death. Ellacuría argues
this entitles us to use the image to draw an analogy between the death of
Jesus and the "crucified peoples" of today.

Ellacuría defines the "crucified people" as that "vast portion of humankind, which is literally and actually crucified by natural, ... historical, and
personal oppressions."[34] And he reminds us that their ongoing crucifixion
has been a defining aspect of "the reality of the world in which the church
has existed for almost two thousand years, [literally] since Jesus announced
the approach of the Reign of God." Ignacio Ellacuría was murdered for
his work on behalf of the crucified people of El Salvador on November 16,
1989, with five other Jesuit priests and two women co-workers at the University of Central America in San Salvador.[35] Jon Sobrino escaped death
because he was traveling in Asia.

Sobrino appropriates and develops this image as the core of his new
Christology, which stands among the most impressive, comprehensive, and
original contextual Christologies written since Vatican II (1965). Both volumes follow what Sobrino calls "the fundamental methodological choice
running right through Latin American Christology: to go back to Jesus in

order to rethink all theological realities in terms of him."[36] But Sobrino's christological project extends far beyond methodology in three key aspects.

First, Sobrino intends to introduce the "crucified people" as a formal christological concept. Second, he sets out to "draw a fundamental analogy"[37] "between the struggles of the *crucified people* to believe and to survive the "world of poverty...today,"[38] and the life, death, and resurrection of Jesus Christ. After reviewing what he calls the factual, historical-ethical, and religious significance of Ellacuría's term, Sobrino writes,

> I wish to add that the term *crucified peoples* is also useful and necessary language in Christology. The *crucified peoples* are those who fill up in their flesh what is lacking in Christ's passion, as Paul says about himself. They are the actual presence of the crucified Christ in history, as Archbishop Romero said to some terrorized peasants who had survived a massacre: "You are the image of the pierced savior." These words are not rhetorical, but strictly christological. They mean that in this crucified people Christ acquires a body in history and that the crucified people embody Christ in history as crucified.[39]

And, third, Sobrino argues that when followers of Jesus take the crucified people down from their cross, they become living signs for the universal church of both the coming of the kingdom of God and the resurrection of the crucified Jesus from the dead.

Each of these three elements points to the overall direction of Sobrino's entire christological project. In a theme that has been consistent throughout Sobrino's career, he says that his latest work "does no more than — starting from Jesus — elevate the reality we are living to the level of a theological concept, to theorize about a Christological faith that we see as real faith." The truth of this statement is reflected when Sobrino apologizes for the delays and the limits of the first volume. He says, "This book has been written in the middle of war, of threats, of conflict and persecution." And, he confesses, "The murder-martyrdom of my brother Jesuits, of Julia Elba, and Celina Ramos, left my heart frozen and my mind empty."[40]

These comments lend perspective to Sobrino's explanation that he is doing Christology from the everyday experiences and faith of the people El Salvador. And they help us to believe him when he claims, "Because of this [people and their faith], in spite of everything, this book is written in hope and joy."[41] Thus, he argues, "The crucified Jesus Christ, so omnipresent, is really good news." Indeed, for the people of El Salvador, "He is truly Jesus Christ the liberator."

Exegetical Hesitations

In 1988 John P. Meier, a leading biblical theologian from the University of Notre Dame, challenged certain aspects of Sobrino's earliest analyses of the historical Jesus. The critique is instructive, for it raises important questions about the legitimacy of the basic analogy that Sobrino is out to establish between the crucified people and the historical Jesus. The exchange between Meier and Sobrino also has bearing on Elizondo's case for the christological implications of the *mestizo Jesus.*

Meier criticized Sobrino's use of the phrase *historical Jesus* in his pre-1988 work. Meier makes three major points that are of particular interest. First, he asserts correctly that "Sobrino's whole presentation of liberation theology claims to be based on the historical Jesus." However, citing Sobrino's earliest work, Meier argues, "Nowhere in the book is there any extended, critical discussion of what the phrase 'the historical Jesus' means or what criteria we are to use to discern authentic material."[42]

Second, Meier offers several important and helpful technical criticisms of Sobrino's use of New Testament texts. He charges that Sobrino makes specific claims about the life of Jesus that can be refuted in light of contemporary historical-critical scholarship. In one telling example, Meier questions Sobrino's postulation that a crisis took place toward the middle or the end of Jesus' life.[43] Specifically, Meier objects that Sobrino imports an "historically dubious"[44] biographical detail from John's Gospel into his very "synoptic" account of the life of Jesus.

Third, Meier criticizes Sobrino for his claim that "Latin American Christology understands the historical Jesus as the totality of Jesus' history."[45] But, as Meier argues, "Of course, that is precisely what the historical Jesus cannot be." This point goes to the substance of Meier's disagreement with Sobrino about the precise nature of the term *historical Jesus.* He asserts that, "the historical Jesus is that which the methods of historical criticism enable us to retrieve of Jesus of Nazareth."[46]

Meier says of Sobrino's view that, "One almost gets the impression that the historical Jesus equals the full reality of the pre-Easter Jesus, with no awareness of the difficulties that simplistic equation involves."[47] Indeed, Meier apparently believes that Sobrino naively confuses phrase *the historical Jesus* (which Meier asserts can only be a scholarly reconstruction) with its first-century object, which Meier prefers to call "the real Jesus." For Meier, "The real Jesus, i.e., the total reality of Jesus of Nazareth as he lived in the first century, is no longer accessible to us by scholarly means." And he adds, "It is this basic insight which touches off a quest for the historical Jesus, and it is this basic insight that is lacking in Sobrino's approach."[48]

Ellacuría's Philosophy of Historical Reality

The work of Ignacio Ellacuría frames Sobrino's entire approach to the crucified people as a formal christological concept. We cannot understand Sobrino's response to Meier's critique without a brief presentation of Ellacuría's philosophy of historical reality, his principle of historicization, and his theology of sign. Ellacuría uses this image to interpret the action-oriented mysticism of the Spiritual Exercises of St. Ignatius and the theology of symbol of his theological teacher, Karl Rahner, from the perspective of Latin American liberation theology and postcolonial thought. One of his concerns is to assist his fellow Central American Jesuits in their post-Medellín option for the poor and their Third World critique of Western colonialism.

Ellacuría's *magnum opus,* published posthumously in 1990, states, "Historical reality is the 'ultimate object' of philosophy."[49] He argues that historical reality has an "all-inclusive and totalizing character," and, as historical, it is the "supreme manifestation of reality."[50] It is important to appreciate that this position emerges from Ellacuría's liberationist and postcolonial perspective on globalization. He states that, while "it is becoming ever so clear that [history] is 'one,'" it is also true that "this unity is ... enormously painful for the majority of humanity."[51] He argues that the fact that "we speak of different worlds (a first world, a third world, etc.)" reveals that, while history is one, it is also "contradictory." Thus, writes Ellacuría, it is painfully obvious that "the time has come to make this one history the object of the various branches of philosophy."

Ellacuría's philosophy of historical reality is a development of the philosophy of science of Ellacuría's mentor, the Spanish philosopher and student of Husserl, Xavier Zubiri. Zubiri says that the proper object of philosophy is the cosmos, understood in the classical sense as "the world or universe as an ordered and harmonious system."[52] Zubiri says that the cosmos-as-system forms "a single complex and differentiated physical unity,"[53] constituted by interactive and progressively more complex subsystems of matter, biological life, sentient life, and human history (in its personal and social dimensions). Ellacuría asserts that the theory of evolution offers "empirical proof" for Zubiri's hypothesis that the cosmos operates as an integrated system.

While philosophy builds on science, however, it has its own unique concerns. Thus, Ellacuría says, "What philosophy does is to conceptualize why it is that one reality is more a reality than another."[54] Accordingly, if philosophy determines that "the degree of reality is measured by the degree of autonomy," then it follows that biological "life is not only a different reality than pure materiality, but it is [a] ... superior form of reality." Here, it must be emphasized that Ellacuría is talking about an autonomy-in-relation. Each subsystem of the cosmos (e.g., matter, biological life, sentient life, human history, etc.) "does not unfold apart from all the anterior moments that make up the process of reality." Rather, "What happens is that ... there is a qualitative increment in reality," so that "the inferior reality ... is always ... made present in the superior forms of reality."[55]

Ellacuría finally asserts that the "last stage of reality in which all other stages of reality are made present, is what we call historical reality." He argues, "In this stage, reality is a 'greater' reality because it contains all anterior reality." And, he asserts, the distinctive characteristic of "the modality we have been calling historical" is that it "manifests itself in the social realm of freedom." For Ellacuría, human freedom "is reality demonstrating its most excellent virtues and possibilities."[56]

Historical reality, then, is "the totality of reality as it is given in its highest qualitative form, the specific form of which is history."[57] Ellacuría suggests that it is precisely here "where we are given not only the highest forms of reality, but also the field of the maximum possibilities of the real." He asserts that "historical reality . . . includes all other types of reality." And he argues that "there is no historical reality without purely material reality, . . . biological reality, . . . [and] personal and social reality." In the end, however, Ellacuría says "historical reality is where reality is 'more,' . . . where it is both 'more its own,' and 'more open.' " And it is from this point (derived from Zubiri) that Ellacuría develops his most creative efforts.

Historicization

The second factor that shapes Sobrino's treatment of the crucified people is one of Ellacuría's most important innovations, the principle of *historicization* (a more limited term in the work of Zubiri). There are two primary uses of the term in Ellacuría's work. First, in his philosophy of historical reality,[58] Ellacuría uses the term *historicization* to refer to the incorporative and transformative power that human praxis exerts over the historical and natural dimensions of reality. Second, in another article Ellacuría says, "Demonstrating the impact of certain concepts within a particular context is [also] . . . understood here as their historicization."[59] In this secondary sense, historicization becomes a procedure for testing and validating truth claims associated with a concept. Ellacuría holds that the truth of an historicized concept lies in its "becoming reality," so that its "truth can be measured in [its] results."[60] It is this secondary meaning that predominates in the great majority of Ellacuría's occasional pieces.[61]

During the final decade of his life, Ellacuría attempted to historicize U.S. claims to be promoting democracy in El Salvador during the 1980s. Many writings from this period document his discovery that, despite official claims to the contrary, U.S. support for brutal Salvadoran governmental repression of civil society was actually undermining attempts to bring true democracy to El Salvador. Outraged by these reports, gunmen were sent to silence the voice of Ellacuría on November 16, 1989. The United Nations Commission on the Truth for El Salvador reports that the decision was made at the highest levels of the Salvadoran military "to eliminate Father Ellacuría and to leave no witnesses."[62] Shortly thereafter, U.S. policy in the region lost credibility and bipartisan Congressional support, forcing the Salvadoran government to submit for the first time to open elections with true opposition parties.

Theology of Sign

The third factor that shapes Sobrino's treatment of the crucified people is Ella-curía's theology of sign. Ellacuría argues that a theology of sign is needed to articulate the presence and the activity of God in historical reality and the cosmos. This claim reflects the profound influence of Ellacuría's studies (1958–62) with Karl Rahner. But it is also designed to respond to the mandate issued by Pastoral Constitution on the Church in the Modern World from Vatican II: "In every age the Church carries the responsibility of reading the signs of the times and of interpreting them in light of the Gospel" (*Gaudium et spes* 4).

Ellacuría emphasizes that "God is only accessible through the mediation of signs."[63] For Judeo-Christians, salvation history implies that "the fundamental sign for God is history itself, though not all history in the same way." And he asserts, citing *Gaudium et spes,* that Vatican II implies that "the revelation of God in history happens in the...signs of the times."[64] Ellacuría uses these elements to develop a theology of revelation that simultaneously distinguishes, yet links, signs of the times of the present with the ancient deposit of faith (*depositum fidei*) from the past. Thus, he argues, "the signs of the times...bring forth possibilities, new and old, from the hidden treasure [of revelation]."

The basic elements of this theology of sign appear in Ellacuría's first and best-known work in fundamental theology. He writes, "Everything that is presented as salvation in history ... is regarded as a sign of the history of salvation."[65] He adds, "My work tries to demonstrate the connection between the sign and what constitutes it as a sign." In a later commentary he asserts, "Not to have understood this theology of sign that dominates the entire publication (and which I will later say belongs to ... fundamental theology) implies a serious lack of depth in the interpretation and the evaluation of my work."[66]

I would suggest that Ellacuría's sacramental and critical regard for historical reality as the preeminent sign for God embodies the characteristics of what some have called a "Catholic imagination"[67] in a liberating, postcolonial, Latin American form. Nowhere is this more evident than in Ellacuría's original claim that the principle sign of the times "by whose light all the others should be discerned and interpreted...is...the crucified people."[68] For Ellacuría, this refers to those great majorities "from whom the sin of the world continues to take away all human form, and whom the powers of this world dispossess of everything, seizing even their lives, above all their lives."

Jon Sobrino, S.J., Ellacuría's close friend, co-worker, and fellow Jesuit for over forty years, asserts that the personal and intellectual dimensions of Ellacuría's biography converged in a powerful sense of vocation defined by this image or sign. Sobrino recalls, "If anything in Ellacuría forcefully drew my attention from the very first, it was his passion for service. His fundamental, or perhaps transcendental question, was always 'what should I do?' "[69] As a Jesuit, Sobrino says, "This was his historical embodiment of the typically Ignatian desire 'to seek God's will in all things, and carry it out.' " Sobrino asserts, however, that Ellacuría's passion for service reached beyond his vocation to religious life. He says,

> In my opinion, this was the foundation of his life, his vocation as a Jesuit, and deeper still, as a human being: knowing you are called to serve, using all your talents, even your defects, to serve in the best way possible, and staying faithful to the end. With no exaggeration and strictly speaking, his life was a decentered life, a life of service *for* others, and, more and more, service *from the place of* others.

Ellacuría's sense of vocation came to be defined by this sign. Sobrino says that Ellacuría experienced a "vocation within a vocation," one that gradually integrated the varied elements of his identity as a Jesuit, a Christian, and a human being. He asserts that Ellacuría "not only dedicated his life to service," but slowly "came to understand that it was not just any service to which he was called, but a specific service: to take the crucified people down from the cross."[70]

This image, then, bears the sacramental weight of what I have called Ellacuría's Catholic imagination, his philosophy of historical reality, the principle of historicization, and his theology of sign. There is no denying that the image can be uncomfortable.[71] Historically, however, it came to embody the gradual articulation among members of the University of Central America's Jesuit community of a post-Medellín spirituality that learned to recognize the risen Jesus, vibrant and alive, in the crucified people of El Salvador.

Sobrino explains that Ellacuría and his companions (including himself) arrived at this corporate spirituality through a process of personal and intellectual conversion. He emphasizes, however, that "it was not any set of ideas that can explain what happened to us. Rather, we were changed by reality. Finally, it was historical reality that changed us."[72] Sobrino says that, "Ellacuría had a particular talent at conceptualizing [historical reality]." But he insists that "from an existential perspective, what was most decisive for Ellacuría was not simply the exercise of his intelligence — which was truly prodigious — but rather the dedication of himself, and his intelligence, to the service of" this crucified people.[73]

Sobrino's Response

Ellacuría puts us in a better position to understand Sobrino's response to the criticisms raised by John Meier. Volume 1 of Sobrino's two-volume Christology[74] focuses on the historical Jesus: his mission, his faith, and the conflict that led to his death. Sobrino's response to Meier's criticisms can be found here.

Meier's straightforward criticisms of Sobrino's exegesis receive a positive response. Sobrino outlines the historical-critical criteria for his statements about the historical Jesus and agrees that any picture of Jesus (no matter how empowering) must answer to publicly verifiable criteria developed by scholars. He admits that, "Latin American systematic Christology has not distinguished itself in the area of historical criticism." Meier's consideration of his work provoked important improvements and clarifications.[75]

Sobrino goes out of his way to distinguish the concern that "touches off a quest for the historical Jesus" in Latin America from the concern of the Euro-American quest. Quoting his colleague José Ignacio González Faus, Sobrino writes, "In Europe the historical Jesus is an object of investigation, whereas in Latin America he is a criterion of discipleship. In Europe study of the historical Jesus seeks to establish the possibilities and the reasonableness of the act of believing or not believing. In Latin America the appeal to the historical Jesus seeks to confront people with the dilemma of being converted or not."[76]

This basic distinction goes a long way toward clarifying the central interlocking arguments of Sobrino's two books. Volume 1 does not end (unlike Schillebeeckx and others) with a list of claims that believers can reasonably make about the historical Jesus, important as those may be. Rather, it is oriented toward the assertion that faith in Jesus Christ leads his followers to take the crucified peoples of today down from the cross. Volume 2 examines the interaction between the need to remember Jesus and faith in Jesus Christ. Sobrino scrutinizes this interaction between memory and faith in the New Testament, the early ecumenical councils of the church, and the faith of believers in Latin America today. He builds on volume 1 with the claim that followers of Jesus are transformed into living signs of the coming of the kingdom of God and Jesus' resurrection from the dead when they take the crucified people of today down from the cross.

Sobrino clarifies his meaning when he cites a question raised about his early work by Cardinal Joseph Ratzinger, head of the Congregation for the Doctrine of the Faith. Ratzinger compliments yet questions Sobrino's "impressive, but ultimately shocking interpretation . . . that God's gesture in raising Jesus is repeated in history . . . through giving life to the crucified."[77] Sobrino responds, "I hope it is clear that I am not talking of repeating God's action, any more than I talked of bringing the Kingdom of God in the previous volume of this work." Rather, he continues, "What I do insist on is giving signs — analogously — of resurrection and the coming of the Kingdom. And this is what Ignacio Ellacuría meant when he — for the first time, as far as I can establish — used the expression 'taking the crucified people down from the cross' as a formulation of the Christian mission."[78]

These comments serve to highlight the underlying paradigm guiding Sobrino's recovery of the historical Jesus, a paradigm grounded in the work of Ignacio Ellacuría. Sobrino's Christology is driven by his preoccupation with discovering living "signs" that historicize in the present both the lifework of Jesus (establishing the kingdom of God) and its confirmation by God's raising Jesus from the dead. As stated earlier, Sobrino wants to build his Christology on the popular religiosity of Salvadorans who draw an analogy between the life, death, and resurrection of Jesus of Nazareth and the life, death, and resurrection of El Salvador's crucified people. He wants to elevate this analogy from Salvadoran popular religion to the level of a theological concept. For Sobrino, it is this concern that ultimately drives Latin American Christology to ask, "What can we really know about Jesus of Nazareth?" For, "If we could really not know anything about him, or only insignificant things, the claim to produce a Christology based on [analogy to] the historical Jesus would be futile."[79]

This brings us back, then, to Meier's challenge to Sobrino's use of "historical Jesus." Meier argued that Sobrino naively confuses the phrase *the historical Jesus* (for Meier a scholarly reconstruction) with its first-century object, which Meier calls "the real Jesus."

Sobrino addresses the meaning of the "historical Jesus" and the role this concept plays in his Christology in volume 1. "Let me say from the beginning," he writes, "that I have chosen as my starting point the reality of Jesus of Nazareth, his life, his mission and his fate, what is usually called the 'historical Jesus.'"[80] Defining what he means by the concept, Sobrino says "By 'historical Jesus' we mean the life of Jesus of Nazareth, his words and actions, his activity and his praxis, his attitudes and his spirit, his fate on the cross (and the resurrection). In other words, ... the history of Jesus."[81]

In volume 2, Sobrino outlines what he calls the "reality principle"[82] that shapes his use of the New Testament sources. The authors of the various New Testament Christologies clearly believe that "the real and historical subject is still Jesus of Nazareth."[83] Thus, even though individual authors may add titles and other attributes to the story of Jesus, in the end, "Faith is referred back to 'what we have heard, what we have seen with our eyes, what we have looked at and touched with our hands' (1 John 1:1)." Sobrino then argues that the claim of Latin American Christology to be "reevaluating the 'reality' of Jesus of Nazareth, recalling it, and understanding it as 'history'" is grounded in a version of the reality principle.

Sobrino understands the phrase *historical Jesus* to refer to what Meier prefers to call the "real Jesus." However, contra Meier, Sobrino is neither naïve nor uncritical about the provisional status of his conclusions. He does not claim to have fully reconstructed or to have privileged access to the "total reality of Jesus of Nazareth as he lived in the first century." Indeed, he explicitly states that Latin American Christology "accepts the reservations imposed by historical criticism," and that "it knows that it is not possible to gain adequate access to the 'historical' Jesus, but only to a 'historical version' of Jesus."[84] "Nevertheless," Sobrino explains, Latin American Christology "does not share the skepticism of previous periods," and it does not "think it is impossible to know anything about Jesus." Rather, building on the work of biblical scholars, Sobrino "accepts some fundamental data, which allow us access to the basic structure of Jesus' life, about which there seems to be a consensus." And here we should notice the difference between Meier's "total reality," and Sobrino's "basic structure."

It is instructive to substitute Ellacuría's nuanced understanding of *historical reality* for Meier's phrase *total reality*.[85] Sobrino is asking a substantially different question from the one Meier attributes to him. Sobrino wants to know whether it is possible to recover the basic pattern of the choices that shaped the life of Jesus of Nazareth. Following Ellacuría, the historical reality of Jesus has less to do with the number of material details one might assemble about him than with the basic pattern of the way Jesus of Nazareth exercised his human freedom. An epistemological problem remains, but it shifts to the practical and theoretical possibility of accurately discerning the pattern of what Rahner would call the "fundamental option" that shaped the life of Jesus. Rahner, Ellacuría, and Sobrino believe it is possible to discern this pattern. Sobrino argues that the gospels are based on a parallel claim.

This aspect of Sobrino's basic position shares traits with a major trend in biblical scholarship on Jesus. Leading Jesus scholar N. T. Wright asserts that in "the last twenty years or so of scholarship . . . there has been an impressive turning of the tide, away from the 'via negativa' and towards historical realism"[86] in studies of the historical Jesus. Wright refers to this trend as the "third quest"[87] for the historical Jesus. He places the work of John Meier in this category. While I would largely agree, Meier's notion that "the historical Jesus is that which the methods of historical criticism enable us to retrieve of Jesus of Nazareth"[88] strikes me as standing outside this trend. It looks more like a version of Kantian percept — concept idealism, which must refuse to answer the question whether these images of Jesus achieve what they claim.

Epistemological issues remain. But the substantive issue is whether the gospels put us in touch with the basic pattern of the historical reality of Jesus. Like Kant's much-criticized "thing-in-itself," Meier postulates the existence of a "real Jesus," and then declares him unknowable because he is "no longer accessible to us by scholarly means."[89] He offers a scholarly portrait of the historical Jesus painstakingly constructed by empirical data. But there are philosophical shortcomings at work in his misreading of Sobrino. None of Meier's remarks shows an awareness of the philosophical warrants that link Sobrino's overall approach to that of Karl Rahner, Ignacio Ellacuría, and Xavier Zubiri. He seems to assume that Sobrino's position is philosophically uninformed.

Conclusion

This chapter has introduced the *mestizo Jesus* discovered by Virgilio Elizondo and the root metaphor of crucified people for the suffering yet hope-filled faith of the church of El Salvador. Elizondo's *mestizo Jesus* functions as a powerful and realistic theodicy for many U.S. Latino/a Christians. From the work of Jon Sobrino, I have highlighted his argument that Salvadorans find the analogy between Jesus' crucifixion and their own sufferings to be liberating and empowering. The power of each image, I would argue, is located in their ability to bring followers of Jesus Christ closer to the life, death, and resurrection of Jesus of Nazareth.

Few readers would question the historicity of the theodicies that Elizondo and Sobrino discovered among millions of people living at the margins of the American century. The images of Jesus they offer have an empowering and liberating legacy in communities at the U.S.-Mexico border and in El Salvador. I have tried to identify and address serious questions that arise from the efforts of Jon Sobrino and Virgilio Elizondo to introduce the *mestizo Jesus* and the crucified people as formal christological concepts. Do either of these images of Jesus achieve what they claim? Do they bring believers closer to the historical Jesus, or the "real" Jesus? Do they fit what we know about Jesus and with what the tradition says about Jesus?

Virgilio Elizondo's work on the *mestizo Jesus* has not received widespread consideration. Non-Latino/a theologians fail to consider it in their Christologies. I have emphasized the potential Elizondo's work offers for a contemporary Christology, especially when explored as a theodicy.[90] In my consideration of Sobrino, I have identified questions asked by first-world biblical scholars and theologians as they consider the christological claims raised by these images.

In this regard, I have tried to show how Sobrino's three basic christological claims regarding the crucified people are grounded in the theology of sign, the concept of historical reality, and the principle of historicization developed by Ignacio Ellacuría. I would submit that Sobrino is asking a substantially different question from the one attributed to him. Sobrino does not claim that his investigation of the historical Jesus refers to "the total reality of Jesus of Nazareth as he lived in the first century."[91] Rather, he is interested in the truth of his reconstruction of the basic pattern of the choices that shaped the life of Jesus of Nazareth. An epistemological problem remains, but it shifts to the more modest practical and theoretical possibility of discerning the truth of what Rahner might have called the "fundamental option" that shaped the life of Jesus. I have tried to briefly summarize the reasons Jon Sobrino thinks it is possible to discern this pattern.

My hope is that the reader will be drawn to explore the *mestizo Jesus,* and the image of the crucified people as promising icons for Christology. I have introduced the category of theodicy to explain the power of Elizondo's recovery of the role of *mestizaje* and the *mestizo Jesus* in Latino/a popular Catholicism. I have suggested the promise that Jon Sobrino's use of the work of Ignacío Ellacuría offers to other contextualized and intercultural approaches to Christology. And I have explained why I regard these images as two of the most promising breakthroughs of the last twenty years for those seeking to understand the multiple meanings of Jesus Christ for a global church. In the end, however, the efficacy of the *mestizo Jesus* and the crucified people is grounded in their ongoing role in sustaining the luminescent faith, hope, and communal solidarity of the popular Catholicism that has helped desperate communities to survive and thrive amid the onslaught of the American century. They illustrate how the struggles for human dignity at the end of an era of colonialism have religious creativity of marginalized Christians and pointed the way for a postcolonial church.

For Further Reflection

1. In what ways is the christological concept of *mestizo Jesus* relevant *in* and *beyond* the specific cultural context of U.S. Hispanic/Latino/as?

2. In what different ways do Elizondo and Sobrino tie their Christologies to the historical Jesus?

3. In your opinion, does the "real Jesus" differ from the "historical Jesus," and how does your understanding of these terms compare to Meier's?

4. How might the christological images discussed here — the *mestizo Jesus* and the crucified people — speak to a "postcolonial" world?

5. What is a theodicy, and how does the author argue that the christological images function as theodicies?

For Further Reading

Elizondo, Virgilio. *Galilean Journey: The Mexican-American Promise*. Maryknoll, N.Y.: Orbis Books, 2000 [1983].

Ellacuría, Ignacio. *Teología política*. San Salvador: Ediciones del Secretariado Social Interdiocesano, 1973. Trans., *Freedom Made Flesh: The Mission of Christ and His Church*. Maryknoll, N.Y.: Orbis Books, 1976.

Sobrino, Jon, S.J. *Jesus the Liberator: A Historical-Theological Reading of Jesus of Nazareth*. Maryknoll, N.Y.: Orbis Books, 1993.

Meier, John. *A Marginal Jew: Rethinking the Historical Jesus*. Vol. 2, *Mentor, Message, and Miracles*. Anchor Bible Reference Library. New York: Doubleday, 1991.

Goizueta, Roberto. *Caminemos con Jesús: Toward a Hispanic/Latino Theology of Accompaniment*. Maryknoll, N.Y.: Orbis Books, 1995.

Part Three

CHRIST AND
SOCIAL TRANSFORMATION

Christ in *Mujerista* Theology

Ada María Isasi-Díaz

Identifícate con Nosotros

The *Kyrie Eleison,* a well-known prayer heard for centuries in the Roman Catholic Eucharistic liturgy, becomes a very different cry for mercy when it is uttered by those of us who are marginalized by society and suffer discrimination. A petition to an almighty and sovereign God to show mercy and forgive us our sins is transformed, in the *Misa Nicaragüense,* into a cry to Christ Jesus to identify himself with us and to be in solidarity with us instead of with those who destroy us.[1] Vague requests for mercy become concrete: Christ Jesus, acknowledged as Lord but also addressed as a personal God — *Dios mío* — is asked to stand with us, to become one with us.[2] This request for him to join our ranks is not born out of a desire for personal solace and comfort. A private need would not result in a call for solidarity, which usually refers to a public stance taken to identify with and support others. What is at stake in this *Kyrie* is the need of the community for peace, the opposite, in this song, of being "squelched and devoured" by the oppressive class.[3]

What Is *Mujerista* Theology?

This prayer, this song, points to the *mujerista* understanding that theology is a praxis — that is, reflection-action that in a spiraling motion integrates the faith of Latina women with the struggle for liberation-fullness of life in which we are engaged in our daily living. Our religious beliefs direct and support action on behalf of liberation for ourselves and our people. Our actions, in turn, lead us to clarify what we believe: what it means for us in our everyday struggles against oppression to believe, for example, in Jesus as the Christ. *Mujerista* theology, recognizing the importance of religious beliefs in the lives of Latinas, seeks to elaborate a theology that does not ignore the political and social realities of our life as a marginalized community within the United States. This reality of being marginalized within the most powerful country in the world nowadays is not simply a matter of location, of our mailing address. The marginalization of Latinas plays a substantial role in our theological-ethical enterprise and provides key elements to our theological praxis. Who is God for us who are pushed to the margins? How do we encounter God at the margins? Who is Christ for us, and how do we present Christ from the margins and to the margins?

What Latinas believe about Christ is not a matter of an applied doctrine, an application of what the churches teach. Our Christology is a praxis: what we believe about Christ comes out of our reality as marginalized Latinas, which is one of struggle for fullness of life. What we believe is, at the same time, a force that sustains this struggle. It is from within this praxis that *mujerista* Christology seeks to answer the question Jesus posed to his disciples, "Who do you say that I am?" (Mark 8:29). Jesus' insistence on a personal answer from his disciples makes clear that what we must elucidate are not christological dogmas but rather the meaning Jesus has for Latinas in our daily lives at the beginning of the twenty-first century. Our Christology, as all Christology whether stated or not, is a historical one. We know Jesus is with us because he joins us in our struggle for liberation-fullness of life.

Our insistence on the historical character of *mujerista* Christology and on Christology as a praxis, leads to a third understanding: Christology, as with all religious beliefs, follows our ethical stance. In other words, human beings, previous to any religious thinking, form ideas about what is right and what is wrong, what is good and what is bad, or, in religious language, what is sin and what is grace. Our consciences begin to be shaped well before the so-called "age of reason," usually set around the age of seven. From a very early age we begin to learn from those around us what is good and what is bad. By the time we begin to include the simplest understanding of Jesus in our thinking, the main patterns by which our consciences judge what we are supposed to do are already formed. These understandings "shape" what we believe about Jesus.[4] In other words, when we begin to explicitly think religiously, we ascribe to Jesus or to God or to whatever concept of the divine we are beginning to form, the ideas we have elaborated about the good. At the personal level answers to questions like, "Who is Jesus?" "What does Jesus want me to do?" "What would Jesus do if he were here?" are not based on our knowledge of Jesus. It is the other way around: the answers we give these questions reveal to us what it is that our consciences are telling us. In this sense, what we believe about Jesus is a mirror for our consciences. For Christians this translates into the claim that, regardless of our protests to the contrary, belief follows practice, belief follows the patterns of goodness that have been deeply sown in our hearts and minds and that guide our daily lives.

A fourth understanding of *mujerista* theology is made explicit by the old custom of melding "Jesus" and "Christ" into one word: *Jesucristo.* The traditional understanding among theologians, although not among the common folk, is that "Jesus" refers to the historical person and "Christ" to what the church has taught us to believe about that Jesus. I propose that we take seriously the fusion of the two "names" and that we abandon the thought that we can find in the past what we need to know and believe today about Jesus and about Christ. In *mujerista* Christology we try to move away from the naïve understanding that we can historically reconstruct who Jesus was, how he understood himself, and what he did. We also try to move away from making normative those christological formulae from the past so heavily laden with historical and cultural understandings. We are indeed respectful of church teaching about Christ, but that is not our emphasis. The custom of folding into one word the name Jesus and the title Christ — *Jesucristo* — provides *mujerista* theology with the creative space needed to elaborate a Christology that responds to what Latinas believe about the message of Jesus of Nazareth. It does so precisely because it sustains and motivates us in our everyday struggles against what limits liberation-fullness of life and for all that promotes justice and peace.

In this we follow the established tradition of the gospel writers who created narratives about Jesus that responded to the questions and issues that were alive in the communities for which they wrote. Our attempt to elaborate a *mujerista* Christology is part of our work to provide Latinas with a religious narrative that can help us not only to understand our Christian faith but also to deal with the struggle for liberation-fullness of life that we face everyday. This struggle calls us to be creative, to offer explanations of who *Jesucristo* is for us in ways that have a certain logical flow and coherence. We have always refused to spend time deconstructing theological approaches or church teachings. The precariousness of our communities is such that we feel an urgency to create understandings that are useful in the work of liberation rather than thinking about what was conceptualized in the past. *Mujerista* Christology listens carefully to the voices of grassroot Latinas knowing that they are admirably capable of reflecting on what they believe and of explaining it in ways that contribute to liberation-fullness of life.

Our Christology revolves around three key elements that emerge from the daily praxis of Latinas in the United States, that is, they are rooted in the way Latinas face everyday struggles for their fullness of life. First, Latinas hunger for deep, personal relationships to sustain us in our daily struggles. Second, we need God to help us take care of our people, not expecting God to solve our problems but rather asking God to be our faithful companion in our struggles. Finally, we know that only in so far as we become part of God's family can we really say that we believe in *Jesucristo.*

Familia de Dios — The kin-dom of God

The concept of the kingdom of God has undergone many transformations since it was first conceived by the Jewish people. Initially it was a concept based on the kingships that had enslaved them, Egypt and Babylon. It was the Iranian influence that provided "a transcendent feel, with the introduction of the end time, the idea of justice, and right living, which would bring about the security of the nation [Israel]."[5] Originally this understanding of transcendence did not project the "kingdom" — a new world order — into a different-world reality. "However, by the end of the first century C.E., a clear distinction emerged between this world, its end, and the setting in place of a new world order. For many people things that were believed to be possible in this world became transposed onto another place and time that were eternal and unchanging."[6] This change in the way the kingdom of God was understood actually added to the despair about its realization in this world that followed the destruction of the Temple in Jerusalem in 70 C.E. Furthermore, projection of the realization of the kingdom of God into the next world allowed it to be conceived of as achievable only by God and achievable once and for all. "The psychic landscape changed significantly from a circle of hope, committed action, change, and back to hope for divine intervention and unchanging absolutes."[7] As a result, from then on, the kingdom of God became an excuse for "nonengagement with the real stuff of life."[8]

Unfortunately the split this created between this-world reality and the kingdom of God (kidnapped from this world and taken to a world yet to come) became useful for those in charge of the newly developing church. They determined the meaning and correct interpretation of all that was "Christian." When in 313 C.E. the Edict of Milan legalized Christianity, the new religion began to gain political and economic power in addition to the religious and moral power over consciences it already held. The church became the only access to the kingdom of God in the world to come and its most powerful symbol in this world. Placing itself above the reality of this world and insulating itself against the vast majority of its members, the church came to link its life with the life of the established order, which it grew to resemble. Though it repeatedly claimed that its role was only religious, the church throughout its history has legitimized and supported those who have social, economic and political power. Historically it has become more and more a tool in the hands of the dominant groups in society. And the image and understanding of Christ have been affected sadly in the same way. Historically the image of Christ proclaimed by the church has seemed to float above human reality, nullifying the most precious meaning of the incarnation of God in Jesus of Nazareth. Christ little by little came to resemble monarchs and pontiffs with absolute power to whom the people only had access on bended knees. This Almighty Lord Jesus Christ was more like a feared judge demanding ever more from the people than he was like a loving mother welcoming and nurturing her children. It was only with the Second Vatican Council in the second half of the twentieth century that one finds meaningful movement in redrawing the meaning of the church and of the kingdom of God, with its great implications for Christology. The most relevant statement from the Second Vatican Council in reference to the relationship between the natural order and the supernatural order where the "kingdom of God" had been ensconced is found in *Gaudium et Spes,* no. 39. The text does not go far enough in relating the growth of the kingdom of God to temporal progress but, at least, the conciliar document affirms "a close relationship between temporal progress and the growth of the Kingdom.... Those engaged in the latter not only cannot be indifferent to the former; they must show a genuine interest in and value it."[9] This step taken by Vatican II opened the door for considering theologically "temporal progress as a continuation of the work of creation" and, therefore, for seeing temporal progress as linked to the redemptive act of the life and mission of Jesus of Nazareth.[10]

The theological understanding that "the human work, the transformation of nature, continues creation only if it is a human act, that is to say, if it is not alienated by unjust socio-economic structures,"[11] developed by Latin American liberation theology, opens the possibility for rescuing the "kingdom of God" from the supernatural order. Various liberation theologies elaborated in the second half of the twentieth century make it clear that *kingdom of God* was the expression that Jesus used as the central metaphor for talking about his mission, for which he died on the cross. Every aspect of the life of Jesus related by the gospels, every word ascribed to Jesus by the gospels gyrates around the kingdom of God. In what he did and in what he said Jesus was always announcing the kingdom of God or denouncing the antikingdom, that is to say, the conditions that not only could not be present in the kingdom of God but that make the realization or coming of the kingdom of God impossible. Liberation Christologies, on the whole, tend to make of Jesus the "definitive mediator of the Reign of God," claiming that he was "the person who proclaims the Reign, who posits signs of its reality and points to its totality."[12] To claim that Jesus was the definitive mediator, they have to posit that who Jesus was and what Jesus said and did are central to the kingdom of God. But much more, it is not only a matter of Jesus and his life being central but also that they are essential. The claim is often made that only Jesus could grasp and live to the fullest what it means to be human. His role as definitive mediator, then, is not outside the realm of what is human but rather is "the fullness of the human."[13] And this is precisely what we mean when we say that Jesus is Christ: that he lived to the fullest his humanity and the mission that it entailed. Because what Jesus did in reference to the kingdom of God is within the human realm, other persons can also be mediators, can also be Christs. As a matter of fact, to understand what Jesus meant by the kingdom of God and how he worked to make it a tangible reality, we have to understand that he stood in line with many other mediators of the kingdom, from Adam and Eve to his own mother, Mary of Nazareth. Furthermore, to understand Jesus and the kingdom of God he proclaimed with his life and deeds, we have to look carefully at the mediators of the kingdom that have lived since Jesus, who have committed themselves irrevocably to the kingdom of God, from the early men and women who were deacons, martyrs and confessors, to contemporary witnesses of the faith martyred or still alive.

All who commit themselves to proclaim with their lives and deeds the kingdom of God are mediators of the kingdom. Each and everyone of us has the capacity and possibility of being another Christ, an *alter Christus*. Whether we are mediators of the kingdom of God does not have to do with our capacity to be mediators but rather with the choices we make in our lives, with our commitments, and also with the circumstances in which we live. Our mediation of the kingdom of God is related to the fact that understanding reality always includes dealing with reality. The kingdom of God does not exist apart from us who believe in it, nor does it "pass" through us without being affected by us and affecting us as well. All reality that we come into contact with is changed in some way by how we deal with it or ignore it because all that we do helps "to sustain a conception of the world or to modify it."[14] And the same is true of the kingdom of God.

How does *mujerista* theology deal with the understanding that Jesus was the definitive mediator of the kingdom of God? If this claim indicates that no one can do it as he did it, then we can only agree for no one can be someone else or do what others do the way they do it. But we can likewise claim that no one else, including Jesus, can do what each of us can do in mediating the kingdom of God. In this sense each of us is unique, as Jesus was. Each of us also mediates the kingdom of God in an essential way and in a way that would not happen without us. This is so because each and every one of us is an image of God or *imago dei*: each and every one of us carries seeds of divinity that make who we are capable of being and what we are capable of doing essential to the unfolding of the kingdom of God. This is precisely one of the key reasons why we can rescue the kingdom from the other world and incarnate it once again in our midst. This is one of the most important reasons why we see our struggles in this world as part of the overall work of creation of God. It continues in us and with us.

In the first century Jewish world the metaphor of kingdom was the best way Jesus and his early followers found to indicate how people could encounter a benevolent God, one who would rule in their favor and for their sake. Kingdom was the best way in which they could talk about what values were determinant factors in the life of Jesus' followers. But in today's world the metaphor of the kingdom has become irrelevant because the reality that grounds the metaphor, actual kingdoms, rarely exists any more. Thus, the reference point of the metaphor is foreign to the experience of vast numbers of persons. For this reason alone church officials and theologians should use a different expression to signify the purpose of Jesus' life and mission. However, there is more. The metaphor of kingdom is not only irrelevant; as it has traveled through time, it has lost much of the meaning it had for Jesus and his early followers, often providing room for antikingdom values. In *mujerista* theology we believe that the metaphor of kingdom is not appropriate since obviously it refers only to male sovereigns and reinforces once more the male image of God, still the most prevalent one in the church. In *mujerista* theology we believe kingdom is an ineffective and dangerous metaphor for it suggests an elitist, hierarchical, patriarchal structure that makes possible and supports all sorts of systemic oppressions. Given this reality, one of our tasks is to suggest other metaphors that speak cogently and effectively to twenty-first-century persons.

To change root metaphors, one has to go into the content of the original one: what were the values ensconced in the metaphor kingdom of God when Jesus and his early followers used it? It was Jesus' way of speaking about *shalom,* about fullness of life. *Shalom* was not a private reality that each individual had to find or construct. Rather, *shalom* was a reality for which people needed to work together. Therefore Jesus made love of neighbor central to life in the kingdom of God. Love is communal, the task of a people and not solely of individuals. *Shalom* — fullness of life — then, is the value at the heart of the metaphor that Jesus used and therefore has to be the central value in any metaphor we use to talk about Jesus' understanding of his life and mission. Today, in *mujerista* theology, *shalom* goes by the name of liberation — a holistic liberation that happens at all levels of life: socially, politically, personally, spiritually.[15]

In *mujerista* theology we suggest replacing *kingdom* with *kin-dom.* We suggest moving from a political metaphor to which we have hardly any way of relating to a more personal metaphor that lies at the core of our daily lives. The idea of kin-dom of God, of the family of God, we suggest, is a much more relevant and effective metaphor today to communicate what Jesus lived and died for. This suggestion of the kin-dom of God is in many ways a response to the ongoing concern for the loss of family values and the loss even of a true sense of family in present-day society. Kin-dom of God as the core metaphor for the goal of Jesus' life will help us to reconstitute our sense of family. Moreover, the picture of kin-dom of God that Jesus gives us is a broad one that has to do not exclusively with blood-relatives but also with those who are united by bonds of friendship, of love and care, of community. *Mujerista* theologians bemoan the loss of family but we do not bemoan the loss of what has been called the traditional nuclear family. This so-called traditional nuclear family represents a very private and individualized group more set on defining and protecting its boundaries than in relating and welcoming all those that make life possible and pleasant for its members. The traditional nuclear family is a patriarchal setting where the man is considered the head, the one (perhaps the only one) most capable of representing and defending the family, of guiding and deciding for the family. This is why it is so difficult for society to imagine a family without a man or without a woman to complement the man. This is why we seem incapable of imagining same-sex parents or other than a biological parent carrying out the responsibilities of parenting. The traditional nuclear family in this highly technological industrial period in the United States in the first years of the twenty-first century is a family where relationships are less important than production and accumulation of capital and where if children are not better off economically than their parents, it is presumed that the family has failed. In *mujerista* theology we do not bemoan the disappearance of the traditional nuclear family.

The sense of *familia* that we have in mind when we talk about God's family, the kin-dom, is one in which a true sense of home exists, a sense of belonging and the safety to be and become fully oneself. *Familia* provides for us a sense of unity and cohesiveness that promotes a healthy sense of self-identity and self-worth so important for the development of the person. *Familia* for us "is the central and most important institution in life."[16] Whether personally *familia* is a life-giving structure for us, or unfortunately not a valuable one for whatever reason, *familia* is one of the key markers of our Latina communities. *Familia* is a marker not only of our position in life but also provides a clear indication of how we face life. *Familia* for us is a duty but also, for most of us, it is a never-failing support system. From a very young age, Latinas begin to understand that because of our families we do not have to face the world alone. We are also taught that precisely because the *familia* stands with us, we have a moral responsibility to each of its members who have invested so much in us by claiming us as their own. Who we are and what we do has personal repercussions for them. It is in the midst of *familia* and because of *familia* that at a very young age we are introduced to the ethical world of responsibilities and obligations, a world where one is because one is in relationship to others. In our families we learn that persons are more important than ideas and that, therefore, we have to take time and care to cultivate relationships.

Latinas' sense of *familia* is an expansive and broad one, extending into the community in a formal way. Through the institution of *compadrazgo* and *comadrazgo* a system of relationships is established between godparents and their godchildren and the parents of their godchildren. But this system reaches beyond religious occasions, such as baptisms and confirmations, to secular activities and enterprises. Sponsors of dances, businesses, and sports teams are called *madrinas* (godmothers) and/or *padrinos* (godfathers) for they not only provide monetary support but also supply vital connections with others to protect and promote the well-being of their godchildren. The *compadrazgo* and *comadrazgo* institution creates and sustains an effective infrastructure of interdependence that has the family at the center and extends family values such as unity, welfare and honor in all directions into the community.

Familia relies on interdependence, not subsuming the person but making one realize that the members of our families enable us to be who we are. *Familia* provides the security needed to extend ourselves into the community and form the kind of personal relationships that are vital to us without losing our sense of self. In our families we learn that "as in a prism, ... reflection is also a refraction ... [and that] the identity of the 'we' does not extinguish the 'I'; the Spanish world for 'we' is *'nosotros,'* which literally means 'we others,' a community of *otros* [and *otras*], or others."[17]

It is true that Latina families are not perfect and that some of its characteristics are misguided and can cause damage to its members. We are not setting up Latina families and their relationships as the criteria for the biblical *shalom*. We are simply insisting on the need to change the metaphor traditionally used to refer to what Jesus' life and mission was all about. Kin-dom of God points to what many would say is the central institution of all societies. Kin-dom embraces understandings and values that are intrinsic to liberation-fullness of life. To create and sustain an institution where we can be ourselves in a safe way, where our well-being is of primordial importance, where a new order of relationships excludes all exploitation and abuse — this is indeed the kind of family all persons would welcome, and relate to goodness, to blessedness, to God.

To the question "Who do you say that I am?" Latinas answer Jesus, "You are my brother, my sister, my mother and my father, my grandmother, aunt, uncle, *comadre* and *compadre,* who stands with me and who struggles with me. You are amazingly special to me because I am amazingly special to you. You are my big brother protecting me, and you are my little sister whom I protect. You are my husband, my wife, my partner, my significant other for whom I am precious and who loves me unconditionally. You and I are family, Jesus. What more can you be for me? What more do you want me to be for you?"

Jesucristo me acompaña siempre — Jesus Christ as Faithful Companion

In the kin-dom of God faith in *Jesucristo* rests squarely on the belief that, supported and encouraged within *familia*, Latinas can begin to live in a

166 Ada María Isasi-Díaz

different manner, in a just and loving way. Such a *familia* is open and welcoming of all, even though some may choose to exclude themselves. *Jesucristo* and the other Christs of the family are committed to live into the future reality: we are willing to work as hard as we can to establish a way of life which does not erase differences but considers them enrichments so that all can be part of the kin-dom of God. This preferred way of life is not a preconceived notion but rather a path that we create as we travel together. Cutting this path through the intricacies of life, both at the personal and at the sociopolitical level, struggling for justice and liberation in every aspect of our lives, so that everyone can live fully — that is what salvation is all about. What we learn from *Jesucristo,* our oldest sister and little brother, is that salvation is the responsibility of this whole family. Yes, if we truly believe that the purpose of Jesus' life and mission was to begin to create the kin-dom of God, then we can embrace the notion that salvation is not the exclusive task of *Jesucristo.* It is the task of all of us who have Christ as our last name. Allow me to give you an example from the world of Latinas' popular culture of what salvation looks like, of what belonging to and extending the kin-dom of God is all about.

One of the central characters of a soap-opera called *Bendita Mentira* (Blessed Lie), televised in the United States a few years ago, was Esperanza — the typical long-suffering mother who sacrifices everything for her children.[18] What is important to note was the interpretation Esperanza herself gave to her actions.[19] She never talked about sacrificing herself for her children but rather always saw what she was doing as loving her children. She saw sacrifice as merely a side effect of what she did, something indeed present but not necessarily valuable. She continually talked about love and allowed her children to live their lives, regardless of all the trouble they got into, standing with them through thick and thin. Two things about Esperanza started me thinking about her as a splash of paint that we can use in our understanding of what it means to embrace the mission that Jesus died for. First, Esperanza confessed to killing the lover of her daughter, a crime she did not actually commit, because she wanted to spare her daughter, whom she thought guilty of the crime. "Greater love has no man [*sic*] than this, that a man lay down his life for his friends."[20] A famous lawyer defended Esperanza at her trial. He said to the judge that Esperanza's love for her daughter *"me reconcilió con la humanidad"* — "reconciled me with humanity." Is this not what salvation is about, about being reconciled with humanity? Is it not "living with God" — and what else is the life of Christian faith? What else does it mean to be part of the *familia* of God? "Therefore, if anyone is in Christ, he is a new creation; the old has passed away, behold, the new has come. All this is from God, who through Christ reconciled us to himself and gave us the ministry of reconciliation; that is, in Christ God was reconciling the world to himself, not counting their trespasses against them, and entrusting to us the message of reconciliation."[21]

In another episode of the *novela*, Esperanza's daughter was talking with a friend. This daughter, for whom Esperanza had sacrificed so much, used to "hate her mother" but later realized all that her mother had done for her and came to love her. The friend asks Esperanza's daughter what made her change her attitude toward her mother. The daughter answered, *"Yo no sabía querer y ella me enseñó"* — "I did not know how to love and she taught me." The daughter then explained that Esperanza had taught her how to love by what she did, not by what she said. Is this not what salvation is about? Isn't salvation about loving neighbor without measure, loving neighbor not in word but in deed? "Jesus...having loved his own who were in the world, he loved them to the end....By this all men [*sic*] will know that you are my disciples, if you have love for one another."[22] Didn't Esperanza behave like a most worthy member of the Christ family?

Is it heretical to say that salvation is not exclusively the task of Jesus? I do not think so. This understanding of being co-redeemers with Jesus is what "the following of Jesus" or "discipleship" means. In the context of the kin-dom of God, what does it mean to be disciples of Jesus? First of all, in *mujerista* theology we try to take seriously the intrinsic link that exists between what has traditionally been called the "object" of our faith and the "act of faith." As Christian believers we do not create the "object" of our faith but believe that the object of our faith is a gratuitous "self-bestowal on us" made by God. This gift of self made by God, however, remains inoperative or ineffectual unless it occasions an act of faith. Therefore, the fact that we believe, which itself depends on God's self-bestowal, "testifies to a reality believed in and is an existential help to understanding what the concrete content of this reality [in which we believe] is."[23] To understand God we need to believe. To be able to know enough about ourselves as members of the *familia* of God we need to be specific about what it means to believe.

Belonging to the *familia* of God, like belonging to any family, means being committed to the values and understandings specific to that family. This is why loyalty becomes such an important virtue in maintaining and enriching the links among family members. But family values are more than the mere transmission of what has been. Values exist principally as virtues; that is to say, values do not exist as abstractions but rather as practices. Without ignoring or denying totally what the values of the *familia* of God have been in the past and what these values are today, we believe that how they are effectively practiced is always in the process of being defined. This, of course, is rooted in our claim that all theology is historical. But this claim that values are always in the process of being defined follows a central consideration of pastoral theology: the present situation has to be taken into account. The difference is that in *mujerista* theology we make concerns of the present operative not only at the level of pastoral care, at the level of implementation, but also at the level of understanding who God is and what God is about, that is, at the level of theology. In other words, our understanding of the practice of discipleship — what it actually means to say we are followers of Christ — informs our theology. How we live our faith is intrinsic to our Christian faith.

When one talks about a Christology that emerges from the practice of faith and the personal experience of being a disciple of Jesus, one may be accused of embracing a free-for-all and an everything-goes attitude. This criticism sets relativity over against what is absolutely right. However, in *mujerista* theology we do not understand relativity as noncommitment to what is right but rather as recognizing the centrality of struggling for liberation-fullness of life, in which faith and religion play a vital role in the theological enterprise. The kind of relativity we have adopted is a "responsible relativity,"[24] a way of dealing with reality that takes seriously everyday experience. For us Latinas being a disciple of Jesus means precisely to struggle to live each day in a way that promotes liberation-fullness of life and to become worthy members of the *familia* of God. This is why we insist on the fact that Christology follows ethics, that what we believe about Jesus follows how we conduct our lives. This is why when it comes to being followers of Christ, what we have in mind above all is the right way of acting and being instead of right belief. Again, it is not that belief is not important; it is rather that what we believe about Christ follows our practice of discipleship.

Responsible relativity then allows us to free ourselves from objective universals about the meaning of Christ that often have undergirded structures of oppression. It is precisely because responsible relativity recognizes the presence of subjectivity in all human thinking and knowing that we insist on the historicity of our christological understandings, unmasking so-called objective understandings as being mere subjective pronouncements of those who have the power to impose them as normative. Responsible relativity helps us to see that what we insist is "the" truth is only one of the possible explanations of reality and that the different explanations are not necessarily exclusive of each other but often, on the contrary, agree with each other, at least partially. This is why our christological understandings do not necessarily eradicate traditional ones or those elaborated by other communities. Responsible relativity also makes us be clear about the fact that endorsing a certain version of Christology demands accountability in specific and concrete ways for such a version and the consequences it brings. Lastly, when it comes to Christology, responsible relativity encourages the development of understandings and beliefs that are not offensive to other communities. This makes it possible to have a common point of reference that allows Latinas to join with other communities in the struggle for liberation. One thing is certain: our stance regarding responsible relativity in Christology insists on beliefs about Christ, salvation, the kin-dom of God, and discipleship that do not promote the liberation of some at the expense of others.

Discipleship for us Latinas is a practice of faith related to living as a worthy member of the kin-dom of God. Discipleship has to do with belonging, and belonging is not a static condition but rather an engagement in creating and sustaining relationships. Being family requires a certain way of being and doing. From a *mujerista* perspective, the "how" of this being and doing emerges from what it means to be a member of the family of God as well as from what we have to contribute to this family. In other words, it is in being family that we come to understand what family is. We cannot know the *familia de Dios* unless we throw ourselves whole-heartedly into being an active member of the kin-dom of God. Christology deals with what it means that *Jesucristo* is our sister and our brother; discipleship deals with what it means that I am a sister or a brother of *Jesucristo*. It is only in our efforts to be in a sisterly or brotherly relationship with *Jesucristo* that this meaning takes flesh. "In other words, it is in praxis, and not in the pure concept that the existence and reality" of the kin-dom of God appears and is known.[25]

What does discipleship consist of? What does being a member of the *familia de Dios* look like? It means being committed to liberation-fullness of life. It means insisting on nonobjectifying relationships. It means being adamant about including others instead of seeking to exclude them. It means being *familia* first and foremost with the poor and the oppressed. If you are oppressed, what does it mean to be part of the *familia* of God? It means keeping hope alive — hope in the possibility of justice, hope in being able to be agent of one's life, in being able to contribute to one's own fullness of life and the fullness of life of others in our *familia*.[26] But hope has to be grounded in actual possibilities or it becomes a destructive illusion. Often the poor and the oppressed have no way of making hope operative in their lives for there is no material reality on which to anchor it, no material reality that can sustain their hope and nourish it. For the poor and oppressed to be part of the *familia* of God means insisting at all times on their right to hope, to have others join with them in bringing about at least the most basic material conditions they need to be able to move from despair to hope. The poor and the oppressed contribute to making present the kin-dom of God in our world by insisting on the need to change radically oppressive structures instead of seeking to participate in them. And for the oppressors? What do the oppressors (and here we do well to remember that the vast majority of us are oppressors in some way or other) need to do to become worthy members of the *familia* of God? Radical conversion is what is called for. Today another word for radical conversion is solidarity with the poor and the oppressed. To be *familia* of God the oppressors have to come to understand that their privileges and well-being depend almost always on the misery and anguish of the vast majority of people in our world. To denounce such a stance and move away from it, oppressors have to realize the interconnections that exist among all human beings, and between human beings and the animal world and the biosphere that sustains us. Once this interconnection is understood, the hope of the poor and the oppressed becomes the hope of the oppressors: fullness of life for oppressors will not happen unless there is also fullness of life for the oppressed.

What role does *Jesucristo* play in all of this? *Jesucristo* together with the other members of the *familia* of God struggles to sustain the poor and the oppressed, to give them a reason to hope by working to create the material conditions they need to begin to move ahead in their lives. *Jesucristo* together with the other members of the *familia* of God struggles to make the oppressors among the family members and beyond understand that they are a threat to their own liberation; that no one will be able to experience fullness of life unless all are given what they need. *Jesucristo*, as other big sisters and little brothers do, cajoles, begs, encourages, demands, and cheers us on in our daily struggles for liberation. One of the most luminous understandings among Latinas about who *Jesucristo* is and what role he plays is that *Jesucristo* simply is with us in the midst of the ordinariness of life, that he simply walks with us. This is why among grassroots Latinas one rarely senses a crisis of faith, despite all the suffering and ills present in their personal lives and in our communities. *Jesucristo* is not thought of as a magician who solves or should solve all the problems we face and free us from all of our troubles. Repeatedly we hear from our *abuelitas* (grandmothers) and other older Latinas that what we need is not to be freed from the struggle but to be given the strength to face the harsh reality of our world. As long as we have the strength to struggle, *Jesucristo* is with us. What is primordial about our Christology is the kind of following of *Jesucristo* that is nothing else but walking with him because he walks with us. *Jesucristo* always accompanies us, and that is why he is the redeemer, the savior, the messiah, the Christ. And how do we know that he always accompanies us? Because we know he is *familia*, we are not alone. He is never alone.

Jesús mío — Personal Relationship with the Divine

We were sitting in a big circle with grassroots Latinas discussing embodiment and sexuality. All of a sudden, Lola, one of the quiet ones in the group, spoke out of turn. In a hardly audible voice she told us a little about her intimate relations with the man who was her common-law husband for many years. With her face wrinkled by pain and folding her body as if to protect herself, she finished by saying, *"Nunca tuvo para mí un gesto o una palabra de ternura"* — "he never had for me a tender gesture or a tender word." As she finished talking she lowered her eyes and folded her arms over her chest as if signaling her unwillingness to let anyone else ever hurt her again. She had been wounded to the core of her being by being denied tenderness, that mode of love that can only happen at the most intimate levels of relationship.

Last December I arrived early at my small church, which sits in the midst of a housing project in East Harlem. Originally it was an almost exclusively Puerto Rican community, but more and more Mexicans have been moving into "El Barrio," as this area is called. The priest had agreed to celebrate the feast of Our Lady of Guadalupe, the invocation used in Mexico for Mary, the Mother of Jesus. Mexicans consider themselves daughters or sons of Guadalupe, so it is very important for the community here in New York City to celebrate her day. For Guadalupe's feast, the smell and sight of red roses filled the church. I sat where I could watch the people going up to the side altar where a picture of Our Lady of Guadalupe had been placed. A continuous procession of people made their way up to the altar, knelt, and lifted their eyes to the image of the Virgin. Anyone could see the love for Guadalupe that was reflected in their gestures, in the respect of their demeanor, in the tenderness with which they gazed at Guadalupe's picture. I closed my eyes and tried to understand why Guadalupe is so important in the lives of these people who approached her that day to renew their love for her, their commitment to her as her children. All of a sudden it came to me. Guadalupe is an image of the divine that looks like the Mexican people: her features are those of the Mexican indigenous population. That divinity resembles them means that the divine is not so far removed from them, yes? Gradually I came to understand something very important that I confirmed later on with my friends in the church. Women are used to loving others, to caring for others. So, in many ways, this side of the relationship with Guadalupe was not exceptional. But, as I looked at a middle-aged woman holding on to three little ones while lifting her eyes to Guadalupe, I realized that the difference in this relationship from other relationships is that the people believe that Guadalupe does care for them. She loves them back, with the tender love of a mother. These people might not be important to others but they know they are important to her. In our Latina culture, personal relationships are at the center of our lives, at the center of the institutions and organizations — like *familia*, for example — that we create and use in our daily lives. No matter what problem we have and despite the fact that in our highly industrialized society benefits depend on the bureaucracy, Latinas believe that the best way to proceed always is by contacting someone who has personal connections and can vouch for them. Latinas depend on relationships and thirst for deep connections with others not only because we need them as intercessors but also because we need them to be fully ourselves.

It is unthinkable for us Latinas to conceive God in any other way than as a person with whom we have or can have a deep, intimate relationship. Thinking of God as a force of nature or as an energy or power in the universe is not understandable to us and certainly leaves us cold. The divine for us is personal; the divine is incarnated time and again in Jesus, in Mary his mother, in the holy people of past generations that the church has proclaimed saints, in our ancestors, in the people of the community that during their lives have worked for the benefit of that community. The divine is not far from us in the churches where we worship. The divine is with us at all times. This is why we wear medals with images of the divine, why we have images of the divine hanging from the rearview mirrors in our cars, why we have home altars crowded with statues of Jesus, Mary, the saints, and pictures of all those who have done good and, therefore, are connected to the divine. When asked, Latinas answer that, "of course," their dead *abuelitas* are not God, Our Lady of Guadalupe is not God, St. Martin de Porres is not God, St. Barbara is not God. But Latinas know and say that all of these people have access to the divine; that they share in the divine as *alteri Christi* — other Christs.

A few stories illustrate how these *alteri Christi* function for us. In a workshop with a group of Mexican and Mexican-American women in El Paso, I asked the women to whom they prayed in times of trouble. One of the *abuelitas* in the group blurted out, "To Guadalupe." When I asked her how come she did not pray to God, she said to me, "He is a man and he does not understand what happens to us women." Years later when I asked another group of women the same question in Bay City, Michigan, one of them assured the group that she prayed to God. Later that night she came to my room. "Earlier today I told you I prayed to God in times of trouble because I thought that was the right answer. But now I cannot fall asleep without coming to tell you that the truth is that I pray to Guadalupe." And she proceeded to tell me that when her family had a car accident on a slippery highway, as the car was about to hit a cement wall on the side of the road, she screamed, "*Virgen de Guadalupe*, protect my children." Then I think about my own life of prayer. When I am in really difficult circumstances I pray to my *abuelita*. Knowing how much she loved me and cared for me when she lived with me on this earth, I have no doubt that she helps me in countless ways from wherever she is with God.

The divine is with us and among us but it is so important to notice who is the divine for Latinas. The God whom the churches have proclaimed is an ominous God whose majesty and power confine Him [*sic*] to a pedestal. He is a God to whom adoration is due but from whom one can expect nothing but what is due to us because of our sinfulness. He is a God that demands like a stern parent. This God is in many ways controlled by the church, for the church insists that it alone can tell us who God is and what God is like.

In contrast to this far-removed God, Latinas find nothing but love and wel-coming and help from our *abuelitas* and the saints. What about Jesus? Jesus is often seen only as God and, therefore, not too accessible to us. But then there is the very human *Jesucristo* suffering on the cross who touches our hearts and who understands our suffering because he too has suffered. And this is the *Jesucristo* we turn to, the *Jesucristo* who walks with us. Often theologians chide us Latinas — and our Latin American sisters and broth-ers — for concentrating so much on the Jesus hanging on the cross. Pointing to our lack of understanding of the importance of the resurrection of Jesus, these theologians fail to understand the importance of the personal in the lives of Latinas. They fail to see that for a true relationship with Jesus or with anyone there has to be mutuality — and mutuality needs commonality to exist. It is precisely the Jesus who suffers as we suffer, who is vulnerable as we are vulnerable — that is the *Jesucristo* to whom we can relate.

In my church, on the right-hand sidewall toward the front, there is a huge cross on which hangs a bloody body of Jesus crowned with thorns. I have noticed how some people always get on the right-hand side line for communion and simply stay there no matter how long that line is. I watch how each time they receive communion and, on the way back to their pews, they stop by the crucifix. Placing their hands on the nailed feet, they lift their faces to *Jesucristo*. *"Lo trato de consolar,"* — "I try to comfort him," one of the women said to me one day. She did not say much more, but I realized the importance for her of being able to do something for *Jesucristo*, the importance of being able to feel that she could take care of this *Jesucristo* who is her very own, her *"Jesús mío."*

Can we humans have true relationship with God? To do so we have to be able to be much closer to God than common church practice and theological explanations allow. The divine has to be much more approachable, and we have to struggle to be real members of the *familia* of God if we want to come close to the divine. And here is where the work for justice comes into play, starting for us at home. Latinas struggle for their families, to make life possible for their children, to take care of the elderly in their communities, and to find at least a tiny space for themselves to flourish. They believe themselves to be good in so far as they do this; they are good precisely in so far they take care of others.[27] This doing for others, being good, and being in a relationship with *Jesucristo* are very much intertwined. Though indeed the majority of Latinas would not express it this way, their relationship with *Jesucristo* and the other *alteri Christi* grounds their lives. Talking particularly to older Latinas, one senses this: how a profound relationship with the divine has transformed them, allowing them to see beyond what is observable, to counsel and comfort beyond their natural ability and expertise. Some of this has to do, undoubtedly, with the wisdom that experience brings, but I believe that much of this depends on their relationship with the divine.

Often objectified by society, often considered by exploitative husbands as cogs in a machine used to produce care and satisfaction for them, often not appreciated by their children who demand from them the material goods so valued by society, Latinas long for deep personal relationships. Often they have nowhere to turn but to the various expressions of the divine that have become so important in their lives. This relationship with the divine, which in turn makes it possible for them to be in relationship with themselves, is what gives Latinas the strength to struggle for justice for themselves and others; it is what gives them the wisdom to survive.

Latinas are very emotional. We feel deeply, and in our culture we are not required to hide our feelings. We are taught, by example more than by anything else, to honor our feelings for we grasp intuitively early in life that feelings are "a source of imaginative insight" and a motivation for our daily struggles.[28] Emoting, expressing how we feel, is indeed central to the way we relate, for it is in feeling and in allowing ourselves to feel that we come to know more deeply than is possible with only our minds.[29] But if feelings are to carry us beyond what we can grasp intellectually, they have to be intense and passionate; and for passion to exist, one's emotions have to have resonance. Mutuality is an absolutely essential element of a true relationship. Outside the mutuality of true relationships passionate emotions can consume us and destroy us. Often, then, Latinas seek with the divine the passionate relationships they do not find with partners because we know that if we do not feel deeply, we are not living fully. In such relationships mutuality is essential, so it is not surprising that we conceptualize the divine in a way that allows for true mutuality to exist. "*Jesucristo* needs me," we Latinas tell ourselves. "He needs me to comfort him in his sufferings, he needs me to help him bring people to the *familia de Dios*. God knows I need him! I need *Jesucristo* for I know that I am precious for him."

This is Latinas' way of admitting and insisting on the centrality of relationships, on the need we have for mutuality. The divine has to be accessible to us, *Jesucristo* has to understand us, and we have to be able to contribute to the understanding of who *Jesucristo* is in our world today. We turn to *Jesucristo* whom we love passionately for our salvation, to *Jesucristo* as "the source of creative, relational energy."[30] And frequently he is the only one with whom we can establish a true relationship, one in which we are not exploited but valued for who we are, a relationship that nourishes us, that saves us in a very personal and holistic way.

Living Our Christology

That many questions in life go unanswered is one of the most important things I have learned from grassroots Latinas. Many questions are nothing more than dilemmas, inexorable conundrums, and illogical realities. We can only accept them as part of our daily lives for we do not have the means to deal effectively with them. For us Latinas, *Jesucristo* is not the one who gives us answers but the one who sustains us when there are no answers. Perhaps *Jesucristo* is actually more present to us in the questions, for they often keep us reaching further, stretching our understandings, enabling us to hope and to commit ourselves more and more to liberation-fullness of life for ourselves and for those for whom we are responsible.

As a consequence of this way of looking at life and because of what *Jesucristo* means for Latinas, *mujerista* theology does not seek to provide answers but rather to help us to go deeper in our questions about God and the divine presence in our lives. There is no single answer to Jesus' question, "Who do you say that I am?" What we Latinas have and, therefore, what *mujerista* theology can offer, is some hint of who *Jesucristo* is, some markers along the way for those who are open to seeing them, markers that show us where and how *Jesucristo* is present to us and with us in our daily lives. Sometimes the only way to understand who *Jesucristo* is for us and how he is present in our lives is through stories. Three stories come to mind.

The story of Helen Prejean, a Roman Catholic nun who has spent a large part of her life ministering in the United States to prisoners on death row, is told in the book *Dead Man Walking*. She describes the day she was accompanying Pat Sonnier, a man in Angola Prison, thirty-six hours away from being executed, hoping for a stay. After praying with him, Helen said to Pat, "If you die, I want to be with you." He answered, "No. I don't want you to see it." Then she said to Pat, "I can't bear the thought that you would die without seeing one loving face. I will be the face of Christ for you. Just look at me."

Ivone Gebara, a leading Latin American ecofeminist theologian, told me this story. One evening, when Ivone was returning to her house in a poor neighborhood in Brazil, a woman who lives near and whose son was very sick stopped her and excitedly told her, "God visited me today." Ivone was surprised and started talking to the woman trying to find out what had happened. A neighbor had turned over to the woman the money she had earned that day so she could buy medicine for her sick son. For Ivone's friend this neighbor had become God, had become Christ. This generous neighbor did not merely "represent" Christ but was indeed Christ made present in a poor neighborhood of Brazil in our own days.

Not long ago in New York City, where I live, a mother, helped by the grandmother, poisoned her daughter and simply disposed of the little body in a garbage can. They did it, they said, because the little girl was possessed by evil spirits. While the city authorities looked for the girl's body in the city's garbage dump, I was having a profound crisis of faith. "Where is *Jesucristo?*" I kept asking myself. "Why did God abandon this innocent little girl?" Then I realized it: that little girl was *Jesucristo* nailed on the cross. In her murder, as in the murder of Jesus of Nazareth, "there is salvation and there is light."[31] That little nameless girl was indeed *Jesucristo!*

For Further Reflection

1. What is different about doing theology "from the margins"? How is theology understood in a *mujerista* theology?
2. What does it mean to say that Jesus is the Christ in a *mujerista* theology? Is this designation exclusively for Jesus? How are we mediators of salvation and co-redeemers with Christ?
3. What were the chief consequences of the church's alignment with the Emperor Constantine in the fourth century C.E.? What happened to the image of Christ?
4. What is the problem with the word *kingdom*? Why change it? To what? What is the difference between the patriarchal family and the *familia* valued by *mujerista* theology?
5. Does history matter in a *mujerista* Christology if "moving away" from the scholarly historical reconstruction of Jesus is important? In your view, is historical research important for faith? Why or why not?

For Further Reading

Aquino, María Pilar, Daisy L. Machado, and Jeanette Rodríguez, eds. *A Reader in Latina Feminist Theology.* Austin: University of Texas Press, 2002.

Espín, Orlando O., and Miguel H. Díaz, eds. *From the Heart of the People: Latino/a Explorations in Catholic Systematic Theology.* Maryknoll, N.Y.: Orbis, 1999.

Isasi-Díaz, Ada María. *En la Lucha/In the Struggle: Elaborating a* Mujerista *Theology.* Tenth anniversary edition. Minneapolis: Fortress, 2003.

———. *Mujerista Theology: A Theology for the Twenty-First Century.* Maryknoll, N.Y.: Orbis, 1996.

Isasi-Díaz, Ada María, and Fernando F. Segovia, eds. *Hispanic/Latino Theology: Challenge and Promise.* Minneapolis: Fortress, 1996.

How can you be respectful when your basic premise is the OTHER is wrong.

FAITH DENOTES SOME FORM OF ACTION.

Salvation FIXED PT AT JESUS DEATH RES. OR Salvation begun at and is ongoing creative Proleptic

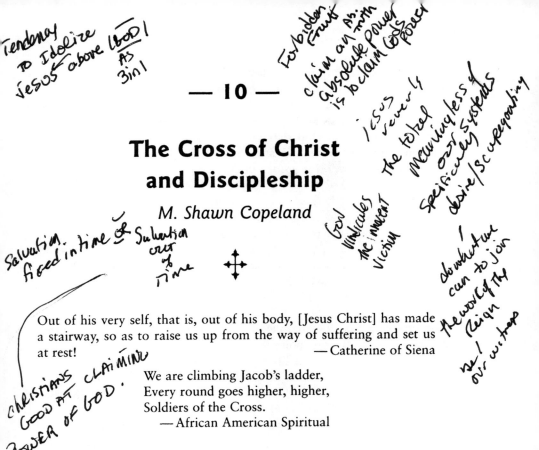

The Cross of Christ and Discipleship

M. Shawn Copeland

> Out of his very self, that is, out of his body, [Jesus Christ] has made a stairway, so as to raise us up from the way of suffering and set us at rest!
> — Catherine of Siena

> We are climbing Jacob's ladder,
> Every round goes higher, higher,
> Soldiers of the Cross.
> — African American Spiritual

To Live at the Disposal of the Cross

Standing in the laundry room of her apartment building, the theologian fidgets as the rinse cycle of the washing machine slows to an end. She bends to clear away a thick wad of lint from the dryer; absently, she looks out of the window. In the parking lot below, a black woman picks through the building's refuse dumpster. Mesmerized, the black woman doing laundry cannot but watch: the woman below works systematically, opening and inspecting small white bags, setting some aside and discarding others. It is difficult from the eighth floor to see precisely what the black woman below selects, but the black woman above wonders if the woman has found the remains of her half-eaten roasted chicken or salad or bread or cheese.

Uncomfortable, angry, and sad, I turn away and put my things in the dryer. I take the elevator to my apartment. I sit down at the computer

First published as "To Live at the Disposal of the Cross: Mystical-Political Discipleship as Christological Locus," in *Christology: Memory, Inquiry, Practice,* the annual publication of the College Theology Society, vol. 48, edited by Anne M. Clifford and Anthony J. Godzieba (Maryknoll, N.Y.: Orbis Books, 2002), pp. 177–98. Reprinted with permission.

where I am struggling to complete an essay on discipleship and the cross of Christ. I am unnerved: writing on such a theme, after such looking, provokes recognition and dis-ease. The woman in the parking lot below is no one other than Christ. Such glimpses of him beg for a theology of the cross, a theology of discipleship that makes both his presence and a praxis of concrete solidarity and compassion more visible in our time. What sort of christological reflection is needed in our situation? What can it mean to tell the woman who searches my garbage that God in Jesus is also alienated, a stranger, a despised "other"? Can memory of his passion and death unmask our pretense to personal and communal innocence, to social and religious neutrality before structural evil and suffering? What sort of christological reflection can do justice to Jesus of Nazareth, to his radical freedom and profound consciousness of God and neighbor, to his desire for life, to his acceptance of the cross? What sort of christological reflection can address adequately the meaning of the cross to children, women, and men brutalized by social suffering?

In this brief essay, I want to explore these questions by sketching discipleship as a *locus* or starting point from which to understand Jesus of Nazareth as the absolute meaning of life for the world. This topic, discipleship as a christological locus, can make no claim to novelty; it forms a conspicuous strand in Christian tradition. Scholars suggest that the word *disciple* (*talmî*) appears rarely in the Hebrew scriptures, but its usage was part of the fabric of the ancient world. However, in the gospel narratives, Jesus of Nazareth invests the relationship of teacher (*rabbi*) and disciple (*mathētēs*) with new and remarkable meaning. For, rather than appeal solely to his acquired knowledge and presumptive authority, conventional prerogatives of the rabbi, Jesus invites and nurtures in his disciples faith in *who* he is and in the "good news" he is sent to proclaim. Yet, Jesus tests their faith: to follow the "way" he teaches requires that Jesus' disciples take up a new and different "way" of being *in* and *for* the world. Thus, they face a commanding and paradoxical challenge: "If any want to become my followers, let them deny themselves and take up their cross and follow me. For those who want to save their life will lose it, and those who lose their life for my sake, and for the sake of the gospel, will save it. For what will it profit them to gain the whole world and forfeit their life?" (Mark 8:34–36; Luke 9:23–25; cf. John 6:35–51).

For our purposes, the Lukan account of the story of the life, death, and resurrection of Jesus of Nazareth will provide the basic performative meaning of discipleship. Biblical exegetes have identified the theme of discipleship almost exclusively with the Markan Gospel. To borrow a term from Ched Myers, scholars have read this gospel as a kind of "catechism" on discipleship.[1] But, since the whole of the New Testament stands as an invitation to radical discipleship, the Lukan account need not be excluded from reflection on this theme. Further, Luke's account of the story of Jesus strategically adverts to and incorporates Torah texts that foreground the tradition and customs of "jubilee," that is, the complex of cyclical practices concerned with restorative justice, reparation and release, healing and re-creation (Lev. 25). These references, coupled with parables in which Jesus describes the reign of God, underscore the importance of justice in the Lukan narrative.

At the same time, feminist scholars have called into question the treatment of women in Luke-Acts, for while the writer shows an interest in women, it is an ambiguous interest.[2] Clarice Martin writes that the Lukan writer demonstrates "redactional and apologetic tendencies [that] actually restrict women's prophetic ministry in some instances, reinforcing women's conformity to conventional, culturally prescribed roles of passivity, submission, silence, and marginality."[3] Turid Karlsen Seim concurs, yet alerts us to the possibility that the Lukan gospel may carry a "double message . . . [with] an ironic twist." While the very structure of the narrative may enable male domination and cooptation of women, nonetheless, it "preserves extraordinary traditions about the women from Galilee . . . [who] were indeed capable and qualified, but the men suspected and rejected them. The male consolidation of power occurs against a story in which the men have shown weakness and failure rather than strength."[4]

In order to tell the story of Jesus, Luke must tell the story of the women from Galilee. Silenced by male power, they "continue to speak." Moreover, the women and their roles in the story of the life, death, and resurrection of Jesus of Nazareth constitute a "dangerous remembrance."[5] Through faith, commitment, and service, these women teach us what it means to be a disciple of Jesus.

Scholars date the writing of Luke-Acts in the final decades of the first century, and Sharon Ringe argues that Luke wrote for a community of mixed economic and social standing. Textual evidence suggests that Luke sought to address strained relations between the poor and the nonpoor. But, as Ringe states, he "pulled his punches": Luke speaks *about* the poor, but he speaks *to* the rich; he emphasizes charity, but not change in repressive political and economic arrangements.[6] Certainly, for us Christians living in nations of wealth and power, the privileged of the "first world," Luke's gospel presents a challenge: How can we live as disciples of Jesus? Will we speak truth to power or pull our punches?

To live as Jesus' disciple means to live at the disposal of the cross — exposed, vulnerable, open to the wisdom and power and love of God. A lived response to Jesus' call requires a praxis of solidarity and compassion as well as surrender to the startling embrace of Divine Love. Christian discipleship as a lived mystical-political way forms the locus for the fundamental grasp of who Jesus of Nazareth is and what following and believing in him means.

This thesis will be elaborated in four sections. The first section, "The Way of Jesus," sketches his ministry and the demands he places on those who would follow him. The second section, "The Cross," draws on the work of Martin Hengel to retrieve the horror and disgust felt by the men and women of the ancient world toward crucifixion. I want to suggest some of the shock they would have experienced at Jesus' summons to "take up your cross and follow me." This discussion prepares the background for the next section, "The Cross as a Condition of Discipleship." For the women and men drawn to his prophetic praxis, Jesus offered a new and compelling "way" of being for God's people that included, even demanded, the cross. The fourth section, "The Way Jesus Is," offers a meditation on the crucified Jesus as the way through the Spirit to union with the Father. This section draws on insights gleaned from reflection on the mystical experiences of Catherine of Siena and of enslaved Africans in the United States. There is, I suggest, a resonance in these experiences that disclose what being caught up in love of God means. They capture what it means to understand that the power of God in the cross is the power to live and to love — even in the teeth of violence and death.

The Way of Jesus

In the Lukan account, the ministry, that is, the teaching, preaching, and healing through which Jesus of Nazareth met his death on the cross, began in a small synagogue in his home town. Jesus takes the scroll from the attendant and reads: "The Spirit of the Lord is upon me, because he has anointed me to preach good news to the poor. He has sent me to proclaim release to the captives and recovering of sight to the blind, to let the oppressed go free, to proclaim the year of the Lord's favor.... Today this scripture has been fulfilled in your hearing" (Luke 4:18–19, 21; Isa. 61:1–2; 58:6).

The narrator portrays the congregation as reacting with pleasure and pride: "All spoke well of him and were amazed at the gracious words that came from his mouth. They said, 'Is not this Joseph's son?'" (Luke 4:22). But Jesus' evocation of Elijah (Luke 4:25–26) stings the conscience, and neither the cautious nor the cynical can tolerate the concluding coda — an irruption of messianic time that hints at the meaning of who Jesus is. Appreciative amazement pitches into anger and attempted violence: "They got up, drove him out of the town, and led him to the brow of the hill... so that they might hurl him off the cliff" (Luke 4:29).

Almost from the outset of the Lukan narrative, Jesus is identified with the prophecy. His ministry signs the in-breaking of the reign of God: he is sent to those who are wounded and impaired; who are possessed by demons; who are poor, broken-hearted, and despised; who are imprisoned by occupation or disfigurement and, thereby, rendered incapable of ritual purity. These children, women, and men are without choice, without hope, and without a future. Jesus announces to these "least" the comfort and judgment of the reign of God. He pledges that God is *for* them and *with* them.

Jesus eats and drinks with women and men of questionable character — tax collectors, prostitutes, outcasts, and public sinners. When questioned about his associates, he replies, "Those who are well have no need of a physician, but those who are sick; I have come to call not the righteous, but sinners to repentance" (Luke 5:31–32). Women — Mary Magdalene, Joanna, the wife of Herod's steward, Susanna, Mary the mother of James (Luke 8:1–3) — form part of the band of disciples who travel with Jesus to various cities and villages and share in his ministry. Jesus does not shy away from talk and debate with women; he heals them, forgives them, and takes them and their experiences seriously. When a woman named Mary sits at his feet as a disciple, Jesus affirms her agency over against narrow and constricting roles set for women by culture and society (Luke 10:38–42). Finally, the proclamation of the resurrection itself is entrusted to women; their remembrance of the very words of Jesus grounds their witness (Luke 24:9–10). Through his audacious proclamation of the reign of God and his astonishing healing power, Jesus attracts crowds and, eventually, disciples. The men and women who would follow him (Luke 8:2–3) are challenged to sever all ties with the past (Luke 5:11), to address God intimately in prayer, to fast without ostentation, to practice self-examen (Luke 11:1–4; 6:42), and to allow no familial obligation, no cultural custom, no ritual observance to turn them to another way (Luke 14:26–27; 9:57–62; 12:22–23).

Through word and deed, Jesus taught his disciples to center themselves *in* and *on* the God whom he knew and loved with all his heart, all his soul, all his strength, and all his mind (Luke 10:25–27; 11:1–13). He enjoined them to love others — particularly the poor, outcast, and despised children, women, and men — concretely and without reservation, to act on behalf of these "little ones" for restoration to God and to community (Luke 10:29–37).

The proclamation of the reign of a God "merciful and slow to anger" (Jon. 4:2) formed the core of Jesus' preaching. In parables and sermons, he drew a vivid portrait of life lived under the reign of this God. What would this new life be like? Like the watchfulness of a farmer at harvest, like the consolation of acceptance, like a lavish and festive feast for those who can neither return the honor nor provide a comparable meal, like the joy at rescuing a stray lamb in the parched wilderness, like the relief at recovering lost funds, like the unshakable love of a broken-hearted parent for a wayward child, like the fruitfulness of the mustard seed and the capaciousness of its tree, like the force of leaven (Luke 8:4–18, 44–48; 14:12–14; 15:4–10, 11–16; 13:18–21). Jesus envisioned life lived under the reign of this God as a realization of truth and love, holiness and grace, justice and peace. More-over, this God staked the gift of that reign *in us* and *in* present existential reality (Luke 17:21). Finally, Jesus taught his followers to pray that the reign of God might come — and to pray for its coming in the way in which God wills it. The disciples are to pray for that reign of justice and peace which, while not yet realized, is seeded in the here-and-now, the point of change where the old order yields to God's dream (Luke 11:2–4).

Jesus cultivated in his disciples a desire, a yearning, an expectation for the coming of God's reign. He led them through the "narrow gate" to glimpse the secrets of living for God (Luke 13:24), to discern just what was required of those who would enter the way (Luke 12:22–48), to grasp the purity of heart and action its realization needed (Luke 12:49–53; 16:13; 14:26). Jesus granted his disciples a share in his healing power; the miracles they worked were a sign for him that the reign of God was breaking through.

But the ministry of Jesus is a dangerous ministry. Discipleship costs. The praxis of compassionate solidarity that he inaugurated on behalf of the reign of God disrupted social customs, religious practices, and conventions of au-thority and power. Without hesitation, Jesus made the cross an undeniable condition for discipleship (Luke 9:23; 14:27). By his own death on the cross, Jesus incarnated the solidarity of God with abject and despised human per-sons. The disciples who heard and responded to his word and the deed of his life came, even if haltingly, gradually, fitfully, to dedicate their lives and their living to the concerns, commitments, and compassion of the God of Jesus. In this way, they placed their lives at the disposal of the cross.

The Cross

From the beginning of his ministry, Jesus taught a "way" of life that not only offered a distinctive "understanding [of] the fulfillment of Israel's hope," but substantively "radicalized [his religious] tradition."[7] In his prophetic "performance" of parable, sign, and deed, Jesus broke open "the prevailing worldview and replace[d] it with one that was closely related, but signifi-cantly adjusted at every point."[8] But it is his crucifixion, his brutal death on the cross (Luke 23:33; John 19:18), that set "the way" apart from other religious movements in the ancient world.

The cross was the mark of shame, the sign of the criminal and the slave. Martin Hengel delineates this point in his monograph *Crucifixion in the Ancient World and the Folly of the Message of the Cross.*[9] To accept the message of the cross, first-century Jews would have had to overcome deep-seated religious, cultural, and political sensibilities toward the very act of crucifixion, while, at the same time, they would have had to grapple with a new notion of the meaning of messiah. Recall the injunction in the Torah: "for anyone hung on a tree is under God's curse" (Deut. 21:23).

In the Hebrew scriptures, the promise of a messiah is bound up with the covenant established by God with the chosen people. Yet, as N. T. Wright argues, during the Judaism of Jesus' day, there was no single or uniform conception of the messiah. The various messianic movements shared no common notion of the messiah and exhibited "considerable freedom and flexibility" toward the "idea of Israel's coming king."[10] However, these movements shared the expectation that with the arrival of the messiah Israel's divinely ordained destiny would be realized: the Roman occupation, colonization, and defilement of sacred land would end and a new age would begin.

The conflicting aspirations of long-subjugated women and men were projected onto the notion of messiah. He would lead the final victorious battle against the enemies of Israel. Not only would he bring about the political liberation of the people and the transformation of their historical situation, the messiah would transform history itself. The messianic age would bring an end to suffering, alienation, and exile. God's chosen people would be gathered — in to their ancestral home. A *crucified messiah,* a messiah who would die dishonored as a criminal, was unthinkable. A crucified messiah was not, could not be the *true* messiah. Paul's message of the cross (1 Cor. 1:22–24) was offensive, monstrous; it could not be tolerated. A crucified messiah would have to be rejected on the grounds of fidelity to religious orthodoxy.

Gentile groups also would have been scandalized by the notion of a crucified God. For these women and men, religious revulsion at the cross was joined to intellectual objections. Potential converts, particularly sophisticated Romans and Greeks, held the notion of a crucified God and of any who would follow such a God in contempt."[11] In the *City of God,* Augustine preserves an oracle of the Greek god Apollo as recorded by the philosopher Porphyry nearly two hundred years earlier. A man petitions the oracle about how to dissuade his wife from Christian belief. The god replies: "Let her go [continue] as she pleases, persisting in her vain delusions, singing in lamentation for a god who died in delusions, who was condemned by right-thinking judges, and killed in hideous fashion by the worst of deaths, a death bound with iron."[12] Belief in a crucified God was deemed madness, mania.[13]

Given the disgust that both Jews and Gentiles felt toward crucifixion, Paul's proclamation of the cross, as Hengel explains, "ran counter not only to Roman political thinking, but to the whole ethos of religion in ancient times."[14] The contemporary Christian remains equally perplexed. There is little in modern or postmodern life to assist us in comprehending the shame that crucifixion denoted in the ancient world. The supreme Roman penalty, crucifixion was a military and political punishment primarily used against insurrectionists, murders, and robbers, and reserved in nearly all instances for men and women of the lower classes, slaves, and subjugated peoples.

Crucifixion was intended to intimidate by example and subdue by spectacle; it was high state theatrical violence. Crucifixion called for the public display of a naked victim in some prominent place — at a crossroads, in an amphitheater, on high ground. Often the condemned was flogged, then made to carry a cross-beam through the streets to the place of execution. The victim's hands and feet were bound or nailed to the wood. If, after this torment, the victim were still alive, he could expect to die by suffocation: unable to support the weight of the body with torn hands, the upper body pressed down, and slowly crushed the diaphragm. Further dishonor and insult accompanied death: the crucified body was left to wild beasts and rot or, sometimes, as Tacitus reports, "when daylight faded, [they] were burned to serve as lamps by night.[15] Jesus was spared this last indignity, although the very manner of his death confounded the claim of divinity. By his death on the cross, Jesus demonstrated the cost of discipleship, even as the cross hallowed in him the capacity for radical resurrection-life.

Whatever resurrection means, the disciples "saw" the risen Jesus. If the sight of him left them dazed, they remained gripped by an unshakable certainty that the Jesus of Nazareth who had been crucified was, by the power of the God of Israel, raised from the dead. The body in which Jesus is raised does not belong to this world; his resurrected body is a new and different reality and signals a new and different mode of living. Not to be confused with resuscitation, resurrection breaks radically with material reality as we experience it. Yet, the appearances on the road to Emmaus (Luke 24:13–32) and in Jerusalem (Luke 24:33–43) are characterized by an insistent corporeality. Jesus eats with the disciples, invites them to examine his hands and feet, to touch him, to feel flesh and bone. "Touch me and see!" (Luke 24:39). The recognition of the heart is grasped by the senses and confirmed by the mind.

Resurrection is an event for Jesus; something radical has happened to him. Resurrection is also an event for the disciples. Jesus' postresurrection appearances awaken in them the embers of a bold witness that the gift of the Spirit will fan into flame. Even as resurrection characterizes the destiny of Jesus, it is not a private destiny intended for him alone; it is the beginning of the absolute transformation of all creation. Resurrection breaks through, formally and materially, the cosmic, psychic, and moral disorder brought about by the reign of sin. Resurrection signals eschatological healing and binds a marred and broken creation back to the heart of God.

The appearances of the Risen Lord to the disciples are gratuitous and, as such, remind us that the resurrection is not primarily about the sight of Jesus, but rather about *insight* into his mission. Real, transformative encounters with the Risen Lord, these appearances refine for the disciples (and for us) just what it costs to live the way of Jesus, to confess him as the absolute meaning of life for the world. At the same time, the death of Jesus discloses

God's own struggle against the powers and principalities of this world and manifests God's desire to emancipate those ensnared in psychic or religious or cultural or social bondage. The crucified Jesus is the sign of the cost of identification with poor, outcast, abject, and despised women and men in the struggle for life. He incarnates the freedom and destiny of discipleship.

The Cross as a Condition of Discipleship

With this background, perhaps, we now may be able to grasp the astonishment of the disciples and the people gathered around Jesus when he said, "If any want to become my followers, let them deny themselves and take up their cross and follow me" (Mark 8:34). Given the humiliation associated with crucifixion, these words could scarcely have been inviting. Surely, more than once, these ordinary women and men of the ancient world had witnessed the barbaric rite of crucifixion: the brutalized man dragging the cross-beam through the streets, the staggering arrival at the place of execution, the torture and mutilation, and, finally, impalement.[16] The summons to such imitation ("take up your cross") surely provoked incredulity and bewilderment; they wanted no part of it. Perhaps, more than once, these ordinary women and men had joined a mob watching the spectacle — feeding on the terror, amazed by their own relief: it is finished. Now, listening to the rabbi from Nazareth ("take up your cross and follow me"), these ordinary people are, at once, attracted and repulsed.

In the third Gospel, the Lukan Jesus puts the cross as a condition for discipleship quite starkly:

> Whoever does not carry the cross and follow me cannot be my disciple. For which of you, intending to build a tower, does not first sit down and estimate the cost, to see whether he has enough to complete it? Otherwise, when he has laid a foundation and is not able to finish, all who see it will begin to ridicule him, saying, 'This fellow began to build and was not able to finish.' Or what king, going out to wage war against another king, will not sit down first and consider whether he is able with ten thousand to oppose the one who comes against him with twenty thousand? If he cannot, then, while the other is still far away, he sends a delegation and asks for the terms of peace. So therefore, none of you can become my disciple if you do not give up all your possessions. (Luke 14:27–33)

Jesus demands that his disciples go the distance, walk the entire "way." His illustrations here are simple, but striking. He teaches a lesson designed to drive home the necessity of self-examen, sacrifice, personal resolve, and love. The prosperous builder and the successful military strategist meet their goals through painstaking attention to detail, thorough planning, and meticulous assessment. The outcomes of such exacting preparation earn admiration. The lesson the disciples must absorb is sharpened by contrast: "the children of this age are more shrewd in dealing with their own generation than are the children of light" (Luke 16:8).

Jesus entrusts to them (and to us) a venture of absolute importance — his own mission, that is, announcing and preparing a context for the coming reign of God. If a builder or military strategist can succeed, certainly his disciples can muster similar dedication, sacrifice, and personal resolve. But the reign of God is no utopian project, it is a very different kind of reality. Over time and in time, the disciples (we as well) learn that they (and we) can and must prepare a context for its advent, but it is most fundamentally God's gratuitous gift. Moreover, this absolute endeavor calls not merely for planning, self-examen, sacrifice, and personal resolve but for love unmeasured, unstinting, overflowing, fearless, passionate. Thus his mission on behalf of the reign of God required of Jesus something bold: that he stake his whole life and very personhood on being absolutely directed toward God in love without measure.

The Way Jesus Is

The foremost lesson of Christian discipleship is that Jesus is the way, and the way Jesus is is the way of the cross. While walking that way is, at once, the same, it is also distinctive for each woman and man who would follow him; it will include privation, intense longing, an acute awareness of emptiness and failure, confusion and loss. Following the way of Jesus, the disciple is exposed, humbled, and opened to the wisdom and power of the Spirit. Just as the cross hallowed in Jesus a capacity for resurrection-life, so too it hallows in the disciple a kind of infinite desire and capacity for life in and with God.[17]

Catherine of Siena knew more than a little about the way of Jesus. In the *Dialogue,* she tells us that to draw us into God's extravagant love, Christ makes a bridge and a staircase of his very crucified body.[18] So eager is God for our love, for union with us, that the Son is sent to demonstrate that love through the sacrifice of his own life on the cross for love of us.[19] Catherine writes:

> The first stair is the feet, which symbolize the affections. For just as the feet carry the body, the affections carry the soul. My Son's nailed feet are a stair by which you can climb to his side, where you will see revealed his innermost heart.... Then the soul, seeing how tremendously she is loved, is herself filled to overflowing with love. So having

climbed the second stair, she reaches the third. This is his mouth, where she finds peace.[20]

The disciple scales the tree of life, moving upward in love and virtue, seeking the fruit of union. At each phase of the ascent, the disciple is drawn on by great desire to know and love as Jesus knew and loved. Just as a mother nurses her child, so too Christ nourishes the disciple: "Through the flesh of Christ crucified, we suck the milk of divine sweetness.[21]

Like the roots of the tree, the nailed feet secure the disciple in the initial stage of the climb. At the first stair the disciple confronts and comes to know self to know and love Christ. In a letter to cloistered women religious, Catherine comments on the significance of reaching the heart of the crucified Jesus in the second stage of the climb. His great heart, she writes, is "open and utterly spent for us."[22] Immersed in the heart of Christ, the disciple is nourished for a praxis of solidarity and compassion. At the final stage of the climb, the disciple reaches the mouth of Christ and "learns to savour souls... [to] become a true shepherd ready to lay down [her or his] life" for [the little ones].[23] The disciple is *for* others. Yet, the disciple flames with desire for the very God who with unimaginable love has looked upon us and fallen in love with us.[24]

"Jacob's Ladder," the familiar African American spiritual, has a strong metaphorical resonance with Catherine's image of the body of the crucified Christ as a staircase. The spiritual conflates and fuses the story of Jacob's vision (Gen. 28:10–17) with the cross of Jesus.

> We are climbing Jacob's ladder, / We are climbing Jacob's ladder,
> We are climbing Jacob's ladder, / Soldiers of the cross.
>
> Every round goes higher, higher, / Every round goes higher, higher,
> Every round goes higher, higher, / Soldiers of the cross.
>
> Sinner, do you love my Jesus? / Sinner, do you love my Jesus?
> Sinner, do you love my Jesus? / Soldiers of the cross.
>
> If you love Him, why not serve him? / If you love Him, why not serve
>   him?
> If you love Him, why not serve him? / Soldiers of the cross.[25]

As simple as the spiritual is, it is more than simplistic repetition, call and response; it engages singer, listener, and disciple in a meditative dialogue about growth in the life of the spirit, knowledge of God, and discipleship.

In Genesis, Jacob, fearful and yearning, dreams of a ladder that reaches upward from earth into the heavens and upon which angels ascend and descend. Jacob is gifted with both *a disclosure* of God's identity ("I am the Lord, the God of Abraham your father and the God of Isaac" [Gen. 28:13]) and *a promise* ("I am with you and will keep you wherever you go... I will

not leave you until I have done what I have promised you" [Gen. 28:15]).
The first and second stanzas of the spiritual offer a thematic statement of the
ladder's direction toward God and its end in God. But unlike Jacob, those
of us who would be disciples are awake; we sin even as we seek. We climb
toward the God who is our destination, but the weight of sin slows our
ascent. The makers of the spiritual invoke soldierly virtues of courage and
fortitude, but these are not enough. Love must be added to the list. The first
stanza discloses our true end, union with God; the final stanza calls those
who profess to love God to love neighbor, to take up a praxis of solidarity
and compassion.

The spirituals give us access to the "experience[s], expression[s], moti-
vations, intentions, behaviors, styles, and rhythms" of African American
religio-cultural life.[26] They open a window onto the lives of the enslaved
peoples and shed light on their religious, social, aesthetic, and psychological
worldview. They emerge from the people's wrestling with and surrender to
the power of the Spirit that set them on the "way."

A former slave become a minister of the gospel, Josiah Henson provides
an example of similarly committed discipleship. In his autobiographical
narrative, first published in Boston in 1849, Henson vividly recalls his conversion to Christ. Urged by his mother to go to hear preacher John McKenny,
young Henson obtained permission to do so from the slaveholder Isaac
Riley. Henson reports that he walked three or four miles to the place of
the meeting, but upon arrival was barred because of his race from entering
the building. After some effort, Henson positioned himself near the open
front door to hear and see McKenny. Henson recalls:

> I saw [Mr. McKenny with his hands raised] and he said: "Jesus Christ,
> the Son of God, tasted death for every man; for the high, for the low,
> for the rich, for the poor, for the bond, the free, the [N]egro in his
> chains, the man in gold and diamonds." I stood and heard [the ser-
> mon]. It touched my heart, and I cried out: "I wonder if Jesus Christ
> died for me."[27]

McKenny preached Jesus' "tender love for mankind, his forgiving spirit, his
compassion for the outcast and despised, his cruel crucifixion" and reminded
congregations that the message of salvation was universal. Jesus Christ died
not for a select few but for all. Henson writes that these, indeed, were "glad
tidings" and they were for

> the slave as well as the master, the poor as well as the rich, for the
> persecuted, the distressed, the heavy-laden, the captive; even for me
> among the rest, a poor, despised, abused creature, deemed by others fit
> for nothing but unrequited toil — but mental and bodily degradation.
> Oh, the blessedness and sweetness of feeling that I was loved!...I

kept repeating to myself, "The compassionate Savior about whom I have heard, 'loves me,' 'He looks down in compassion from heaven on me....'" I thought... "[Jesus will] be my dear refuge — He'll wipe away all tears from my eyes." "Now I can bear all things; nothing will seem hard after this...." Swallowed up in the beauty of the divine love, I "loved my enemies and prayed for them that did despitefully use and [mistreat] me."[28]

Meditating on this message as he returned to the plantation, Henson tells us he grew so excited that he turned into the woods nearby, knelt down, and prayed for guidance and aid. From that day forward, Henson set himself the task of climbing "Jacob's ladder" and leading others in that ascent. He soon began to gather other enslaved women and men, to speak with them about the love of the crucified Jesus, to pray with them, to exhort them, and to comfort them.

Separated by centuries, Catherine of Siena and Josiah Henson are united in committed discipleship. Both understood that Jesus of Nazareth is the absolute meaning of life for the world. He offered them a love that drew them to himself, and their love of him flowed over into a praxis of compassionate solidarity on behalf of women and men in need. Loving as Jesus loved, Catherine challenged a warring society and a fragmented church with a message of peace and reconciliation. Loving as Jesus loved, Henson confronted a slaveholding society and church with a demand for justice and transformation. Catherine and Henson took up the time-shaped challenge to love Jesus, to follow him, to live his command, to share the good news of his love, to stand in solidarity and compassion with others.

Conclusion

In this essay, I have attempted to tease out what it means to follow Jesus of Nazareth, to be his disciple, to stand as he stood at the disposal of the cross. I began with the sad spectacle of a black woman combing through the refuse bins of my apartment building. Here is a woman whose back is against the wall; her situation imposes on Christian discipleship. What can it mean to tell her that God in Jesus is also alienated, a stranger, a despised "other"? What word, what compassionate act of solidarity do we Christian disciples have for her? Moved by sight of her, I went on to examine the terrifying spectacle of the crucifixion of Jesus of Nazareth and to interrogate the cross as an indispensable condition of Christian discipleship. The experiences of Catherine of Siena and of Josiah Henson testify *both* to the unity of the mystical-political for the Christian disciple *and* to discipleship as the locus, the site, in which Christ makes himself present.

This exploration took the performative meaning of discipleship from the Lukan narrative of the story of the life, death, and resurrection of Jesus of Nazareth. Even with its ambivalent attitudes toward women, Luke's gospel affords those of us who belong to privileged groups (for example, whites or black theologians) an occasion for critical self-examination: How do we understand the relation of our own social locations to the coming reign of God? How often do those of us who belong to privileged groups conveniently overlook the incriminating criticisms of the privileged, which the narrator of Luke's gospel places in the mouth of Jesus? How often do we excuse ourselves from human communion with poor, despised hungry women and men? These are questions that any of us who would be disciples must follow to find the Christ of God, questions to be answered by living in search of the One whose great love for us gives absolute meaning to life.

Throughout this essay, I have kept the cross at the forefront, but in concluding I want to shift a bit. My starting point for working out the meaning of discipleship as christological locus was the sad spectacle of a black woman searching garbage. I choose the word *spectacle* deliberately, since the image of the woman leaning into stench and filth seized me, suffused my senses, entered into my theologizing, and remains vivid and authoritative in my memory. I know nothing about her: She may have fallen through the gaping cracks of the so-called safety-net established by the state of Wisconsin in its haste to eliminate welfare. Or she may have been homeless and simply, terribly hungry. Or perhaps she was poor and refrained from eating to feed her children. How hungry and desperate she must have been to stand in the morning sun opening bags of garbage. How hungry she must have been to endure the stares of disgust and condescension from passers-by. But to this woman scraping the dregs for life, the Lukan Jesus offers reassurance: "Blessed are you who are poor, for yours is the kingdom of God. Blessed are you who are hungry now, for you will be filled" (Luke 6:20–21).

The spectacle of a woman searching through rot for food cannot but point the Christian disciple toward the Bread of Life. This phrase, "bread of life," belongs in a special way to the Johannine Jesus, but the Lukan Jesus (like the Jesus of the Synoptics) blesses, breaks, and identifies bread with himself before he completes his way to the cross. In this gospel, the breaking of bread is the gesture that clears the tear-filled eyes of those forlorn disciples who met a stranger on their way to Emmaus (Luke 24:30–31). In *Seeing the Lord*, Marianne Sawicki comments on Luke's association of hunger with the possibility of understanding resurrection life and of recognizing the resurrected Lord.[29] This recognition, I would add, is crucial for mystical-political discipleship and for an authentic praxis of compassion and solidarity.

In Luke 14, we find Jesus on a Sabbath at table, a dinner guest of a Pharisee. Jesus bluntly tells his host: "When you give a banquet, invite the poor, the crippled, the lame, and the blind. And you will be blessed, because they cannot repay you, for you will be repaid at the resurrection of the righteous" (Luke 14:13–14). Jesus is insisting that we make space in our hearts, at our tables, in our communities for the little ones. Perhaps to drive home the point, Jesus reiterates this lesson in the parable of the great banquet. Someone invites guests to a wonderful meal, then sends a servant to summon them when all is ready. But the guests retort with excuses and rebuff his hospitality. Angry, the householder tells the servant, "Go out at once in the streets and lanes of the town, and bring in the poor, the crippled, the blind, and the lame." The servant does so and returns to report that there is still room at table. Again the host sends the servant "out into the roads and lanes, and compel people to come in, so that my house may be filled. For I tell you, none of those who were invited will taste my dinner" (Luke 14:15–24).

Hunger constitutes a possibility for mystical-political discipleship and an authentic praxis of compassion and solidarity. If we would be disciples of Jesus, we must be willing to recognize and alleviate hungers — whether for food or truth or justice, whether our own or those of others.[30] A praxis of compassionate solidarity, justice-love, and care for the poor and oppressed is a sign that we are on the "way" of Jesus. The resurrected Lord himself sends us into streets and alleys, shelters and schools, homes and hospices to find and feed those who are despised, abused, and marginalized. These children, women, and men are the only sure sign of his presence among us in our efforts to prepare a context for the coming reign of his God.

At the same time, the parable of the great banquet reiterates a warning thrown down earlier by the Lukan Jesus: "Woe to you who are full now, for you will be hungry" (Luke 6:25a). All who would be his disciples, especially those of us who have the luxury to stand and watch hungry women and men, are called to critical self-examen and a praxis of compassionate solidarity. In Luke's narrative arrangement, this parable precedes those forceful words about the fundamental condition of discipleship: "Whoever does not carry the cross and follow me cannot be my disciple" (Luke 14:27). The cross rises between the meal that Jesus shares with his disciples before he dies and the bit of grilled fish that he eats with them in Jerusalem (Luke 24:41–43). At the Passover meal, Jesus declares to his friends that he shall not eat or drink again until the kingdom of God comes (Luke 22:16–18). He promises them that when the kingdom does come, they shall sit with him at his table in places set specially for them, eating and drinking with joy (Luke 22:28–30). If we would sit at his table, we too must live in solidarity with the little ones and live at the disposal of the cross.

For Further Reflection

1. How is discipleship a valuable starting point for Black Christology?

2. What is the benefit of using the Gospel of Luke to discuss the meaning of discipleship?

3. What, in the author's view, does it mean "to live at the disposal of the cross"?

4. What was the significance of Jesus' putting the reign of God at the center of his ministry?

5. What is the relationship between the "way" of Jesus and the cross?

For Further Reading

Blount, Brian K. *Go Preach! Mark's Kingdom Message and the Black Church.* Maryknoll, N.Y.: Orbis Books, 1998.

Dunn, James D. G. *Jesus' Call to Discipleship.* Cambridge: Cambridge University Press, 1992.

Hayes, Diana L. *And Still They Rise: An Introduction to Black Liberation Theology.* Mahwah, N.J.: Paulist, 1996.

Hayes, Diana L., and Cyprian Davis, O.S.B. *Taking Down Our Harps: Black Catholics in the United States.* Maryknoll, N.Y.: Orbis Books, 1998.

Lamb, Matthew L. *Solidarity with Victims: Toward a Theology of Social Transformation.* New York: Crossroad, 1982.

Wimbush, Vincent L. *The Bible and African Americans: A Brief History.* Minneapolis: Fortress Press, 2003.

Christology, Ethics, and Spirituality

Lisa Sowle Cahill

The Interdependence of Christology, Ethics, and Spirituality

All Christology begins in life — in communities of human persons trying to express the reality that, in encountering Jesus, they have encountered the one true God.[1] Over three decades ago, Reformed theologian James M. Gustafson wrote that Christian moral teaching takes on meaning within a "life of trust in God, expectation of His Kingdom, reliance on His goodness," and on the basis of "a proclamation of a God who loves both the neighbor and the self." A readiness to love one's neighbor is thus "both required and enabled in the followers of Jesus."[2] More recently, a Catholic theologian, Roger Haight, has drawn similar connections among the Christian's understanding of who God is and how God is present in Jesus Christ ("Christology"); the imaginative world and dispositions of the believer in relation to God and neighbor ("spirituality"); and a life of action in the world ("ethics").[3]

Concepts and symbols for God and the concrete Christian life, as spiritual practices, communal rituals, and moral action, are interdependent. Representations of God create a mode in which God is imagined for prayer and liturgy, provide an orientation for practical living that is reinforced by spirituality, and challenge pieties and patterns of action that may be unfaithful. Since any adequate christological formulation must arise from and make sense of the actual experience of salvation, then ethics, spirituality, and christological concepts are symbiotic. At times Christology, spirituality, and ethics reinforce and mutually shape one another; at other times, one of these dimensions will provoke a correction or development in another.

Liberation Ethics and
Christology from Below

One of the most important developments in Christian ethics in the past century or so has been the emergence of a social conscience and social commitment as intrinsic to a Christian way of life. In contrast to earlier "spiritualizing" interpretations of the kingdom or reign of God, late nineteenth- and twentieth-century theologians stress that God's presence in Jesus Christ and his resurrection signify that a new way of human life is possible now. It is true that God's reign will only be realized fully in the eschaton or final fulfillment of history as a result of God's own decisive action. "Resurrection life" will never be fully available in history itself. Nevertheless, theologians of the nineteenth-century Protestant "social gospel," popes of the same era who inaugurated the tradition of Catholic social encyclicals, and liberation theologians who later advocated a "preferential option for the poor," all agree not only that Christians have the *obligation* to challenge sinful social structures but that Christians can *hope* that social transformation is really possible in light of what God has done in Christ.

Haight is representative when he says that an intrinsic part of the meaning of salvation is "a participation in the movement to resist all forms of dehumanizing institutions and behavior patterns."[4] Gustavo Gutiérrez put this insight in christological perspective when, in his groundbreaking *A Theology of Liberation,* he wrote that "Salvation — the communion of human beings with God and among themselves — is something which embraces all human reality, transforms it, and leads to its fulfillment in Christ."[5] Similarly, the feminist biblical scholar Elisabeth Schüssler Fiorenza insists that passive, individualist, ahistorical interpretations of the reign of God are not adequate to the way the Bible portrays Jesus' own teaching. Instead, biblical interpretation should "become accountable to and promote the well-being of all inhabitants of the global village."[6]

These and similar understandings of salvation are all grounded in the same christological shift. Since the Middle Ages, salvation in Christ has been seen primarily as personal liberation from sin and damnation, bought by the sacrificial death of Christ, who by substituting for us in the atonement, repaid a debt owed God (Anselm). In recent times, salvation in Christ has come to be seen as social and not only personal liberation from corrupt and unjust relationships to other persons and to God. This liberation is inaugurated concretely by God's historical presence in Jesus of Nazareth and confirmed and promised for fulfillment in the world to come by the risen Jesus proclaimed as Christ. While "spirituality" on the older model signifies personal piety and penance in preparation for the life to come, "spirituality" on the new one signifies personal and communal renewal by the power of the Spirit.

The new, more social understanding of salvation is connected to a rediscovery of the life and teaching of the "historical Jesus," especially as focused on his preaching of the kingdom or reign of God. The reign of God, already in Jesus' ministry, incorporates sinners and the righteous, the noble and the lowly, the rich and the poor, and peoples of every religious or ethnic background. The early Christian baptismal formula found in one of Paul's letters is often invoked to communicate the way the first Christians appropriated Jesus' "good news" of salvation in life and liturgy: boundaries and dominations expressed in ethnic-religious, class, and gender divisions are overcome by unity in the Lord (Gal. 3:28). Christologies that begin with the life of Jesus challenge older Christologies, beginning with theological definitions of the incarnation, for failing to connect the symbols of Christian faith with the concrete demands of love of neighbor, healing the effects of sin on human society.

A growing sense that social hierarchy is not immutable has been enabled by discovery, travel, colonization and decolonization, and the emergence of democratic forms of government. Since the Enlightenment, Western philosophy, politics, and cultures have increasingly recognized individual dignity or "equality." Worldwide communication has increased awareness of global differences and global interdependence. This has made it possible for the socially radical implications of Jesus' teaching, always latent in the New Testament, to be newly appreciated and put into practice. The reality of social change, especially in the last century, has sponsored new confidence that actual change in social structures can be brought about by Christian action.

The new approach to Christology entailed by seeing the events in the life of Jesus of Nazareth as a constant resource and referent for Christian spirituality and ethics is often called a "Christology from below." This contrasts to a "Christology from above," focused not on the earthly career of Jesus Christ, but on a vision of Christ identified with the preexistent Logos (as in the Gospel of John), or on the doctrines about Christ formulated at Nicea (one in being with God) and Chalcedon (a true human nature and a true divine nature). In a famous essay, Karl Rahner distinguished these two christological approaches as really two perspectives on the same events and faith. What is understood on the basis of a "saving history" Christology can obviously be re-expressed later in terms of doctrine and a more "metaphysical" approach.[7] The perspective and emphasis are different. For the first, "ascending," Christology, the point of departure "is the simple experience of the man Jesus, and of the resurrection in which his fate was brought to its conclusion." For the second, "metaphysical" or "descending," Christology, it is assumed that the words of Jesus himself warrant that "the pre-existence of the Logos, his divinity, his distinction from the Father, the predicate 'Son of God,' " can all be ascribed to Jesus from the first.[8]

Virtually all scholars would agree that these two christological approaches are complementary. However, the current predominance of Christologies from below testifies to the power of "the historical Jesus" to speak concretely to the reality of evil in the world, human suffering, the sinful complicity of human beings in the structures that create suffering and evil, and the need for renewal here and now. As Roger Haight sees clearly, "Christology must address the humanly caused and systemically ingrained human suffering that so characterizes our world situation today." Christology cannot avoid the problem of "needless human suffering"; indeed, "Jesus cannot be the Christ and salvation cannot be real without having some bearing on this situation."[9]

In the next section we shall examine ways in which liberation theologians, including feminist theologians, have proclaimed the life and example of Jesus, especially his death on the cross, so as to address, challenge, and begin to transform the countless situations in which human beings suffer in our world. In so doing, they also challenge traditional christological expressions that see Christ's suffering and death as the consequence of a divine demand for "satisfaction," hence portraying human suffering as an unavoidable and even salutary form of participation in the redemptive process. Such theologies, they would claim, serve too easily to subdue victims, placate reformers, and bolster the authority of those who benefit from the deprivations of others. However, looking further, we will see that the "Christologies from below" invoked by liberation theologians also go on to incorporate aspects of key doctrinal affirmations usually thought to have been protected best in traditional "Christologies from above." Such aspects include faith in the bodily resurrection of Christ and of the believer, the two natures of Christ, the three persons of the trinity, the "pre-existent" Logos Christology of John's Gospel, and the Anselmian connection of Christ's death with satisfaction for our sins.

While Christian ethics, in the form of transformationist social and political movements, challenges traditional Christologies, these same movements also rely on and are occasionally challenged by the contours and parameters of historic christological affirmations. The christological hermeneutic is always dynamic and circular (from experience to theory and doctrine, and back to experience, then on to reformulated theologies). Christologies from above and below are complementary; moreover, any so-called Christology from above once had its origin in Christian experience and will be tested for continuing relevance to it.

The Voices of Suffering and a Theology of the Cross

Liberationist and feminist theologians seek alternatives to Anselmian Christologies that see Christ's suffering on the cross as a substitutionary penalty for sin, a penalty willed by God. This theological framework encourages social attitudes and practices that blame victims for their own suffering, accept human suffering as God's will, and discourage attempts to change the human reality as we know it. Instead, many thinkers propose variations on a paradigm in which the suffering Christ discloses God's presence to, in, and with those who suffer. Inasmuch as Christ is still suffering in the suffering of the victims of history, Christian faith and theology furnish a powerful motivation to change the historical situation of needless human misery.

The historical Jesus likewise suffered, given his innocent condemnation as a criminal and revolutionary, his agony and expressions of distress and abandonment as he confronted his death, the confusion and fear of his disciples and family, and Jesus' faithfulness to his mission and obedience to God up to and including the events of his torture and execution. The recorded experiences of Jesus as risen and as present in the Spirit do not provide a rationale for nonresistance to human suffering in this life but empower the virtues of compassion, solidarity, courage, and hope.

A classic statement of this kind of activist Christology is voiced by Leonardo Boff:

> God assumes the cross to be in solidarity with those who suffer — not to sublimate and eternalize the cross, but to enter into solidarity with those who suffer on the cross and thus transform the cross into a sign of blessing, a sign of suffering love. Love, then, is the motive for this assumption of the cross by God. . . . In this vision, courageous poverty, decision, outrage, and suffering win a divine dimension — not to numb our awareness in the struggle with the passion of the world, but to say that only in solidarity with the crucified can we struggle against the cross, only in identification with the victims of tribulation can there be real liberation from tribulation. And this was Jesus' road, the path of God incarnate.[10]

For Boff, the cross does not symbolize a penalty for sin, exacted by a just God but mysteriously (or paradoxically) paid by a merciful God with the life of his innocent Son. Instead, the overwhelming meaning of the cross is compassionate love, evoking a spirituality of imitation of Christ and self-offering identification with the oppressed, giving rise to social action.

Mary Solberg similarly envisions a theology of the cross as inspiring ethical struggle, based on her work with the poor of El Salvador. The cross makes it possible to see, even from within suffering, that God's purposes lead beyond "the systems and ideologies" that "thrive on racism, sexism, heterosexism, and gross maldistribution of economic resources and political power within nations and across international boundaries in all directions."[11] Conversion includes acceptance of accountability and a commitment to work for change in solidarity with the suffering of the poor.

Jacquelyn Grant recounts slave narratives showing the identification of Black people with Jesus in his suffering. "As Jesus was persecuted and made to suffer undeservedly, so were they. His suffering culminated in the crucifixion. Their crucifixion included rape, and babies being sold."[12] Shawn Copeland declares that "a theology of suffering in womanist perspective repels every tendency toward any ersatz spiritualization of evil and suffering, of pain and oppression." Instead, a womanist Christology remembers, resists, and redeems by remembering and retelling the experiences of African-Americans, understanding them in the light of "the liberating Word and deed of God in Jesus of Nazareth."[13]

It is widely agreed among liberation theologians, then, that the life of Jesus and his death on the cross condemn historical injustice and reveal God's compassion for its victims.

Resurrection

Some "historical-Jesus" scholars eschew any christological trajectory of interpretation of the significance of the man Jesus of Nazareth as unduly "supernaturalizing" Jesus beyond the reliable historical evidence.[14] Liberation theologians see social history and sociology as important resources for understanding the social and political ramifications of Jesus' preaching of the reign of God. However, they do not see any need to reduce Jesus to a prophetic figure who championed social outcasts, confronted unjust power, and was true to his values to the death.

Without necessarily asserting the "literal" truth of every detail of the resurrection stories, they see the raising of Jesus by God, his presence to believers in a transformed, resurrected state, and God's promise of resurrection to those who are united with the risen Jesus in faith, as essential to Jesus' ultimate significance as the Christ. Jesus not only suffers as other human beings suffer; his resurrection is a vindication of his mission. God promises real liberation to those who are united with Jesus Christ in suffering. As Gerald O'Collins expresses it, "The God who is always and everywhere the very ground of being acted with loving and life-giving power in Jesus' resurrection."[15] This power has ethical implications; in fact it is verified in the conversion to transformed personal and social life experienced by Christians.

The resurrection makes the life and death of Jesus "a story where death is not the ultimate answer to human life, irrespective of all appearances to the contrary." It is to be converted and empowered in the conviction that "Jesus is the stronger one, stronger than any forces of evil, more powerful than any horrible problems that imprison and distress us."[16] In Christ, "Salvation means being delivered from death, absurdity and hatred, and being redeemed for life, meaning, and love."[17] The movement of theology "from below," in Christian experience, is what ultimately gives power and significance to the idea of resurrection. The credible testimony of believers and theologians, that in and through faith in Jesus Christ, the poor and oppressed not only struggle but do survive, is essential to the "truth" of the story of resurrection today. As Grant says, although "the condition of black people today reflects the cross of Jesus...the resurrection brings the hope that liberation from oppression is immanent."[18] Elizabeth Johnson eloquently elaborates on the significance of this reality:

> At the very heart of Christianity, therefore, is an experience and a claim. The experience is one of transforming, transcendent, personal power within communities that can be expressed in shorthand as 'the gift of the Holy Spirit.' The claim is that this power comes from Jesus, who was crucified but who now lives by the life of God. . . . Experience and conviction together form the primordial "resurrection experience" that founds the Christian movement and continues to ground it today. As Paul also says, "If Christ has not been raised, then our preaching is in vain, and your faith is in vain" (1 Cor. 15:14).[19]

Yet, for a theology that takes seriously the deepest suffering that afflicts and sometimes destroys human beings, resurrection faith cannot be naïve or superficial. Its theological or christological expression, certainly, will never be coherent and secure beyond the possibility of any deconstruction. Johnson confronts this fact squarely: "Evil is indeed the surd which shatters every rational system of thought. Anyone who works out a rational way to integrate evil and radical suffering in an ordered fashion into a total intellectual system of which God is a part thereby justifies it." The available alternative to a fully coherent theoretical Christology is a "praxis of hope" oriented by the faith of those who do suffer profoundly and by the narratives of the suffering God who brings them not only compassion but life.[20]

Nicea and Chalcedon

A Christology from below that warrants, motivates, and accomplishes confident social engagement does not stop with the claim that God has raised the man Jesus from the dead, nor even that through his death and resurrection the human being Jesus of Nazareth was given an exalted status at the hand of God. Rather, the ground of Christian hope, grounded in the most grueling experiences of the oppressed, is that, in Jesus, it is *God* who is our companion in radical *human* suffering. It was exactly because Jesus was not only a man but "God incarnate," according to Jacquelyn Grant, that identification with his suffering lifted Black people above the enslaving system controlled by white people and gave them resources to resist and survive that system.[21] Their experience of God was strengthened, not annihilated, by their suffering. Elizabeth Johnson's christological paradigm likewise accentuates that empowerment and "salvation" come with the knowledge that *God* suffers with human beings. If God "is in compassionate solidarity with suffering people in history, a future is thereby opened up through even the most negative experience." A suffering God "can help by awakening consolation, responsible human action, and hope against hope in the world marked by radical suffering and evil."[22]

The Council of Nicea was a reaction to the Arian heresy that Jesus Christ, as the "Son of God," is a creature. Although there are still unresolved questions in the debates over what it means for the Son to be "begotten" and yet coequal with the Father, Nicea set an important parameter for later expressions of the Christian experience of God. According to Nicea, God did not send any lesser being as an intermediary to participate in the human condition; the love of God for humanity was great enough to draw God directly into humanity's own being, marred though it is by sin and death. It is God alone who can and does save us from this condition. If human life is so united to God that it is lifted into the very reality of God, then transformation of our condition is possible. As Roger Haight states it, Nicea can make sense "from below," and not only as a doctrinal authority from the past: "the point is that Jesus must be considered divine because God is encountered in and through him for human salvation."[23]

Agreeing that "Christian experience of faith" is "the generating matrix about God as triune," Elizabeth Johnson highlights the christological and soteriological significance of the doctrine of three persons in God. First, Jesus mediates to human beings the liberating reign of God; human liberation and reconciliation come from God, and in the experience of Jesus, God is truly encountered.[24] Second, following the groundbreaking work of Catherine LaCugna in feminist trinitarian theology,[25] Johnson affirms that "being in communion constitutes God's very essence" and that the unity of God is constituted by the mystery of personal love in relationship.[26] Liberation for human persons "in the image of God" is also, then, liberation for mutuality, equality, and love.

Against what was at the time a consensus about the divinity of Jesus, Chalcedon, in the century after Nicea, drew Christian attention back to the reality of Jesus as a vulnerable and suffering human being. The doctrine of Chalcedon affirms that Jesus is truly human and truly God, without, however, clarifying exactly how these two natures coexist in the one person, Jesus. A Christology "for today" must not lose sight of the biblical narratives about the "real" Jesus, nor turn the identity of Jesus into a metaphysical abstraction. As it is for Nicea, the ultimate test for Chalcedonian doctrine is the crucible of Christian experience. Chalcedon as a standard for contemporary Christology means that resurrection, salvation, and personal conversion can and do take place only if and because God is present fully within what is still authentically human existence. "Over against the kingdom of evil and the forces of death, Jesus reveals a way of life. The power of

God for life and salvation is realized concretely in his own life; Jesus makes God present in a saving way especially in his acts in the power of God as Spirit."[27]

A Role for Christology from Above?

The Christian tradition has known many Christologies; the New Testament itself is pluralistic in its interpretations of Jesus as the Christ.[28] In recent decades, "low Christologies," those that are grounded primarily in the gospel accounts of Jesus' earthly life and ministry, including his death on the cross, have enjoyed particular favor among theologians and ethicists, as well as in popular piety and spirituality. In particular, Christologies that make central Jesus' preaching of the reign of God and his ensuing crucifixion by the political and religious authorities, correlate very effectively with the historical experiences of suffering, oppression, solidarity, commitment, and liberation. The resurrection and the proclamation of Jesus as "Christ" then function to empower conversion and renewed relations with God and others in the church and in society. For example, Roger Haight proposes a "Spirit Christology" that centers on New Testament portrayals of God as Spirit present in Jesus and in his ministry; and of the risen Jesus as present and alive with God, sending his Spirit or as being himself present as Spirit in the Christian community.[29] While not seeing Jesus as "merely a holy man" or a "prophet," a Spirit Christology begins with and keeps its focus on the earthly life of Jesus and the way the first Christians experienced Jesus historically and interpreted his life after the resurrection event.

Although not eliminated or refuted by such approaches, the contrasting Logos-centered Christology from above that presents Jesus as having pre-existed with God before the world began and that has been associated with the Prologue to John's Gospel (and with Paul[30]) has been displaced. Logos Christology has fallen out of favor as too abstract, overly tradition-bound, hard to connect with ordinary religious experience, and not particularly inspiring for spirituality and ethics today. After examining some of the origins of this Christology, we shall take a second look at its usefulness for feminist and liberationist ethics and spirituality.

While John's Christology incorporates many strands, the most comprehensive and developed is a view of Jesus as "the one sent from above to reveal the Father, take away the sin of the world, and give life to those who receive him." John identifies Jesus as the fulfillment of the Torah, "the creative Logos that was in the beginning with God," and the "Wisdom of God" that personified God and dwelt among God's people.[31] According to John, Jesus is "a preexistent who came into this world from another, heavenly realm, where he had been with the Father."[32] There are many parallels between the Logos of God and the Wisdom of God portrayed in the Books of Wisdom, Proverbs, and Sirach.[33] Wisdom is a feminine personification of

God ("Lady Wisdom"), present with God and serving as an agent of creation, present with Israel throughout her history, and instructing, inspiring, and saving Israel's people.

Logos Christology, identifying Jesus as a preexistent being, was the basis of the Nicene formulation calling Jesus the "eternally begotten Son of God." Roger Haight points out that this doctrine creates a certain "clash of images" between Christology ("from above") and critical reconstructions of the historical figure of Jesus, especially of his full humanity and fully human consciousness.[34] The Synoptic Gospels, in contrast, do not portray Jesus as a "divine person," but "as one like us relating to the transcendent God, his heavenly Father."[35] According to Haight, the moral and spiritual issues of the modern age, especially the mandate to liberate the oppressed, have created a shift in the christological "problematic." The issue is no longer how to explain Christ's divinity but how to be faithful to his true humanity. The premise is not so much "an eternal Logos" but rather "Jesus of Nazareth."[36] An adequate Christology simply cannot be abstracted from Jesus' humanity and real human subjectivity.

The prophetic power and practice of liberation spirituality and ethics leave no room to deny that final claim. However, the fact is that liberationist Christologies from below that take their cue from Jesus' ministry have become so widespread and authoritative in contemporary theology, spirituality, and ethics that they now amount almost to a new version of Christology from above — a "dogmatic" formulation of the meaning of Jesus that is an unquestioned starting point and standard of control. Yet any hegemonic paradigm runs the risk of overwhelming new, dissenting, or qualifying interpretations of Christ that might emerge in different aspects of contemporary Christian experience, shedding new light on what the controlling formulation protects. Can the twentieth-century christological "dogma" of the revelatory humanity of Jesus be complemented by a creative reaffirmation of Jesus' divinity, one that likewise arises from and is validated by spiritual and moral experience, that is validated in the New Testament's plural Christologies, and that reclaims aspects of a Logos Christology?

Karl Rahner's and Roger Haight's proposals that Christologies from above and below are complementary paves the way to take another look at mutually critical views of Christ, in feminist liberation theology, for example. Elisabeth Schüssler Fiorenza[37] and Elizabeth Johnson are foremost among those who have invoked the identification of Jesus with Wisdom or its Greek equivalent Sophia to counteract patriarchal appropriations of Jesus and salvation. Johnson specifically argues that a christological distortion occurs when Jesus' mediation of divinity and his salvific power are linked in an essential way with his human maleness.

In other words, the reality of the earthly Jesus of Nazareth, even if he is empowered and empowers us by God's Spirit, needs to be transcended in an interpretation of Jesus that relativizes his human characteristics without ever denying them. In Johnson's view, a problem with so-called traditional Christologies was not that they denied or underplayed Jesus' humanity but that they made it normative in the wrong way. Hence, "the fact that Jesus was a man is construed to strengthen not only a patriarchal notion of God but also an androcentric anthropology," in which the male sex is accorded special dignity and an exclusive right to represent Christ in the ordained priesthood and on the altar. Men are supposedly by nature "Christomorphic" or capable of imaging Christ in a way that is impossible, by nature, for women. Women's redemption is even implicitly put in jeopardy, since, according to the early Christian saying, "what is not assumed is not redeemed."[38]

The grip of androcentric Christology is broken by going beyond the historical reality of the man Jesus of Nazareth, drawing on other images in Bible and tradition, and expanding his meaning for believers. This "expansive" movement begins even within the New Testament, as early believers search for ways to say that their experience of salvation in Christ comes from God. Refusing to "collapse the totality of the Christ into the human man Jesus, biblical metaphors such as the Pauline body of Christ (1 Cor. 12:12–27) and the Johannine branches abiding in the vine (John 15:1–11) expand the reality of Christ to include potentially all of redeemed humanity."[39] Shedding special light on the fact that Jesus is Christ by virtue of a unity in his person of divine and human (male and female) is the New Testament association of Jesus with the personification of God as Lady Wisdom (see 1 Cor. 1:22–24; and Matt. 11:19, especially, where the reference to Wisdom is most overt).

Wisdom Christology is not necessarily a "preexistence Christology," but it is a Christology from above. Its key referent is not the man Jesus of Nazareth as such but an experience of relation to God made possible in and through Jesus as a human incarnation of the divine. Wisdom Christology challenges and corrects an "experiential" interpretation of Christ that stays too close to the parameters of his particular human embodiment. An inauthentic Christology from below misrepresents the reality of the Christ event by making maleness as crucial to the identity of the Christ as it is to that of the man Jesus.

All experiences (and doctrines) of Jesus Christ are limited and prone to distort the mysterious reality of God. Jesus has a transcendent and universal significance (whether or not an exclusive significance) that, along with his historical particularity and humanity, is a valid and necessary referent for Christology. The larger sense of incarnation gives a proper perspective to the Christian relationship to God, relations to others, and to the connections between our love of God and right relations with our neighbors. Biblical imagery for Jesus that goes above and beyond his historical reality can nourish a spiritual orientation and a practical commitment to challenge provisional explanations of Jesus' meaning that rely too heavily on human limits, customs, and expectations.

Sin

Because the christological orthodoxy of today affirms a central place for human liberation from historical conditions of suffering, it has decentered the Anselmian view that salvation is to be understood as redemption from the penalty of sin, won by the death of the God-man on the cross. The Anselmian view has had unfortunate effects that need to be overcome: "spiritualizing" salvation, accepting or even glorifying suffering on this earth as a participation in Christ's sacrifice, and — most problematic — finding the cause of human suffering in the sin of those who suffer. The interpretation of the crucified Christ as the embodiment of God's solidarity has had the positive effect of consoling, encouraging, and empowering the oppressed; of challenging the status quo that causes suffering; and of calling those who cooperate with oppressive institutions to account and to conversion.

Strikingly, however, not all the "victims" of historical oppression are as eager to eliminate the understanding that Christ died for our sins as are some liberation theologians and ethicists. Jacquelyn Grant quotes an old slave woman, who with nothing to offer him, implores Jesus to come to her people. She remembers how he carried his cross up Calvary for them. She promises that if Jesus visits the slaves, they will "pick out de torn, de prickles, de brier, de backslidin' and de quarrel and de sin out of you path so dey shan't hurt Ooner pierce feet no more." Though they have not even cool water to offer, they "gwine to take de 'munion cup and fill it wid de tear of repentance, and love clean out of we heart. Dat all we hab to gib you, good Massa."[40]

Enslavers of any stripe, having been resistant to recognizing their own sin, may with good reason avoid Christologies and soteriologies that ascribe basic sinfulness to those whom they have wronged. It is true nonetheless that the Christian tradition has always upheld the universality of sin.[41] Sin means domination, violence, and "massive dehumanization" — but it also and as pervasively means the "major and minor ways we sabotage our personal relationships and fail those who would love us without reserve."[42] Remarking the ways Christian conceptions of sin have been used to denigrate women, Serene Jones still believes "the much disdained topic of sin" has "great resonance with feminist theory."[43] "At the heart of the Christian story lies this insistence that sin is pervasive in scope, debilitating in force, and stubbornly persistent."[44] She enumerates the mundane ways in which even those who are the victims of structural sin perpetuate the evil fruit of oppression in destructive actions provoked by the very institutions against which they struggle.[45] Ultimately the Christian doctrine of sin is a way to affirm a transformation that comes from outside our experience and is capable of transforming what human beings seem unable to resist. The theology of sin nurtures our awareness of grace, strengthens our faith, and prompts us in love.[46]

Cynthia Crysdale voices a theology of the cross from the perspective of those in the grip of "inner demons" created by abuse or addiction. Even when suffering has "external" causes, persons are often complicit in their own suffering and that of others. Therefore, it is important to understand how the cross brings redemption and empowerment as a response to our own sin as well as to that of "oppressors." God's love is necessary for redemption, but so is the conversion of human freedom. The death of Jesus, "accepted by Jesus in union with God's will," shows that God does not solve the problem of evil by circumventing or "dominating" human freedom. Jesus accepted his suffering as the price of love and faithfulness, he did not choose it. What God accepted was the possibility that his offer of relationship and communication, made in Jesus, could be rejected. Thus, "to follow Jesus means embracing pain, choosing to love, forgiving others, letting go of justice as revenge." For one to become "an agent of God's communication," one must resist sin in all its forms but at the same time be willing realistically to accept that the process of salvation follows the crucified Christ and does not exclude Christ's suffering.[47]

Discussing the fact that substitutionary theories of the atonement have become virtually obsolete in contemporary Christology, and perhaps even more so in spirituality, Mark Heim comments that "Most people are no more likely to regard Christ as a sin-offering who removes our guilt than they are to consider sacrificing oxen on an altar in the neighborhood playground as a way to keep their children safe."[48] Still, when all transactional elements have been subtracted to create "atonement lite," major parts of scripture and tradition remain unappropriated.[49] As Paul writes to the Romans, "There is no distinction; all have sinned." Yet all are justified "through the redemption in Christ Jesus, whom God set forth as an expiation, through faith, by his blood" (Rom. 5:24–25). Such texts are not easy to interpret, and they do not necessarily require all that Anselm proposed. Still, while the sacrificial images of Christian faith may need to be reinterpreted, they are too central and too provocative to be abandoned. Just how best to accomplish this at this point remains a standing challenge of the tradition to the new Christologies (and spiritualities) of liberation and social change.

Spirituality

Far from being a unique, personal, even interior relationship to divinity, Christian spirituality is an experience of God formed in community and expressed in action. Spirituality, as active, practical love of God, is intimately connected to love of neighbor, though not identical with it.[50] Christology is essential for spirituality because the former provides the images and understandings of God that contour worship, prayer, and mode of action. According to Roger Haight, "Christology is not only the center of Christian self-understanding and understanding of all reality, it is the ground of Christian spirituality which in its most elementary form is a conception of the Christian life."[51]

Christologies focused on the historical Jesus, so crucial for liberation and feminist theologies, mediate a God whose reign is concretized through the surprising images of the prodigal Son's Father, the Good Samaritan, and the woman caught in adultery who is forgiven by Jesus. Prayer to and worship of a merciful, forgiving, compassionate, generous God whose love overturns human standards can form Christians for action that serves, includes, and empowers those who have suffered domination and violence.

William Spohn entitles a book on spirituality and ethics, *Go and Do Likewise,* recalling the instruction Jesus gave, after telling the parable of the Good Samaritan, to the young man who asked, "Who is my neighbor?" (Luke 10:29–37).[52] According to Spohn, "those who engage in the practices of intercessory prayer, meditation on scripture, discernment, baptism, and Eucharist do so to deepen their friendship with God. As they do, they will see that these practices necessarily imply 'a life worthy of the gospel.' "[53] The connection between biblical stories and ethics is made by thinking analogically within a community whose spiritual and liturgical practices train members in discernment. Christian moral reflection considers the biblical text in relation to its world, and draws an analogy to today's Christian community in relation to its own world.[54] Christians do not always do exactly what is illustrated or commended in biblical narratives, but they do what will have a similar key meaning and effect. Spiritual practices reinforce the association of biblical images and the Christian's disposition to act in a certain way. The Lord's Supper or Eucharist is identified as the spiritual practice that above all fosters a relational identification with Christ. Those who "share the life and table of Jesus" should create a fellowship that includes sinners and outcasts. The fact that elitism and divisions in the church so often occur is to be expected, given that the same thing happens in the New Testament (e.g., Gal. 2:12–13, or 1 Cor. 11: 17–22). This reminds us that forgiveness and solidarity, especially with the poor, are also part of the meaning of Eucharistic practice.[55]

Bruce Morrill has developed the significance of liturgy for ethical formation, using the political theology of Johann Baptist Metz. Morrill uses the term *anamnesis* (from the Greek biblical word, *anamnesin*) to refer to eucharistic sharing as an event of active remembering and reappropriation of Christ's salvific act.[56] Participation in the Eucharist keeps alive — indeed continues to live out — "the Christian faith as the dangerous memory of

Christ's passion, death, and resurrection."[57] This living memory has political consequences. The Christian who is poor or oppressed or who is in solidarity with those so placed "experiences the acute absence of God" in the sinfulness of the situation. Since human suffering "contrasts negatively with the divine love for humanity one has known in prayer, liturgy and contemplation," the Christian acts to end or resist injustice and alienation.[58]

Morrill notes that the base communities of the poor in the Third World celebrate the word of God by reflecting on texts in relation to their own experienced struggles. Thus their social sufferings are assimilated into their liturgies and become part of an integrated narrative of the Christian life. Experiences of suffering are brought into contact with and transformed in light of the "mystical" dimensions of worship and liturgy, those dimensions in which the immanence and transcendence of a personal, loving, and redeeming God are experienced.[59] Perhaps the "crisis" both of faith and of liturgical meaningfulness in European and North American Christianity is due at least partly to the fact that Christian institutions and practices have grown too remote from the practical Christian message:

> Christians need to know a way of living in relation to God, humanity, and all creation that can transform what they — due to arrogance, selfishness, indifference, resignation, or despair — already know and take for granted about the way the world is.... In other words, giving oneself over to the radical otherness, the transcendent, messianic, and eschatological content of the liturgy, changes the way one perceives and prioritizes all aspects of life — interpersonal, economic, familial, political.[60]

Liturgy should be inspired by and reenact the incarnation, which illumines the world as created to participate in the life of God (the Logos), and whose brokenness is redeemed in union with Jesus Christ. Sin hides the true life of the world. Communal worship also participates in and reveals life in the kingdom of God as made possible by union with the risen Christ, beginning with the church, extending through Christian action into society, and anticipating fulfillment in a world to come, a culmination of history that breaks in from beyond it.[61]

In Conclusion

Recent liberationist movements act in Christian faith on the experience of a God who not only judges but redeems and transforms human suffering. They challenge Christology to incorporate, as central elements, the inbreaking of God in the earthly ministry of Jesus, his cross, and his resurrection, as experienced by the first Christians and recounted in the gospels. In turn, certain traditional formulations of Christian faith, also grounded in authentic experiences of God, provide resources for a continual renewal of Christology, spirituality, and ethics. Today these include breaking the boundaries of an exaggerated focus on the male characteristics of Jesus as mediating salvation and a resurgence of interest in the significance of Christ's sacrificial death as part of human redemption from sin.

A key function of a Christology from above is to moderate or sublimate emphasis on the historical particularity of Jesus. The Second Person of the trinity, Son of God, and Word are metaphors or images of divinity that capture what is not reducible to that person. A key function of a Christology from below is to refocus christological faith on the realities of human existence shared by Christ. These two approaches are always in creative tension, if not balance. Perhaps the reason Christianity has an authoritative scripture as its foundational text, rather than an authoritative systematic theology, is that scripture comprises a richness of symbolic and metaphorical meaning that better conveys the mystery of God and the profound complexity of human experience. Scripture challenges both the average believer and the theologians to live and think within its creative tensions, ambiguities, and facets. Therefore, different New Testament Christologies and different historical interpretations can continue to serve as hermeneutical resources, even if it is true that these different imaginative and conceptual "explanations" cannot easily be reduced to common terms.

Both types of Christology can be useful in addressing social concerns and the need for spiritualities that nourish social commitment as well as religious experience. One new direction in feminist and liberationist Christology is the redemption of the planet from the ecological devastation wrought by human sinfulness. How does this challenge current Christologies and prompt the renewal of more traditional ones? First of all, environmental concern arises from human experience. Turning to Christian resources to address it, we might employ a Christology from below. We could draw on imagery of the human Jesus telling parables replete with references to nature or healing the human body or interacting with the sea of Galilee, the wheat fields, and the local plains and hills.

On the other side, new Christologies from above might inquire how to imagine and symbolize a participation of creation in God through Christ, analogous to the participation of humanity in divinity through Jesus Christ's personal union of two natures. As has been remarked already, Chalcedon did not spell out the precise manner and mode of this union, nor what it meant experientially for Jesus. Moreover, the basic insight of Nicea is that Jesus Christ is not one among other "creatures." This means that the meaning of Jesus as the Christ is not constrained by the limits of what one could say if one were to focus only on a human being as such (the man Jesus of Nazareth). It implies that the divinity of Jesus, imaged in language reflecting the Prologue to John's Gospel (only-begotten Son, one in being with the Father) expands in some way beyond and before the Christ event, as a specific manifestation of God in history.

Why not develop theologically the "Christic" and redemptive presence of God in the natural world in general, as well as in humanity?[62] Beyond the creation of human beings, John says that "all things" came into being through the Word that was with God "from the beginning" (John 1:2–3). Johannine imagery of God as the Word through which all creation comes into being and which is present within the creation in history can be combined with imagery of Wisdom as present at the beginning of creation (Prov. 3:19; 8:22–31) and active throughout all creation (Wisd. 8:1). Also contributing to a Christology that goes beyond the man Jesus to see God's redemptive presence through Christ in the creation is Pauline imagery of creation awaiting salvation in Christ. According to Paul, even "the creation waits with eager longing for the revealing of the children of God" (Rom. 8:19); "the whole creation has been groaning in labor pains until now" (Rom. 8:22). Through Christ, "the creation itself will be set free from its bondage to decay and will obtain the freedom of the glory of the children of God" (Rom. 8:21). If creation is to obtain the glory of God's children, perhaps the divine is redemptively united with it in a way analogous to (not the same as) the union of divine and human in Christ. Though these few suggestions about Christology and ecology are loose ends and threads rather than positions or conclusions, I hope they may exemplify or stimulate the kind of new thinking about Christ — from below and above — that both responds to and challenges the experiences of contemporary Christians. These and other richly hued threads wait to be woven into a creative new christological perspective. The tapestry of Christology, spirituality, and practice will no doubt be as rich and colorful in the twenty-first century as it has been in the past.

For Further Reflection

1. What is Christology from below vs. Christology from above?

2. How do the abstract terms of Christology relate to practical ethics and to spirituality?

3. Why and how is the issue of *suffering* a problem for Christology? What approaches to the problem does the author propose?

4. What, to your mind, should be the social importance of the christological framework we choose?

5. What advantages and disadvantages does the author find in retrieving a Christology from above?

For Further Reading

Cahill, Lisa Sowle. *Sex, Gender, and Christian Ethics.* Cambridge and New York: Cambridge University Press, 1996.

Crysdale, Cynthia S. W. *Embracing Travail: Retrieving the Cross Today.* New York: Continuum, 2001.

Johnson, Elizabeth A. *She Who Is: The Mystery of God in Feminist Theological Discourse.* New York: Crossroad, 1994.

Solberg, Mary. *Compelling Knowledge: A Feminist Proposal for an Epistemology of the Cross.* Albany: State University of New York Press, 1997.

Spohn, William C. *Go and Do Likewise: Jesus and Ethics.* New York: Continuum, 1999.

Notes

Preface

1. Cited in Philip Hefner, "Modern and Postmodern Forms of Unbelief," *Christian Century* (January 26, 2000): 89. The Nobel laureate in physics and recipient of the National Medal of Science, Steven Weinberg, made this comment in a speech to the American Association for the Advancement of Science in 1999.

Chapter 1. Thinking of Christ (Tatha Wiley)

1. On creeds, see J. N. D. Kelly, *Early Christian Creeds,* 3rd ed. (New York: David McKay, 1972).

2. Two of the most significant councils for Christology were the Councils of Nicea in 325 C.E. and Chalcedon in 451 C.E. See Christopher M. Bellitto, *The General Councils: A History of the Twenty-One Church Councils from Nicaea to Vatican II* (New York: Paulist Press, 2000), esp. 17–34.

3. In Bernard Lonergan's terms, this development requires a differentiation of consciousness, a shift from commonsense apprehension to theory. See Bernard J. F. Lonergan, S.J., *Method in Theology* (New York: Herder and Herder, 1972), 335–53 and 235–66.

4. Ibid., 347; cf. 350.

5. See Reinhold Niebuhr's now-classic work, *Moral Man and Immoral Society: A Study in Ethics and Politics* (New York: Charles Scribner's Sons, 1932). Also his *magnum opus, The Nature and Destiny of Man,* vols. 1 and 2 (New York: Charles Scribner's Sons, 1941–43).

6. Larry Rasmussen, ed., *Reinhold Niebuhr: Theologian of Public Life* (Minneapolis: Fortress Press, 1991), 19.

7. Ibid.

8. "Slaves, obey your earthly masters with fear and trembling, in singleness of heart, as you obey Christ: not only while being watched, and in order to please them, but as slaves of Christ, doing the will of God from the heart" (Eph. 6:5–6). See also Colossians 3:18 and 1 Timothy 6:1–2. These texts also portray resistance to gender domination as sin. In 1 Timothy, see 2:11–14. On slavery in the ancient world, a seminal book is Orlando Patterson, *Slavery and Social Death* (Cambridge, Mass.: Harvard University Press, 1982).

9. Elizabeth A. Johnson, *She Who Is: The Mystery of God in Feminist Theological Discourse* (New York: Crossroad, 1992), 23.

10. Ibid., 157. Inclusive of women as well as men, Jesus "widens the circle of the friends of God to include the most devalued people, even tax collectors, sinners, and prostitutes ... women interact with Jesus in mutual respect, support, comfort, and challenge."

11. Sandra M. Schneiders, *The Revelatory Text: Interpreting the New Testament as Sacred Scripture* (San Francisco: HarperSanFrancisco, 1991), 175.

12. For a brief account of the development of modern biblical scholarship, see Robert L. Wilken, "The Bible and Its Interpreters: Christian Biblical Interpretation," in *Harper's Bible Commentary*, ed. James L. Mays (San Francisco: Harper & Row, 1988), 63.

13. Scholarly agreement regarding the object of Jesus' preaching is noted in Gerd Theissen and Annette Merz, *The Historical Jesus: A Comprehensive Guide* (Minneapolis: Fortress Press, 1998), 240.

14. See, for example, the discussion of *basileia* in Stephen Patterson, *The God of Jesus: The Historical Jesus and the Search for Meaning* (Harrisburg, Pa.: Trinity Press International, 1998), 60.

15. Walter Wink, *The Powers That Be: Theology for a New Millennium* (New York: Doubleday, 1998), 39.

16. Matthew 5:3–12; Luke 6:20–23.

17. Walter Wink, *Engaging the Powers* (Minneapolis: Fortress Press, 1992), 107.

18. On the Christian characterization of Judaism as legalistic, see E. P. Sanders, *Jesus and Judaism* (Philadelphia: Fortress Press, 1985), 337–40.

19. John M. G. Barclay summarizes the history of interpretation in *Obeying the Truth: Paul's Ethics in Galatians* (Minneapolis: Fortress Press, 1988), 3–8.

20. Ibid., 82.

21. Hans Dieter Betz, *Galatians,* Hermeneia (Philadelphia: Fortress Press, 1979), 184–85.

22. Mary C. Boys, *Has God Only One Blessing? Judaism as a Source of Christian Self-Understanding* (New York: Paulist Press, 2000), 10–11.

23. The new perspective was initiated by the seminal article of Krister Stendahl, "The Apostle Paul and the Introspective Conscience of the West," *Harvard Theological Review* 56 (1963): 199–215. A major contribution to the new perspective was E. P. Sanders, *Paul and Palestinian Judaism* (Philadelphia: Fortress Press, 1977) and Sanders's other works: *Jesus and Judaism* (Philadelphia: Fortress Press, 1976); idem, *Paul, the Law, and the Jewish People;* and idem, *Judaism, Practice and Belief, 63 BCE–66 CE* (Philadelphia: Trinity Press International, 1992). Central to the new perspective is the work of James D. G. Dunn. See, for example, James D. G. Dunn, *The Epistle to the Galatians,* Black's New Testament Commentary (Peabody, Mass.: Hendrickson Publishers, 1993); idem, "The Theology of Galatians," in *Pauline Theology,* ed. Jouette M. Bassler, vol. 1 (Minneapolis: Fortress Press, 1991); idem, *The Parting of the Ways* (Philadelphia: Trinity Press International, 1991); and idem, "The New Perspective on Paul," *Bulletin of the John Rylands Library* 65 (1983): 95–122. A summary is given by Frank J. Matera in "Galatians in Perspective," *Interpretation* 54, no. 3 (2000): 233–45.

24. Sanders, *Paul and Palestinian Judaism,* 59.

25. John T. Pawlikowski, O.S.M., "Christology, Anti-Semitism, and Christian-Jewish Bonding," in *Reconstructing Christian Theology*, ed. Rebecca S. Chopp and Mark Kline Taylor (Minneapolis: Fortress Press, 1994), 246.

26. Boys, *Has God Only One Blessing?* 19.

27. Sidney G. Hall III, *Christian Anti-Semitism and Paul's Theology* (Minneapolis: Fortress Press, 1993), x.

28. Johann-Baptist Metz, "Facing the Jews: Christian Theology After Auschwitz," in *The Holocaust as Interruption*, ed. Elisabeth Schüssler Fiorenza and David Tracy, *Concilium* (1984), 26–33. In this same volume, John Pawlikowski deals with postwar Christian interpretations of christological claims in "The Holocaust and Contemporary Christology," 43–49.

29. Rosemary Radford Ruether, *Sexism and God-Talk: Toward a Feminist Theology* (Boston: Beacon Press, 1983), 126.

30. Lonergan, *Method in Theology*, 116–17.

31. Ibid., 115–18.

32. Ibid., 240–44.

33. Bernard J. F. Lonergan, *Third Collection*, Part Two, Lectures on Religious Studies and Theology, "First Lecture: Religious Experience, 121–22. See also, *Method in Theology*, "Religion," 101–24.

Chapter 2. Jesus of Nazareth in Historical Research (Elisabeth Schüssler Fiorenza)

1. It would be too lengthy to list them here. For the discussion of the literature, see my book *Jesus: Miriam's Child, Sophia's Prophet: Critical Issues in Feminist Christology* (New York: Continuum, 1994).

2. N. T. Wright, "The Quest for the Historical Jesus," in *Anchor Bible Dictionary* 3 (1992), 800.

3. See, e.g., Alicia Suskin Ostriker, *Feminist Revision and the Bible* (Cambridge: Blackwell, 1993).

4. See James H. Charlesworth, "From Barren Mazes to Gentle Rappings: The Emergence of Jesus Research," *Princeton Seminary Bulletin* 7, no. 3 (1986): 221–30 with annotated bibliography.

5. I use this broken form to avoid an essentialist depiction of "woman." *Wo/man* here denotes not one simple reality, and I often use it to be equivalent to *people*.

6. *Kyriarchal*, derived from the Greek word for Lord, underscores that domination is not only gender-based but more comprehensive, in all kinds of hierarchical structures of oppression (racial, ethnic, economic, etc.)

7. *Androcentrism* means male-centered.

8. For the historical context of this rhetoric, see Roy A. Harrisville and Walter Sundberg, *The Bible in Modern Culture: Theology and Historical-Critical Method from Spinoza to Käsemann* (Grand Rapids, Mich.: Eerdmans, 1995).

9. Martin Kähler, *The So-Called Historical Jesus and the Historic, Biblical Christ*, trans. and ed. Carl Braaten (Philadelphia: Fortress, 1988).

10. This paper was published by Ernst Käsemann, "The Problem of the Historical Jesus," in his *Essays on New Testament Themes*, trans. W. J. Montague (London: SCM Press, 1964).

11. See Barry W. Henaut, "Is the 'Historical Jesus' a Christological Construct?" in *Whose Historical Jesus?* ed. William E. Arnal and Michel Desjardins (Waterloo, Ont.: Wilfrid Laurier University Press, 1997), 241–68.

12. Marcus J. Borg, *Jesus in Contemporary Scholarship* (Valley Forge: Trinity Press International, 1994), 4.

13. Norman Perrin, *Rediscovering the Teaching of Jesus* (New York: Harper & Row, 1967), 39f., who has labeled the criterion of exclusivity as the criterion of dissimilarity.

14. See, for instance, the dissertation of Helga Melzer Keller, *Jesus und die Frauen: Eine Verhältnisbestimmung nach den synoptischen Evangelien* (Freiburg: Herder, 1997), 440f: "In his sayings, Jesus accepted the patriarchal order as the norm — the traditional behavior patterns and forms weren't disputed or even remotely questioned by him in any way. Even though Jesus primarily sided with the downtrodden, the religiously marginalized, and the socially disadvantaged, he did not subscribe to a reform program or socially revolutionary action. We must draw the conclusion that he had no conscious objection to the unequal distribution of rights between the sexes. Jesus did not acknowledge legal and social discrimination against women or show interest in changing the status quo regarding them." The ideological interests of this text are obvious.

15. See for instance Amy-Jill Levine, "Second Temple Judaism, Jesus, and Women: Yeast of Eden," *Biblical Interpretation* 2 (1994): 8–33, who concedes a "feminist impulse" in Judaism but then in her argument against Luise Schottroff ["Itinerant Prophetesses: A Feminist Analysis of the Sayings Source Q," *Institute for Antiquity and Christianity, Claremont Graduate School Occasional Papers* 21 (1991) and idem, Wanderprophetinnen: Eine feministische Analyse der Logienquelle," *Evangelische Theologie* 51 (1991): 332–44] retreats from it. Instead of researching the emancipatory tendencies in first-century Judaism, she ends up trivializing the textual information and justifying patriarchal religion. See also Kathleen E. Corley, *Wo/men and the Historical Jesus: Feminist Myths of Christian Origins* (Santa Rosa, Calif.: Polebridge Press, 2002).

16. Coinage of the term Third Quest is attributed to Stephen Neill and Thomas Wright, *The Interpretation of the New Testament, 1861–1986* (Oxford: University Press, 1988), 379ff.

17. See the very helpful chart in Gerd Theissen and Annette Merz, *The Historical Jesus: A Comprehensive Guide* (Minneapolis: Fortress Press, 1998), 12.

18. I write G*d in this broken way to emphasize the inadequacy of our language for the divine.

19. For the intent of the Jesus Seminar and the controversy surrounding it, see Mark Allan Powell, *Jesus as a Figure in History: How Modern Historians View the Man from Galilee* (Louisville: Westminster John Knox Press, 1998), 65–82.

20. This hermeneutical circle between a preconstructed image of Jesus and evaluations of individual texts is recognized by Gerd Theissen and Dagmar Winter, *Die Kriterienfrage in der Jesusforschung. Vom Differenzkriterium zum Plausibilitätskriterium* (Göttingen: Vandenhoeck & Ruprecht, 1997), 206: "An applicable historical model is an ideal construction, a limit that we can only approach in the

form of plausibility." Yet they do not critically question the plausibility criterion itself on the basis of this insight.

21. See my *Jesus: Miriam's Child, Sophia's Prophet,* 5–12.

22. See the self-interview of Kwok Pui-Lan, "On Color-Coding Jesus: An Interview with Kwok Pui-Lan," in *The Postcolonial Bible,* ed. R. S. Sugirtharajah (Sheffield: Sheffield Academic Press, 1998), 176–89.

23. Dieter Georgi, "The Interest in Life of Jesus Theology as a Paradigm for the Social History of Biblical Criticism," *Harvard Theological Review* 85, no. 1 (1992): 51–83.

24. Ibid., 76.

25. Ibid., 83.

26. Sandra Harding, *The Science Question in Feminism* (Ithaca, N.Y.: Cornell University Press, 1986), 218, with reference to Edgar Zilsel, "The Sociological Roots of Science," *American Journal of Sociology* 47 (1942).

27. Harding, *Science Question,* 219.

28. Wolfgang van den Daele, "The Social Construction of Science," in *The Social Production of Scientific Knowledge,* ed. Everett Mendelsohn, Peter Weingart, and Richard Whitley (Dordrecht: Reidel, 1977), 38.

29. For such structuring dualisms in Q research, see the forthcoming dissertation of Melanie Johnson-DeBaufre. For a comprehensive interpretation of Q scholarship, see, e.g., Richard A. Horsley, *Whoever Hears You Hears Me: Prophets, Performance and Tradition in Q* (Harrisburg: Trinity Press International, 1999); and Burton L. Mack, *The Lost Gospel: The Book of Q and Christian Origins* (San Francisco: HarperCollins, 1993).

30. See Ronald T. Takaki, "Aesclepius Was a White Man: Race and the Cult of True Womanhood," in *The Racial Economy of Science: Toward a Democratic Future,* ed. Sandra Harding (Bloomington: Indiana University Press, 1993), 201–9; Nancy Leys Stepan and Sander L. Gilman, "Appropriating the Idioms of Science: The Rejection of Scientific Racism," ibid., 170–93; and Nancy Leys Stepan, "Race and Gender: The Role of Analogy in Science," ibid., 369–76.

31. Patricia Hill Collins, *Fighting Words: Black Women and the Search for Justice* (Minneapolis: University of Minnesota Press, 1998), 100–101.

32. Shawn Kelley, *Racializing Jesus: Race, Ideology and the Formation of Modern Biblical Scholarship* (New York: Routledge, 2002), 3.

33. Ibid., 65–66.

34. Kwok, Pui-Lan, "Jesus the Native: Biblical Studies from a Postcolonial Perspective," in *Teaching the Bible: The Discourses and Politics of Biblical Pedagogy,* ed. Fernando Segovia and Mary Ann Tolbert (Maryknoll, N.Y.: Orbis Books, 1998), 76.

35. Grant LeMarquand, "The Historical Jesus and African New Testament Scholarship," in *Whose Historical Jesus?* 161–80.

36. See, for instance, *Women and Christian Origins,* ed. Ross Shepard Kraemer and Mary Rose D'Angelo (New York: Oxford University Press, 1999), for such an approach. They rework most of the materials in my prior work (see note 39 below) in terms of the study of women, gender, and religion. Since they know the broad influence of the first book, it is unfathomable how they can go on to state: "To date, no one has written a comprehensive treatment of wo/men and Christian origins

appropriate for a wide audience ranging from undergraduate to general readers to scholars previously unacquainted with this literature" (3).

37. William Arnal, "Making and Re-Making the Jesus-Sign: Contemporary Markings on the Body of Christ," in *Whose Historical Jesus?* 317.

38. See Elisabeth Schüssler Fiorenza, "Jesus and the Politics of Interpretation," *Harvard Theological Review* 90, no. 4 (1997): 343–58.

39. See Elisabeth Schüssler Fiorenza, *In Memory of Her: A Feminist Theological Reconstruction of Christian Origins,* 10th anniversary edition (New York: Crossroad, 1983, 1994), 102; idem, *Bread Not Stone: The Challenge of Feminist Biblical Interpretation,* 10th anniversary edition (Boston: Beacon Press, 1984, 1995), 114–15.

40. For the impact of such reading, see Janice A. Radway, *Reading the Romance: Women, Patriarchy, and Popular Literature* (Chapel Hill: University of North Carolina Press, 1991).

41. See Bruce Chilton and Jacob Neusner, *Judaism in the New Testament: Practices and Beliefs* (New York: Routledge, 1995), 10–18, for a critique of E. P. Sanders's *Judaism: Practice and Belief, 63 BCE–66 CE* (Philadelphia: Trinity Press International, 1992) and its construct of a single unitary Judaism attested by a coherent canon.

42. Elisabeth Schüssler Fiorenza, "Jesus — Messenger of Divine Wisdom," *Studia Theologica* 49 (1995): 231–52.

43. See Barbara H. Geller Nathanson, "Toward a Multicultural Ecumenical History of Women in the First Century/ies C.E.," in *Searching the Scriptures: A Feminist Introduction,* ed. Elisabeth Schüssler Fiorenza, vol. 1 (New York: Crossroad, 1993), 272–89.

44. Jacob Neusner, *Jews and Christians: The Myth of a Common Tradition* (Philadelphia: SCM/Trinity Press, 1991). See also Arthur Cohen, *The Myth of the Judeo-Christian Tradition* (New York: Harper & Row, 1969).

45. Alan Segal, *Rebecca's Children: Judaism and Christianity in the Roman World* (Cambridge, Mass.: Harvard University Press, 1987).

46. For such a (deliberate?) misreading see Ross Kraemer's reviews of *In Memory of Her* in *Religious Studies Review* 11, no. 1 (1985): 107 and in *Journal of Biblical Literature* 104, no. 4 (1985): 722. See also my response to her in the introduction to the 10th anniversary edition of the book.

47. For a comprehensive review of the meaning of this expression in Judaism of the time, see Anna Maria Schwemer, "Gott als König und seine Königsherrschaft" in *Königsherrschaft Gottes und himmlischer Kult in Judentum, Urchristentum und in der hellenistischen Welt,* ed. Martin Hengel and Anna Maria Schwemer (Tübingen: J. C. B. Mohr, 1991), 45–118. For the discussion of the *basileia* discourse in early Christianity, see Helmut Merkel, "Die Gottesherrschaft in der Verkündigung Jesu," ibid., 119–61. See also Marinus De Jonge, "The Christological Significance of Jesus' Preaching of the Kingdom of God," in *The Future of Christology: Essays in Honor of Leander E. Keck,* ed. Abraham J. Malherbe and Wayne A Meeks (Minneapolis: Fortress Press, 1993), 7: "Notwithstanding the intrinsic difficulties in reconstructing Jesus' message concerning the kingdom, there is a surprising consensus" in

understanding it as meaning "the time and place where God's power and kingly rule will hold sway."

48. For this expression, see Norman Perrin, *Jesus and the Language of the Kingdom* (Philadelphia: Fortress Press, 1976).

49. For a similar account see also Alan F. Segal, "Jesus, the Jewish Revolutionary," in *Jesus' Jewishness: Exploring the Place of Jesus within Early Judaism*, ed. James H. Charlesworth (New York: Crossroad, 1991), 212–14.

50. Schüssler Fiorenza, *In Memory of Her*, 148.

51. Jacquelyn Grant, "The Sin of Servanthood and the Deliverance of Discipleship," in *A Troubling in My Soul: Womanist Perspectives on Evil and Suffering*, ed. Emilie M. Townes (Maryknoll, N.Y.: Orbis Books, 1993), 199–218 and I have problematized servanthood and emphasized discipleship in very similar ways, although we come from quite different social and religious backgrounds. Since Grant does not refer to my theoretical analysis [see my article " 'Waiting at Table': A Critical Feminist Theological Reflection on Diakonia," *Concilium* 198 (1988): 84–94; and my book *Discipleship of Equals: A Critical Feminist Ekklesia-logy of Liberation* (New York: Crossroad, 1993), 290–306], I feel justified in surmising that a comparable multiplicative analysis of kyriarchy results in coinciding theoretical proposals.

52. See Elisabeth Schüssler Fiorenza, *But She Said: Feminist Practices of Biblical Interpretation* (Boston: Beacon Press, 1992).

53. See Robert Holst, "The Anointing of Jesus: Another Application of the Form-Critical Method," *Journal of Biblical Literature* 95 (1976): 35–46; Claus-Peter März, "Zur Traditionsgeschichte von Mk 14,3–9 und Parallelen," *New Testament Studies* 67 (1981–82): 89–112; for a general bibliography on the Passion Narratives, see Raymond E. Brown, *The Death of the Messiah* (New York: Doubleday, 1994), 94–106.

54. See, for instance, the fresco at Dura Europos for the importance of prophetic anointing. See also Warren G. Moon, "Nudity and Narrative: Observations on the Frescoes from the Dura Synagogue," *Journal of the American Academy of Religion* 40 (1992): 587–658.

55. For a discussion of Mark's account, see Marie Sabin, "Women Transformed: The Ending of Mark Is the Beginning of Wisdom," *Cross Currents* 48 (1998): 149–68; Monika Fander, *Die Stellung der Frau im Markusevangelium unter besonderer Berücksichtigung kultur- und religionsgeschichtlicher Hintergründe* (Altenberge: Telos Verlag, 1989), 118–35; for Matthew, see the excellent analysis of Elaine M. Wainwright, *Towards a Feminist Critical Reading of the Gospel according to Matthew*, Beihefte zur Zeitschrift für die neutestamentliche Wissenschaft 60 (Berlin: Walter de Gruyter, 1991), 252–83.

56. Vernon K. Robbins, "Using a Socio-Rhetorical Poetics to Develop a Unified Method: The Woman Who Anointed Jesus as a Test Case," *Society of Biblical Literature Seminar Papers* 31 (1992): 311.

57. James Brownson, "Neutralizing the Intimate Enemy: The Portrayal of Judas in the Fourth Gospel," In *Society of Biblical Literature 1992 Seminar Papers*, ed. Eugene H. Lovering (Atlanta: Scholars Press, 1992), 49–60.

Chapter 3. Classical Christology (William P. Loewe)

1. *Ep.* X, 96.
2. For one survey of primitive Christian creedal patterns, see E. Schillebeeckx, *Jesus: An Experiment in Christology,* trans. H. Hoskins (New York: Seabury, 1979), 404–37.
3. For the analysis that follows, see Bernard Lonergan, *The Way to Nicea,* trans. C. O'Donovan (Philadelphia: Westminster, 1976).
4. For a popular narrative of the Arian controversy, see Richard E. Rubenstein, *When Jesus Became God* (New York: Harcourt Brace, 1999).
5. This account relies chiefly on Aloys Grillmeier, *Christ and Christian Tradition,* vol. 1: *From the Apostolic Age to Chalcedon (451),* trans. J. Bowden (Atlanta: John Knox Press, 1975).
6. R. V. Sellers, *The Council of Chalcedon* (London: SPCK, 1953), 82 n. 6.
7. Norman J. Tanner, English editor, *Decrees of the Ecumenical Councils,* vol. 1 (Nicaea I–Lateran V).(London: Sheed and Ward; Washington, D.C.: Georgetown University Press, 1990), 86.
8. John C. Cavadini, *The Last Christology of the West: Adoptionism in Spain and Gaul, 785–820* (Philadelphia: University of Pennsylvania Press, 1991).
9. See A. Grillmeier, with T. Hainthaler, *Christ in Christian Tradition,* vol. 2, part 2, *The Church of Constantinople in the Sixth Century,* trans. P. Allen and J. Cawte (Louisville: Westminster John Knox, 1995), 282.
10. Thomas Aquinas, *Summa Theologiae,* IIIa, q. 9, art. 4.
11. Ibid., q. 12, art. 4.
12. Ibid., q.14., art. 4; q. 46, art. 5.
13. Ibid., q. 47, art. 2.
14. Karl Rahner, "Current Problems in Christology," *Theological Investigations,* vol. 1, trans. C. Ernst (Baltimore: Helicon Press, 1961), 149–200.
15. Raymond E. Brown, "How Much Did Jesus Know?" *Jesus God and Man* (New York: Macmillan, 1967), 39–102.
16. Schillebeeckx, *Christ.*
17. Hans Küng, *On Being a Christian,* trans. E. Quinn (Garden City, N.Y.: Doubleday, 1976).
18. Walter Kasper, *Jesus the Christ,* trans. V. Green (New York: Paulist, 1976).
19. John Galvin, "From the Humanity of Christ to the Historical Jesus: A Paradigm Shift for Catholic Christology," *Theological Studies* 55 (1994): 252–73.
20. Karl Rahner, *Foundations of Christian Faith: An Introduction to the Idea of Christianity,* trans. W. Dych (New York: Seabury, 1978), 206–28.
21. Bernard Lonergan, "Christology Today: Methodological Reflections," in *A Third Collection: Papers by Bernard J. F. Lonergan, S.J.,* ed. F. Crowe (New York: Paulist, 1985), 74–99.
22. Piet Schoonenberg, "From a Two-nature Christology to a Christology of Presence," in *Christian Action and Openness to the World,* ed. J. Papin, vols. 2–3, the Villanova Theological Symposia (Villanova, Pa.: Villanova University Press, 1970), 219–43; Piet Schoonenberg, "God and Man," *The Christ,* trans. D. Couling (New York: Herder and Herder, 1971), 105–75.

23. Roger Haight, *Jesus, Symbol of God* (Maryknoll, N.Y.: Orbis Books, 1999), 273–98.

24. Lonergan, "Christology Today," 95; John Wright, "Roger Haight's Spirit Christology," *Theological Studies* 53 (1992): 729–35.

Chapter 4. Christ and Redemption (Gerard S. Sloyan)

1. John 4:42, uniquely in the New Testament.

2. Luke 2:38; 21:28; Romans 3:24; 8:23; 1 Corinthians 1:30; Colossians 1:14; the deutero-Pauline Ephesians 1:7, 14; 4:30; Hebrews 9:12.

3. Luke 19:9; John 4:22; Romans 1:16; 11:11; 13:11, and nine other places in Paul's correspondence; five times in the deutero-Pauline writings and fourteen elsewhere in the New Testament.

4. See Ruth 4:7–9.

5. Numbers 35:19.

6. Luke 1:68.

7. Luke 1:69.

8. Job 19:25.

9. Psalm 78:35.

10. Hebrews 9:15.

11. Romans 3:23–25.

12. See Exodus 25:17.

13. See Leviticus 23:2, 14–16.

14. Hebrews 9:12.

15. 1 Peter 1:18–19.

16. See 1 Corinthians 1:30.

17. Colossians 1:20; Ephesians 2:16.

18. See Romans 1:3–4.

19. "My great one," John 1:38; Mark 9:5.

20. See Isaiah 53:12; cf. Wisdom of Solomon 3:12–20.

21. Hebrews 1:2–3.

22. 1 Thessalonians 1:9–10.

23. 5:10.

24. See Romans 7:17.

25. See Galatians 3:19.

26. For a good account of the find, see Bruce M. Metzger, *The Canon of the New Testament: Its Origin, Development and Significance* (New York: Oxford University Press, 1987), 191–201.

27. *To the Ephesians,* 20.1; cf. *Smyrnaeans,* 12.2; *Philadelphians* 8.2; 9.2.

28. *Smyrnaeans,* 6.1; Christ's "flesh and blood," *Trallians,* 8.1; *Romans,* 7.3.

29. *1 Clement,* 36.1; cf. 61.3; the title "high priest" is found also in Ignatius, *To the Philadelphians,* 9.1; Polycarp, 12.2.

30. *To Diognetus,* 9.2. For this, 1 Clement above, and the four citations below, see C. C. Richardson, ed., *Early Christian Fathers* (New York: Macmillan, 1996).

31. *The First Apology of Justin, the Martyr,* ed. J. P. Migne, *Patrologia Graeca* VI; trans. and ed. E. R. Hardy in Richardson, *Early Christian Fathers,* 225–89.

220

Notes to Pages 69–73

32. *The Apocryphon of James,* 6.1–5a, ed. James M. Robinson, *The Nag Hammadi Library in English,* 3rd rev. ed. (San Francisco: Harper & Row, 1988), 32.

33. *The Gospel of Truth,* 26.5, p. 44.

34. Ibid., 16.35, p. 40.

35. See Book I, 1–3, 10–11, 21, 27, of the popularly titled *Adversus Haereses* since only a Latin translation is extant, with snatches of Greek available in Hippolytus, Epiphanius, and other church fathers.

36. *The Apocryphon of John,* II, 15, in Robinson, *Nag Hammadi Library,* 113–15.

37. *The Tripartite Tractate,* Part III, 14. in ibid., 94–95.

38. Ibid., 13, 116, 30.

39. *The Hypostasis of the Archons,* II, 92.18–32, in ibid., 167.

40. *The (First) Apocalypse of James* V.24.15; 33.1, 20–22; 34.1–20, in ibid., 264, 265–66.

41. *The Refutation and Overthrow of the Knowledge Falsely So Called,* V.1–3; 2.2–3; trans. E. R. Hardy in Richardson, *Early Christian Fathers.*

42. Romans 5:12–21; 1 Corinthians 15:20–22, 45–49.

43. *The Refutation* (or *Against Heresies*), V.19; 20.2; 21.

44. *On Repentance,* 7.14.

45. See 5.9.

46. *On Modesty,* 22.4.

47. *Commentary on Matthew 16:8,* at 13.9.

48. Origen, *On First Principles* (*Perì Archō*), trans. Paul Koetschau and G. W. Butterworth; Henri de Lubac, Introduction to the Torchbook Edition (New York: Harper & Row, 1966).

49. Ibid., Book I, Chapter III.8, pp. 38–39.

50. Romans 8:30.

51. *Catechetical Oration,* 22–24.

52. *A Commentary on the Apostle's Creed,* 16, trans. J. N. D. Kelly (Westminster, Md.: Newman Press, 1955), 51, 119–20.

53. *Against the Arians,* 2.61, as quoted by J. N. D. Kelly in *Early Christian Doctrines* (London: A. & C. Black, 1958), 379.

54. *On the Incarnation,* 27–32, Kelly, *Early Christian Doctrines.*

55. *Exposition of the Psalms,* 53.12–13.

56. *Exhortation to Chastity,* 2.5.

57. *Enchiridion on Faith, Hope and Love* 48, ed. and trans. Henry Paolucci (South Bend, Ind.: Regnery/Gateway, 1961).

58. For this development, see the present writer's *The Crucifixion of Jesus: History, Myth, Faith* (Minneapolis: Fortress Press, 1995), 112–14. The lengthy poem of Melito of Sardis, *On the Passion* (ca. 175) and the early Eastern and Roman Liturgies kept Christ's suffering, death, resurrection, and ascension as the one cause of human redemption, but Jesus' glorification did not survive in extraliturgical writings, leaving the cross alone.

59. See Vladimir Lossky, "Redemption and Deification" in *In The Image and Likeness of God* (Crestwood, N.Y.: St. Vladimir's Seminary Press, 1974) for a summary of this tradition. He faults the treatment of the dogma of the redemption in

isolation from the general body of Christian teaching that he finds in Anselm: "The thought of unity with God is forgotten because of our preoccupation solely with our own salvation; or rather, union with God is seen only negatively, in contrast with our present wretchedness," 97–98.

60. From the "Commendation of the Work to Pope Urban II," *Why Did God Become Man?* in *Collected Works,* ed. F. S. Schmitt, vol. 2,42 (Stuttgart, 1968). See E. R. Fairweather's translation in *A Scholastic Miscellany: Anselm to Ockham* (Philadelphia: Westminster Press, 1981).

61. M. B. Pranger, *The Artificiality of Christianity: Essays on the Poetics of Monasticism* (Stanford, Calif.: Stanford University Press, 2003), 177–78.

62. Book 2, chapter VI-IX; Schmitt, *Collected Works,* 150–55.

63. "Why did God become man...when it seems [God] could have done this in some other way?...You have shown that the debt [of sin] was so great that, while man alone owed it, only God could pay it....It is clear that God did not need in any way to do the act we have been speaking of, but that [God's] unchanging truth required it. For while God is said to have done what that Man did, on account of the unity of the person, God did not need to descend from heaven to conquer the devil...by justice to deliver man. But God did require of man...that he who had offended God by sin should make satisfaction by justice....Whatever was required from man was owed to God, not to the devil." Ibid., chapter XVIII, 176–77.

64. *Summa Theologiae* III, 9.48, art. 2. trans. R. T. A. Murphy, O.P., in *Summa Theologiae: Latin Text and English Translation, Introduction, Notes, Appendices, and Glossaries* (New York/London: McGraw Hill, 1965), 79.

65. Jaroslav J Pelikan, *The Christian Tradition: A History of the Development of Doctrine,* vol. 3, *The Growth of Medieval Theology (600–1300)* (Chicago: University of Chicago Press, 1978), 136–57.

66. Ibid., 143.

67. Hans Urs Von Balthasar, "Der Bruder für den Christus Starb," *Lebendiges Zeugnis* (1970), 17–18, in *The Von Balthasar Reader,* ed. M. Kehl and W. Löser, trans. R. J. Daly and F. Lawrence (New York: Crossroad, 1982), 201.

68. Ibid., 202.

69. From *Klarstellungen,* E. T. *Elucidations* (Einsiedeln, 1978), 39–46; in ibid, 199. Shakespeare's recruit Feeble said it well: "A man can die but once: we owe God a death." *Henry IV, Part II,* 2.2.250–51.

70. "The One Christ and the Universality of Salvation," in Karl Rahner, *Experience of the Spirit: Source of Theology, Theological Investigations,* vol. 16 (New York: Seabury Press, 1979), 199. See also "Observations on the Problem on the 'Anonymous Christian,'" Karl Rahner, *Theological Investigations,* vol. 14 (New York: Seabury Press, 1976), 280–94.

71. "The One Christ," 207.

72. Ibid.

73. Ibid., 217.

74. Ibid, 216–17.

75. He waives discussion of "the question of anonymous theism, as was done at the Council" (ibid., 217) but shortly thereafter asks whether faith, as he has been

defining it, "may conceivably contain... an implicit but still genuine presence of Jesus Christ, especially in the case of so-called atheists" (278).

76. Ibid., 219.

77. In Karl Rahner, *Penance in the Early Church, Theological Investigations,* vol. 15 (New York: Crossroad, 1982), 23–53.

78. "One Mediator and Many Mediations" in Karl Rahner, *Writings of 1965–67, Theological Investigations,* vol. 9 (New York: Herder and Herder, 1976), 169–84, at 179.

79. Michael Winter, *The Atonement* (Collegeville, Minn: Liturgical Press, 1995), 101, 114.

80. Parker in Rita Nakashima Brock and Rebecca Ann Parker, *Proverbs of Ashes: Violence, Redemptive Suffering, and the Search for What Saves Us* (Boston: Beacon Press, 2001), 49. The individually authored chapters are autobiographical with reflections like the above interspersed.

81. Ibid., 156. Similar views on the relation between Jesus' violent death and a theology of redemption are to be found in some essays in Joann Carlson Brown and Carolyn R. Bohn, *Christianity, Patriarchy, and Abuse: A Feminist Critique* (New York: Pilgrim Press, 1989). Summarized in Sloyan, *The Crucifixion,* along with the similar views of René Girard and R. G. Hamerton-Kelly on redemption without the cross (187–92).

82. Joel B. Green and Mark D. Baker *Recovering the Scandal of the Cross: Atonement in New Testament and Contemporary Contexts* (Downers Grove, Ill.: InterVarsity Press, 2000).

Chapter 5. Jesus Christ and Religious Pluralism (Roger Haight, S.J.)

1. I do not suggest here that these two positions exhaust the field. The two are chosen because of their stature as Catholic theologians and the depth and range of their theological production. Each has generated in his turn a large, coherent world of theological understanding within which his response to this particularly crucial problem is situated.

2. Biographical data on Karl Rahner can be found in Herbert Vorgrimler, *Understanding Karl Rahner: An Introduction to His Life and Thought* (New York: Crossroad, 1986).

3. Maurice Blondel defined the term *extrinsicism* and the extrinsicist imagination in his essay "History and Dogma" in *The Letter on Apologetics and History and Dogma,* ed., trans., and introduction by Alexander Dru and Illtyd Trethowan (New York: Holt, Rinehart and Winston, 1964).

4. Biographical data on Edward Schillebeeckx may be found in John Bowden, *Edward Schillebeeckx: In Search of the Kingdom of God* (New York: Crossroad, 1983); and Philip Kennedy, *Schillebeeckx* (Collegeville, Minn.: Liturgical Press, 1993).

5. The method of Karl Rahner is represented in his *Foundations of Christian Faith: An Introduction to the Idea of Christianity* (New York: Crossroad, 1994). One can see the logic as I've described it here in most general terms exemplified in the table of contents of the work.

6. See Mary Catherine Hilkert, "Hermeneutics of History: The Theological Method of Edward Schillebeeckx," *Thomist* 51 (1987): 97–145.

7. These ideas are developed during what may be called the middle period of Schillebeeckx's theology. He writes of them in *God the Future of Man* (New York: Sheed & Ward, 1968); and *The Understanding of Faith: Interpretation and Criticism* (New York: Seabury Press, 1974). These are universal structures of experience in human existence.

8. Edward Schillebeeckx, *Christ: The Experience of Jesus as Lord* (New York: Seabury Press, 1980), 731–43.

9. Rahner, *Foundations*, 116–22.

10. Schillebeeckx's theology of creation and its bearing on salvation is concisely analyzed by Dorothy Jacko, "Salvation in the Context of Contemporary Secularized Historical Consciousness: The Later Theology of Edward Schillebeeckx" (Ph.D. diss., University of St. Michael's College, Toronto School of Theology, 1987), 83–136.

11. Rahner, *Foundations*, 142–52.

12. One can find the essentials of Rahner's position on Christ and other world religions in Karl Rahner, "Christianity and Non-Christian Religions," *Theological Investigations* 5 (New York: Seabury, 1974), 115–34; and *Foundations*, 311–21.

13. Rahner explains this causality not simply on the ground of finality and the orientation of the religions to the manifestation of what is going on in them in the Christ event, and not simply in the single incarnation and hypostatic union of the Son in Jesus of Nazareth, but also historically in the response of Jesus to God's self-communication as Word. In a sense the hypostatic union and the saving event are not finally complete until Jesus' complete yes to God in the acceptance of his death. See Karl Rahner, "The One Christ and the Universality of Salvation," *Theological Investigations*, vol. 16 (New York: Seabury, 1979), 199–224.

14. One can find the essentials of Schillebeeckx's position on Christ and other world religions in Edward Schillebeeckx, "The Religions and the Human Ecumene," in *The Future of Liberation Theology: Essays in Honor of Gustavo Gutiérrez*, ed. M. E. Ellis and O. Maduro (Maryknoll, N.Y.: Orbis Books, 1989), 177–88; and Schillebeeckx, *Church: The Human Story of God* (New York: Crossroad, 1990), 159–86. Schillebeeckx's position is concisely analyzed by Diane Steele, "Creation and Cross in the Later Soteriology of Edward Schillebeeckx" (Ph.D. diss., University of Notre Dame, 2000), 252–94.

15. I draw this conclusion not only from Schillebeeckx's performance but also from the section in the Christ book where he provides a schematic outline for his theological vision. See Schillebeeckx, *Christ*, 629–44.

16. "As a consequence of all this we can, may and must say that there is more religious truth in all the religions together than in one particular religion, and that this also applies to Christianity." Schillebeeckx, *Church*, 166.

17. Edward Schillebeeckx, "The Uniqueness of Christ and the Interreligious Dialogue," Address to the Catholic Academy in Munich (April 22, 1997), 4, 16–17, of a manuscript in English translation.

18. Schillebeeckx, "The Religions and the Human Ecumene," 183–84.

19. Schillebeeckx, *Church*, 167.

20. This has been done by Jacques Dupuis in his *Toward a Christian Theology of Religious Pluralism* (Maryknoll, N.Y.: Orbis Books, 1979). I take Dupuis to be expressing an essentially Rahnerian position, but with new emphases, especially relative to the doctrine of the trinity, by drawing out in a more explicit way how God, as Christians speak about God, can be understood to be working in other religions and the whole world outside the Christian sphere.

Chapter 6. The Christ Event and the Jewish People (John T. Pawlikowski, O.S.M.)

1. Rosemary Ruether, *Faith and Fratricide: The Theological Roots of Anti-Semitism* (New York: Seabury, 1974).

2. David Efroymson, "The Patristic Connection," in *Anti-Semitism and the Foundations of Christianity*, ed. Alan T. Davies (New York: Paulist, 1979), 103–4.

3. Origen, *On First Principles*, 4.2.1

4. Ruether, *Faith and Fratricide*, 181.

5. Gustavo Gutiérrez, *A Theology of Liberation* (Maryknoll, N.Y.: Orbis Books, 1973), 161.

6. Clark M. Williamson, "Christ against the Jews: A Review of Jon Sobrino's Christology," in *Christianity and Judaism: The Deepening Dialogue*, ed. Richard W. Rousseau, S.J. (Scranton, Pa.: Ridge Row Press, 1983), 148; Jon Sobrino, *Christology at the Crossroads* (Maryknoll, N.Y.: Orbis Books, 1978). Also see John T. Pawlikowski, *Christ in the Light of the Christian-Jewish Dialogue* (New York: Paulist, 1982), 59–75.

7. Leonardo Boff, *Jesus Christ Liberator* (Maryknoll, N.Y.: Orbis Books, 1978).

8. Ibid., 284.

9. Barbara Bowe, R.S.C.J., "From Guarded Turf to Common Ground: Biblical Terrain and Contemporary Dialogue among Jews and Christians," in *Jews and Christians in Conversation: Crossing Cultures and Generations*, ed. Edward Kessler, John Pawlikowski, and Judith Banki (Cambridge, U.K.: Orchard Academic, 2002), 15–23.

10. See Judith Plaskow, "Christian Feminism and Anti-Judaism," *Cross Currents* (Fall 1978): 306–9; Deborah McCauley and Annette Daum, "Jewish-Christian Feminist Dialogue: A Wholistic Vision," *Union Seminary Quarterly Review* 38, no. 2 (1983): 147–90; Katharina von Kellenbach, *Anti-Judaism in Feminist Religious Writings* (Atlanta: Scholars Press, 1994); Helen P. Fry, "Women's Dialogue, Christology and Liturgy," in *Jews and Christians in Conversation*, ed. Kessler et al., 259–75.

11. Judith Plaskow, "Anti-Judaism in Feminist Christian Interpretation," in *Searching the Scriptures: A Feminist Introduction*, ed. Elisabeth Schüssler Fiorenza (New York: Crossroad, 1993), 1:117.

12. Katharina von Kellenbach, "Anti-Judaism in Christian-Rooted Feminist Theologians" (Ph.D. diss., Temple University, 1990), 57.

13. On Pharisaism, see John Bowker, *Jesus and the Pharisees* (London: Cambridge University Press, 1973); Anthony J. Saldarini, *Pharisees, Scribes and Sadducees* (Wilmington, Del.: Michael Glazier, 1988); Ellis Rivkin, *A Hidden Revolution: The Pharisees' Search for the Kingdom Within* (Nashville: Abingdon, 1978); Louis

Finkelstein, *The Pharisees,* 2 vols. (Philadelphia: Jewish Publication Society, 1962); Asher Finkel, *The Pharisees and the Teacher of Nazareth* (Leiden, Holland: Brill, 1964); Jacob Neusner, *The Rabbinic Traditions about the Pharisees before 70,* 3 vols. (Leiden, Holland: Brill, 1971); Jacob Neusner, *From Politics to Piety: The Emergence of Pharisaic Judaism* (Englewood Cliffs, N.J.: Prentice Hall, 1973); Michael Cook, "Jesus and the Pharisees — The Problem as It Stands Today," *Journal of Ecumenical Studies* 15, no. 3 (Summer 1978): 441–60.

    14. Ruether, *Faith and Fratricide,* 186.

    15. One example can be found in Mediterranean Spain. See Robert I. Burns, S.J., *Jews in the Notarial Culture: Latinate Wills in Mediterranean Spain, 1250–1350* (Berkeley: University of California Press, 1996).

    16. Leuenberg Church Fellowship, *Church and Israel: A Contribution from the Reformation Churches in Europe to the Relationship between Christians and Jews,* ed. Helmut Schwier (Frankfurt am Main: Verlag Otto Lembeck, 2001), 94.

    17. See World Council of Churches, *The Theology of the Churches and the Jewish people: Statements by the World Council of Churches and Its Member Churches,* with a commentary by Allan Brockway, Paul van Buren, Rolf Rendtorff and Simon Schoon (Geneva: WCC Publications, 1988); Helga Croner, ed., *Stepping Stones to Further Jewish-Christian Relations: An Unabridged Collection of Christian Documents* (London: Stimulus Books, 1977); Helga Croner, ed., *More Stepping Stones to Jewish-Christian Relations: An Unabridged Collection of Christian Documents 1975–1983* (New York: Paulist, 1985); Eugene J. Fisher and Leon Klenicki, eds., *In Our Time: The Flowering of Jewish-Catholic Dialogue* (New York: Paulist, 1990).

    18. Gregory Baum, "The Social Context of American Catholic Theology," *Proceedings of the Catholic Theological Society of America* 41 (1986): 87.

    19. Avery Dulles, S.J., "Evangelization and the Jews," with a "Response" by Mary C. Boys, Philip A. Cunningham, and John T. Pawlikowski, *America* 187, no. 12 (October 21, 2002): 8–16; Luke Timothy Johnson, "Beyond Supersessionism," *Commonweal* 130, no. 2 (January 31, 2003): 15–19.

    20. Johannes Metz, "Facing the Jews: Christian Theology after Auschwitz," in *The Holocaust as Interruption,* ed. Elisabeth Schüssler Fiorenza and David Tracy, *Concilium* 175, no. 5 (October 1984): 27.

    21. Gerhard Kittel and Gerhard Friedrich, eds., *Theological Dictionary of the New Testament* (Grand Rapids, Mich.: Eerdmans, 1985).

    22. Gerhard Kittel, *Die Judenfrage* (Stuttgart: Kohlhammer, 1933), 73.

    23. Martin Noth, *The Laws in the Pentateuch and Other Studies* (Edinburgh: Oliver and Boyd, 1966).

    24. Rudolf Bultmann, *Theology of the New Testament* (New York: Scribners, 1951).

    25. Clemens Thoma and Simon Lauer, *Die Gleichnisse der Rabbinen,* vols. 1–2 *Judaica et Christiana* 10, no. 13 (Bern: Peter Lang, 1986–1991); Clemens Thoma and Hanspeter Ernst, *Die Gleichnisse der Rabbinen,* vol. 3 *Judaica et Christiana* (Bern: Peter Lang, 1966), 16; Clemens Thoma, "Differences with the Church in the Rabbinic Parables," in *Reinterpreting Revelation and Tradition,* ed. John T. Pawlikowski and Hayim Goren Perelmuter (Franklin, Wis.: Sheed & Ward, 2000), 51–62.

26. See Dieter Zeller, "God as Father in the Proclamation and in the Prayer of Jesus," in *Standing before God: Studies on Prayer in Scriptures and in Tradition with Essays in Honor of John M. Oesterreicher,* ed. Asher Finkel and Lawrence Frizzell (New York: KTAV, 1981), 117–29. While theologians such as Edward Schillebeeckx relied too heavily on a notion of Jesus' supposed unique "*Abba* experience," I believe one can still argue from the overall context of Jesus' preaching for a unique understanding of his relationship with God the Father.

27. Carlo Cardinal Martini, S.J., "Christianity and Judaism: A Historical and Theological Overview," in *Jews and Christians: Exploring the Past, Present and Future,* ed. James H. Charlesworth (New York: Crossroad, 1990), 19.

28. See Helga Croner, ed., *More Stepping Stones.*

29. See Joseph Cardinal Bernardin, *A Blessing to Each Other: Cardinal Joseph Bernardin and the Jewish-Catholic Dialogue* (Chicago: Liturgy Training Publications, 1996), 78–79.

30. Robin Scroggs, "The Judaizing of the New Testament," *Chicago Theological Seminary Register* 75 (Winter 1986): 1.

31. See Wayne A. Meeks and Robert Wilken, *Jews and Christians in Antioch in the First Four Centuries* (Missoula, Mont.: Scholars Press, 1978); Robert Wilken, *John Chrysostom and the Jews: Rhetoric and Reality in the Late Fourth Century* (Berkeley: University of California Press, 1983); Anthony J. Saldarini, "Jews and Christians in the First Two Centuries: The Changing Paradigm," *Shofar* 10 (1992).

32. Cardinal Carlo Martini, S.J., "The Relation of the Church to the Jewish People," *From the Martin Buber House* 6 (1984): 3–10.

33. Paul van Buren's three major books on the theology of the Christian-Jewish relationship, including the christological question, are: *Discerning the Way* (New York: Seabury, 1980); *A Christian Theology of the Jewish People* (New York: Seabury, 1983); and *Christ in Context* (San Francisco: Harper & Row, 1988). In a posthumously published volume, van Buren seems to back away somewhat from some of his positions in his original trilogy, returning to his early Barthian roots. He also began, just before his death, criticizing some other theologians associated with the Christian-Jewish dialogue for giving up too much of the Christian heritage, especially with regard to the christological question. See Paul van Buren, *According to the Scriptures: The Origins of the Gospel and the Church's Old Testament* (Grand Rapids, Mich.: Eerdmans, 1998).

34. Franz Mussner, *Tractate on the Jews: The Significance of Judaism for Christian Faith,* trans. with an introduction by Leonard Swidler (Philadelphia: Fortress Press, 1984). Also see Franz Mussner, "From Jesus the 'Prophet' to Jesus the Son," in *Three Ways to the One God: The Faith Experience in Judaism, Christianity and Islam,* ed. Abdold Javad Falaturi, Jacob J. Petuchowski, and Walter Strolz (New York: Crossroad, 1987), 76–85.

35. Franz Mussner, *Tractate on the Jews,* 226.

36. See Elliot R. Wolfson, "Judaism and Incarnation: The Imaginal Body of God," in *Christianity in Jewish Terms,* ed. Tikva Frymer-Kensky, David Novak, Peter Ochs, David Fox Sandmel, and Michael A. Signer (Boulder, Colo.: Westview Press, 2000), 239–54.

37. See Jacob Neusner, *Death and Birth of Judaism: The Impact of Christianity, Secularism, and the Holocaust on Jewish Faith* (New York: Basic Books, 1987); Efraim Shmueli, *Seven Jewish Cultures: A Reinterpretation of Jewish History and Thought* (Cambridge/New York: Cambridge University Press, 1990); Hayim Goren Perelmuter, *Siblings: Rabbinic Judaism and Early Christianity at Their Beginnings* (New York: Paulist Press, 1989).

38. See n. 931.

39. See *A Sacred Obligation: Rethinking Christian Faith in Relation to Judaism and the Jewish People* (A Statement by the Christian Scholars Group on Christian-Jewish Relations, Boston College, September 1, 2002).

40. See John T. Pawlikowski, *Christ in the Light of the Christian-Jewish Dialogue* (New York: Paulist Press, 1982); idem, *Jesus and the Theology of Israel* (Wilmington, Del.: Michael Glazier, 1989); and "Christology, Anti-Semitism, and Christian-Jewish Bonding," in *Reconstructing Christian Theology*, ed. Rebecca S. Chopp and Mark Lewis Taylor (Minneapolis: Fortress, 1994). On Cardinal Bernardin's thinking, see n. 29.

41. See the Pontifical Biblical Commission, *The Jewish People and Their Sacred Scriptures in the Christian Bible* (Vatican City: Libreria Editrice Vaticana, 2002). For a positive evaluation of the document, see Donald Senior, "Rome Has Spoken: A New Catholic Approach to Judaism," *Commonweal* 130 (January 31, 2003): 20–23. Some other Catholic and Jewish commentators, such as Elias Mellon, Lawrence Frizzell and Michael Signer have been more critical of the document, especially what they see as an inadequate understanding in the document of postbiblical Judaism.

42. See Cardinal Walter Kasper, "The Good Olive Tree," *America* 185, no. 7 (September 17, 2001): 12–14; idem, "Spiritual and Ethical Commitment in Jewish-Christian Dialogue," in *From the Martin Buber House,* ed. Ruth Weyl, 30 (Summer 2002), 12–20; and idem, "Christians, Jews, and the Thorny Question of Mission," *Origins* 32, no. 28 (December 19, 2002): 457.

43. Kasper, "Christians, Jews, and the Thorny Question of Mission," 464.

44. "Reflections on Covenant and Mission," *Origins* 32, no. 13 (September 5, 2002): 218–24.

45. *A Sacred Obligation,* #7

46. See n. 19.

47. See John Paul II, *On Jews and Judaism: 1979–1986,* ed. Eugene J. Fisher and Leon Klenicki (New York and Washington, D.C.: Anti-Defamation League of B'nai B'rith and United States Catholic Conference Publications, 1987); John Paul II, *Spiritual Pilgrimage: Texts on Jews and Judaism, 1979–1995,* ed. Eugene J. Fisher and Leon Klenicki (New York: Crossroad, 1995).

48. See n. 19.

49. See Cardinal Joseph Ratzinger, "The Heritage of Abraham: The Gift of Christmas," *L'Osservatore Romano,* December 29, 2000; idem, *Many Religions — One Covenant* (San Francisco: Ignatius Press, 2000); and idem, *God and the World: Believing and Living in Our Time* (San Francisco: Ignatius Press, 2002).

50. See John Pawlikowski, "Christology after the Holocaust," in *The Myriad Christ: Plurality and the Quest for Unity in Contemporary Christology,* ed. T. Merrigan and J. Haers (Paris: Leuven University Press and Peters, 2000), 381–97; idem,

From the Unthinkable to the Unavoidable: American Christian and Jewish Scholars Encounter the Holocaust, ed. Carol Rittner and John K. Roth (Westport, Conn.: Praeger, 1997); and *Contemporary Jewish Religious Responses to the Shoah,* ed. Steven L. Jacobs, Studies in Shoah (Lanham, Md.: University Press of America, 1993).

51. Vytautas Kavolis, *Moralizing Cultures* (Lanham, Md.: University Press of America), 1993.

52. James F. Moore, *Christian Theology after the Shoah* 11 (Lanham, Md.: University Press of America, 1993).

Chapter 7. Christology and Patriarchy
(Rosemary Radford Ruether)

1. This argument that women cannot be ordained because they do not image Christ is found in the "Vatican Declaration on the Question of the Admission of Women to the Ministerial Priesthood" (1976), sec. 27. The argument was repeated in the pastoral letter of Pope John Paul II, "The Dignity and Vocation of Women," September 31, 1988, sec. 26; and in the pastoral on women by the American Catholic bishops, "One in Christ: A Pastoral Response to the Concerns of Women for Church and Society" (Second Draft: *Origins,* April 5, 1990, sec. 115, p. 730).

2. For the development of Logos Christology in the New Testament, especially in the Gospel of John, see C. H. Dodd, *The Interpretation of the Fourth Gospel* (New York: Cambridge University Press, 1963), 263–85. For its development in the second century, see Erwin Goodenough, *The Theology of Justin Martyr* (Amsterdam: Philo Press, 1968), 139–75.

3. For a critical exegesis of this passage, see Phyllis Bird, "Male and Female He Created Them: Gen. 1:27b in the Context of the Priestly Account of Creation," *Harvard Theological Review* 74, no. 2 (1981): 129–59.

4. For essays on the historical development of the exclusion and gradual inclusion of women as *imago dei,* see Kari Børresen, ed., *Image of God and Gender Models in Judaeo-Christian Tradition* (Minneapolis: Fortress Press, 1995).

5. Gregory Nyssa, *De Opif Hom.* 16.7; see Rosemary R. Ruether, "Misogynism and Virginal Feminism in the Fathers of the Church," in *Religion and Sexism: Images of Women in the Jewish and Christian Traditions,* ed. R. Ruether (New York: Simon and Schuster, 1974), 153–55.

6. Augustine, *De Trinitate* 7.7.10

7. Aristotle, *De. An.,*729b, 737–38.

8. Thomas Aquinas, *Summa Theologiae,* pt.l, q. 92, art. 1.

9. Mary Jane Sherfey, *The Nature and Evolution of Female Sexuality* (New York: Random House, 1972).

10. For example, see Isaiah 42:13, 14 and 49:14–15. Also Leonard Swidler, *Biblical Affirmations of Women* (Philadelphia: Westminster Press, 1979), 21–50.

11. See Wisdom of Solomon 6–8.

12. Luke 11:49 and Matthew 11:18–19: see James M. Robinson, "Jesus as Sophos and Sophia: Wisdom Tradition and the Gospels," and Elisabeth Schüssler Fiorenza,

"Wisdom Mythology and the Christological Hymns in the New Testament," in *Aspects of Wisdom in Judaism and Early Christianity,* ed. Robert L. Wilken, ed. (Notre Dame, Ind.: University of Notre Dame Press, 1975), 35ff.

13. See Sigmund Mowinckel, *He That Cometh: The Messiah Concept in the Old Testament and Later Judaism* (Nashville: Abingdon Press, 1955).

14. See "Son of Man," in *An Inclusive-Language Lectionary: Readings for Year A,* by the Inclusive Language Lectionary Committee.

15. Luke 1:45–55: See Jane Schaberg, *The Illegitimacy of Jesus* (San Francisco: Harper and Row, 1987), 92–107, for the interpretation of the Magnificat as a statement that God vindicates the most despised of society, the "fallen" woman.

16. In the Synoptic Gospels it is Mary Magdalene who is central to the group of female disciples who are "last at the cross and first at the tomb." Although John puts Mary, Jesus' mother, and John as central figures at the cross, he has the most extended narrative of Mary Magdalene's key role as the first witness of the resurrection. Mary Magdalene plays the key role in the Gnostic claims for women's apostolic authority: see "The Gospel of Mary," in *The Nag Hammadi Library in English,* ed. James M. Robinson et al. (San Francisco: Harper & Row, 1977), 471–74.

17. See Edward Schillebeeckx, *Jesus: An Experiment in Christology* (New York: Seabury, 1979), 703, nn. 31–33.

18. Joel 2:28–32: Acts 2:17–21.

19. Elisabeth Schüssler Fiorenza, "Word, Spirit and Power: Women in Early Christian Communities," in *Women of Spirit: Female Leadership in the Jewish and Christian Traditions,* ed. R. Ruether and E. Maclaughlin (New York: Simon and Schuster, 1979), 39–44.

20. *Didache* 11:3–13:7.

21. Elisabeth Schüssler Fiorenza, *In Memory of Her: A Feminist Theological Reconstruction of Christian Origins* (New York: Crossroad, 1983).

22. The alternative Pauline tradition that sees women as liberated from marriage into itinerant ministry through chastity is expressed in the noncanonical "Acts of Paul and Thecla." For interpretation of this conflict between eschatological and patriarchal Paulinisms, see Dennis R. MacDonald, *The Legend and the Apostle: The Battle for Paul in Story and Canon* (Philadelphia: Westminster, 1983).

23. 1 Timothy 2:11–15.

24. Montanist women prophets were accused of abandoning their husbands, which suggests that they shared the view of the "Acts of Paul and Thecla" that women converts to Christ transcend their marital obligations. Gnostics believed that spiritual rebirth enabled women and men to transcend sex and procreation and enter a state of spiritual androgyny. Both groups supported women in ministry. See Fiorenza, "Word, Spirit and Power," 42; and Elaine Pagels, *The Gnostic Gospels* (New York: Random House, 1979), 48–69.

25. The Council of Elvira, 400 C.E., was the first to mandate clerical continence. The council documents show the connection between clerical sexual continence and obsession with control over female sexuality. See Samuel Laeuchli, *The Emergence of Canon Law at the Council of Elvira* (Philadelphia: Temple University Press, 1972).

26. It became formulaic for fourth-century advocates of asceticism, such as Jerome and Athanasius, to affirm three levels of blessing on female states of life: one hundred-fold for virginity, sixty-fold for continent widowhood, and thirty-fold for marriage. See William Phipps, *Was Jesus Married?* (New York: Harper & Row, 1970), 142–75.

27. See Susan Fonay Wemple, *Women in Frankish Society: Marriage and the Cloister, 500 to 900* (Philadelphia: University of Pennsylvania Press, 1985).

28. The period between 500 and 1500 saw a continuous struggle of celibate women to retain autonomy and ministry, as well as the resistance of the lower clergy to the imposition of clerical celibacy. See Lina Eckenstein, *Woman under Monasticism: Chapters on Saint-Lore and Convent Life between A.D. 500 and A.D. 1500* (Cambridge: The University Press, 1896). Also John Boswell, *Christianity, Social Tolerance and Homosexuality* (Chicago: Chicago University Press, 1980), for the eleventh-century movements to enforce clerical celibacy, seen by married clergy as a monastic, homosexual movement. Also Rosemary Ruether, *Christianity and the Making of the Modern Family* (Boston: Beacon, 2000), 49–50; and Anne L. Barstow, *Married Priests and the Reforming Papacy: The Eleventh-Century Debates* (Toronto: Edwin Mellen Press, 1982).

29. There was some notable resistance to Protestant closing of monasteries by nuns. See Jane Dempsey Douglass, "Women and the Continental Reformation," in *Religion and Sexism,* ed. R. Ruether, 309–14.

30. The Puritan leaders placed major emphasis on the household for defining marriage: see William Perkins, *Christian Economia* (London, 1590); and William Gouge, *Of Domestical Duties* (London, 1622).

31. See Joyce I. Irwin, *Womanhood in Radical Protestantism, 1525–1675* (New York: Edwin Mellon Press, 1979), 179ff. Also Rosemary Ruether, "Women in Utopian Movements," in *Women and Religion in America: The Nineteenth Century,* ed. R. Ruether and R. Keller (New York: Harper & Row, 1981), 46–100.

32. Eusebius, *Oration on Constantine* 10.7.

33. The nineteenth-century Shakers most fully develop the sexual egalitarianism of the mystical-millennialist tradition. See their Bible, *The Testimony of Christ's Second Appearing* (United Society, 1856).

34. The reply of John Adams to his wife's exhortation to "remember the ladies," in the civil rights of the American Constitution, clearly reveals the exclusion, not only of women, but also of slaves, Indians and propertyless white servants from Adams's concept of those persons with civil rights. See Miriam Schneir, ed., *Feminism: Essential Historical Writings* (New York: Vintage, 1972), 3–4.

35. This claim to affirm women's secular equality through the concept of *imago dei* is found both in the pastoral letter on women of John Paul II, and also the Catholic bishops' pastoral letter on women (see n. 1, above).

Chapter 8. Christ and Postcolonialism (Robert Lassalle-Klein)

1. Karl Rahner, "Basic Theological Interpretation of the Second Vatican Council," *Concern for the Church, Theological Investigations,* vol. 20 (New York: Crossroad, 1981), 85. See pp. 83–84 for his comparison with Paul.

2. Roberto Goizueta, "A Christology for a Global Church," *Beyond Borders: Writings of Virgilio Elizondo and Friends* (Maryknoll, N.Y.: Orbis Books, 2000), 150.

3. This is my term. See Robert Lassalle-Klein, "The Potential Contribution of C. S. Peirce to Interpretation Theory in U.S. Hispanic-Latino and Other Culturally Contextualized Theologies," *Journal of Hispanic-Latino Theology* 5 (February 1999): 48–77.

4. For more on this argument see Roberto Goizueta, *Caminemos con Jesús: Toward a Hispanic/Latino Theology of Accompaniment* (Maryknoll, N.Y.: Orbis Books, 1995), ix, 1–17, esp. 7; and 18–46, esp. 19, 29, 30.

5. We will not deal here with the important role Our Lady of Guadalupe has in this pattern.

6. Orlando Espín, "Mexican Religious Practices, Popular Catholicism, and the Development of Doctrine," in *Horizons of the Sacred: Mexican Traditions in U.S. Catholicism,* ed. Timothy Matovina and Gary Reibe-Estrella (Ithaca, N.Y.: Cornell University Press, 2002), 169, n. 6.

7. Orlando Espín, "Popular Catholicism among Latinos," in *Hispanic Catholic Culture in the U.S.: Issues and Concerns,* ed. Jay P. Dolan and Allan Figueroa Deck (Notre Dame, Ind.: University of Notre Dame Press, 1994), 313.

8. Virgilio Elizondo, *Galilean Journey: The Mexican-American Promise* (Maryknoll, N.Y.: Orbis Books, 2000 [1983]), 5.

9. Ibid., 10. See also Virgilio Elizondo, *Guadalupe: Mother of the New Creation* (Maryknoll, N.Y.: Orbis Books, 1997).

10. Elizondo, *Galilean Journey,* 9–13. The following historical account is drawn from Elizondo, 5–16.

11. Ibid., 16.

12. Ibid., 5.

13. This phrase, quoted to Elizondo, is from the monument to "La Raza" in the Plaza de las Tres Culturas in Mexico City. See Virgilio Elizondo, *The Future Is Mestizo: Life Where Cultures Meet* (Bloomington, Ind.: Meyer-Stone Books, 1988), 73.

14. Elizondo, *Galilean Journey,* 5: "The word we shall be using in this book to designate the origination of a new people from two ethnically disparate parent peoples is the Spanish word 'mestizaje' (from 'mestizo, 'mixed,' 'hybrid')." Roberto Goizueta points out links between Elizondo's interpretation of *mestizaje* and the more romantic work of Mexican statesman and philosopher José Vasconcelos (1882–1959).

15. Goizueta, *Caminemos,* 7. Goizueta expands on Elizondo's seminal hypothesis, asserting that, "If the confluence of European and indigenous or African cultures marked our first mestizaje, and the confluence of Latin American and U.S. cultures marks our second mestizaje, then we might begin to speak of a third mestizaje taking place 'between and among' Latino cultures in the United States" (8).

16. The terminology is less important than the historical reality it captures. A recent work expresses a preference for the Nahua term *nepantla* to describe some of the phenomena that Elizondo places under *mestizaje.* See Timothy Matovina and Gary Reibe-Estrella, "Introduction," *Horizons of the Sacred,* 11.

17. Elizondo, *The Future Is Mestizo,* 73.

18. Elizondo, "Preface to the 2000 Edition," *Galilean Journey,* xiv–xvii.

19. Elizondo, *The Future Is Mestizo,* 72–73.

20. Elizondo, "Preface to the 2000 Edition," *Galilean Journey,* xvii.

21. Elizondo, *The Future Is Mestizo,* 76–77.

22. Ibid., 79.

23. Elizondo, *Galilean Journey,* 53.

24. Ibid., 103.

25. Ibid., 91, 103.

26. Elizondo, *The Future Is Mestizo,* 85–86.

27. Elizondo, "Preface to the 2000 Edition," *Galilean Journey,* xvii–xviii.

28. Virgilio Elizondo, *Guadalupe.*

29. Virgilio Elizondo to Dean Jerry Cleland, Barat College of DePaul University, December 20, 2001. Papers of Robert Lassalle-Klein, Evanston, Ill.

30. Goizueta, "Christology for a Global Church," 157.

31. In his famous homily delivered two months after the assassination of Fr. Rutilio Grande, S.J., to the Jesuit's former parishioners in Aguilares, El Salvador, Archbishop Romero stated to the terrorized peasants, "You are the image of the pierced savior." Archbishop Oscar Romero, "Homilia en Aguilares," June 19, 1977), *La voz de los sin voz: La palabra viva de Monseñor Oscar Arnulfo Romero* (San Salvador: UCA Editores, 1980), 208.

32. For a brief sample, see: James H. Cone, "An African-American Perspective on the Cross and Suffering," in *The Scandal of a Crucified World,* ed. Yacob Tesfai (Maryknoll, N.Y.: Orbis Books, 1994), 48–60; Kwesi A. Dickson, *Theology in Africa* (Maryknoll, N.Y.: Orbis Books, 1984), 81–98; Kosuke Koyama, "The Crucified Christ Challenges Human Power," in *Asian Faces of Jesus,* ed. R. J. Sugirtharajah (Maryknoll, N.Y.: Orbis Books, 1993), 156; Chung Hyun Kyung, "Who Is Jesus for Asian Women?" in ibid., 224; Salvador T. Martinez, "Jesus Christ in Popular Piety in the Philippines," in ibid., 247–57; John M. Waliggo, "African Christology in a Situation of Suffering," in *Faces of Jesus in Africa,* ed. Robert Schreiter (Maryknoll, N.Y.: Orbis Books, 1991), 164–80.

33. Ignacio Ellacuría, "The Crucified People," in *Mysterium Liberationis* (Maryknoll, N.Y.: Orbis Books, 1993), 580–604. Trans. from "El pueblo crucificado, ensayo de soteriología histórica," in Ignacio Ellacuría et al., *Cruz y Resurrección* (Mexico City: CTR, 1978), 49–82.

34. Ibid., 580.

35. See Teresa Whitfield, *Paying the Price: Ignacio Ellacuría and the Murdered Jesuits of El Salvador* (Philadelphia: Temple University Press, 1994); Robert Lassalle-Klein, "The Jesuit Martyrs of the University of Central America: An American Christian University and the Historical Reality of the Reign of God" (Ph.D. diss., Graduate Theological Union, 1996); Kevin Burke, S.J., *The Ground beneath the Cross: The Theology of Ignacio Ellacuría* (Washington, D.C.: Georgetown University Press, 2000).

36. Jon Sobrino, S.J., *Jesus the Liberator: A Historical-Theological Reading of Jesus of Nazareth* (Maryknoll, N.Y.: Orbis Books, 1993), 266. Trans. from *Jesu-*

cristo liberador: Lectura historica-teologica de Jesus de Nazaret (San Salvador: UCA Editores, 1991), 443.

37. Sobrino, *Jesus the Liberator,* 254–73; Jon Sobrino, *Christ the Liberator: A View from the Victims* (Maryknoll, N.Y.: Orbis Books, 2001), 3–8. Translated from *La fe en Jesucristo: Ensayo desde las víctimas* (Madrid: Editorial Trotta, 1999). Speaking of the crucified people, Sobrino identifies three "typical situations" of "present-day deaths for God's Kingdom [that] are like Jesus's death" (*Jesus the Liberator,* 268). There are those priests, nuns, catechists, delegates of the words, students, trade unionists, peasants, workers, teachers, journalists, doctors, lawyers, etc. who structurally reproduce the martyrdom of Jesus: "they defended the Kingdom and attacked the anti-Kingdom" with a prophetic voice "and were put to death" (ibid., 269). There are those who die an ethical "soldier's death," defending the kingdom by open struggle using "some sort of violence." He believes such a person may "share in martyrdom by analogy" by "laying down one's life for love" (ibid., 270). Then, "finally, there are the masses who are innocently and anonymously murdered, even through they have not used any explicit form of violence, even verbal." Sobrino notes that, "They do not actively lay down their lives to defend the faith, or even, directly, to defend God's Kingdom." For, "They are the peasants, children, women and old people, above all who died slowly day after day, and die violently with incredible cruelty and totally unprotected." But, he argues "their historical innocence," like that of the suffering servant, shows they "are unjustly burdened with a sin which has been annihilating them" (ibid., 270, 271).

38. Sobrino, *Christ the Liberator,* 4

39. Sobrino, *Jesus the Liberator,* 255. Romero quote: Oscar Romero, *Voz de los sin voz,* 208.

40. My translation of Sobrino, *Jesucristo liberador,* 29–30. See Sobrino, *Jesus the Liberator,* 8.

41. Ibid.

42. John Meier, "The Bible as a Source for Theology" in *Catholic Theological Society of America: Proceedings of the Forty-Third Annual Convention,* Toronto (June 15–19, 1988), ed. George Kilcourse, 53:3. Here Meier is discussing Jon Sobrino, *Christology at the Crossroads: A Latin American Approach* (Maryknoll, N.Y.: Orbis Books, 1976).

43. Sobrino, *Christology at the Crossroads,* 91–95.

44. Meier, "The Bible as a Source for Theology," 6.

45. Ibid., 5. Cites Jon Sobrino, *Jesus in Latin America* (Maryknoll, N.Y.: Orbis Books, 1987), 65.

46. Ibid., 6. Meier also cites Edward Schillebeeckx, *Jesus: An Experiment in Christology* (New York: Seabury, 1979), 67–71. Meier's three-volume study of the historical Jesus contrasts what he calls the "real" and the "historical" Jesus: "In contrast to the 'real Jesus,' the 'historical Jesus' is that Jesus whom we can recover or reconstruct by using the scientific tools of modern historical research." See John Meier, *A Marginal Jew: Rethinking the Historical Jesus,* vol. 2: *Mentor, Message, and Miracles,* Anchor Bible Reference Library (New York: Doubleday, 1991), 4.

47. Ibid., 3.

48. Ibid., 6.

49. Ignacio Ellacuría, *Filosofía de la realidad histórica* (San Salvador: UCA Editores, 1990).

50. Ibid., 42.

51. Ibid., 46.

52. "Cosmos," in *Oxford English Dictionary,* 2nd ed. (Online Edition).

53. Ellacuría, *Filosofía,* 31.

54. Ibid., 39–40.

55. Ibid., 42–43.

56. Ibid., 43.

57. Ibid., 43–44.

58. Ibid., 169.

59. Ignacio Ellacuría, "La historización del concepto de propiedad como principio de desideologización," *Estudios Centroamericanos* 31, nos. 335–36 (1976): 425–50. Trans. as "The Historicization of the Concept of Property," in *Towards a Society That Serves Its People,* ed. John Hassett and Hugh Lacey (Washington, D.C.: Georgetown University Press, 1991), 109.

60. Ibid., 428.

61. It was to this latter project that Ellacuría, the public intellectual, dedicated most of his career. He produced three massive volumes containing hundreds of such articles appropriately titled, *Twenty Years of History in El Salvador 1969–1989.* See Ignacio Ellacuría, *Veinte años de historia en El Salvador (1969–1989): Escritos políticos,* 3 vols. (San Salvador: UCA editores, 1991).

62. United Nations, Report of the Commission on the Truth for El Salvador, *From Madness to Hope: The Twelve-Year War in El Salvador,* March 15, 1993, 50.

63. Ignacio Ellacuría, *Teología política* (San Salvador: Ediciones del Secretariado Social Interdiocesano, 1973), 47. Trans., *Freedom Made Flesh: The Mission of Christ and His Church* (Maryknoll, N.Y.: Orbis Books, 1976), 87. Ellacuría privileges "Jesus Christ," "the Church," and "the chosen people" as historical signs, though not the only ones, for God (*Teología política,* 47–48).

64. Ignacio Ellacuría, *Conversión de la Iglesia al Reino de Dios: Para anunciarlo y realizarlo en la historia* (San Salvador: UCA Editores, 1984), 233. He bolsters this claim with that argument that, while orthodoxy may hold that "the deposit of revelation is closed as a system of possibilities," this implies that the efficacy of those possibilities "will only be seen in their historical realization." (*Teología política,* 52–53; *Freedom Made Flesh,* 97).

65. Ibid., 127.

66. Ignacio Ellacuría, "Repuesta crítica a 'Nota sobre la publicación *Teología política* del Reverendo Padre Ignacio Ellacuría, S.J.,' " Archives of Ignacio Ellacuría (San Salvador: Archbishop Oscar Romero Pastoral Center, April 24, 1974), 6–7.

67. See Andrew Greeley, *The Catholic Imagination* (Berkeley: University of California Press, 2001); Richard Aloysius Blake, *Afterimage: The Indelible Catholic Imagination of Six American Filmmakers* (Chicago: Loyola Press, 2000); Mary Catherine Hilkert, *Naming Grace: Preaching and the Sacramental Imagination* (New York: Continuum, 1997); David Tracy, *The Analogical Imagination* (New York: Crossroad, 1981).

68. Ignacio Ellacuría, "Discernir el signo de los tiempos," *Diakonía* 17 (1981): 58, 59.

69. Jon Sobrino, "Ignacio Ellacuría as a Human Being and a Christian: 'Taking the Crucified People Down from the Cross,' " in *Love That Produces Hope: Essays on the Thought of Ignacio Ellacuría*, ed. Robert Lassalle-Klein and Kevin Burke, S.J. (Collegeville, Minn.: Michael Glazier/Liturgical Press, forthcoming). Jon Sobrino, "Ignacio Ellacuría, el hombre y el cristiano. 'Bajar de la cruz al pueblo crucificado' (I)," *Revista Latinoamericana de Teología* 11, no. 32 (May–August 1994): 134.

70. Ibid.

71. Sobrino uses "the word 'victim,' . . . [for] the more powerful expression 'crucified people,' " both of which are intended to capture "what the term 'poor' used to express." Jon Sobrino, *La fe en Jesucristo*, 14. See also Sobrino, *Christ the Liberator*, 4.

72. Interview with Jon Sobrino by Robert Lassalle-Klein, San Salvador, April 19, 1994, 1. Second quote: Interview with Jon Sobrino by Robert Lassalle-Klein, Santa Clara, California, March 17, 1994, 1.

73. Sobrino, "Ignacio Ellacuría as a Human Being and a Christian," 146.

74. *Jesus Christ the Liberator*. My translation of the Spanish title. Unfortunately, the English version has mistranslated the title as *Jesus the Liberator*.

75. Sobrino responds to Meier by changing his position from Jesus to Gospel. *Mark* shows Jesus persevering in the face of rejection. Sobrino writes, "Whether one calls it a 'crisis' or not, whether it can be dated and located as 'Galilean' or not, is secondary for our purposes here. The important thing is that Jesus is shown being faithful to God to the end, and this fidelity is expressed as going up to Jerusalem, where he is going to meet God, again in a new form, in his passion and cross" (Sobrino, *Jesus the Liberator*, 152).

76. Ibid., 50

77. Cardinal Josef Ratzinger, *30 Giorni* 3, no. 3 (1984): 48–55; quoted in Sobrino, *Christ the Liberator*, 48.

78. Sobrino, *Christ the Liberator*, 48.

79. Ibid., 60.

80. Ibid., 36–63, esp. 36.

81. Ibid., 50.

82. Ibid., 225.

83. Ibid., 225, 228.

84. Sobrino, *Jesus the Liberator*, 61.

85. The statement would read, "the real Jesus, i.e., the [historical reality] . . . of Jesus of Nazareth as he lived in the first century, is no longer accessible to us by scholarly means." See, Meier, "The Bible as a Source for Theology," 5–6.

86. N. T. Wright, *Jesus and the Victory of God* (Minneapolis: Fortress Press, 1996), 11.

87. Wright, *Jesus*, 83–124.

88. Meier, "The Bible as a Source for Theology," 6. For his three-volume study of the historical Jesus, Meier writes: "In contrast to the 'real Jesus,' the 'historical Jesus' is that Jesus whom we can recover or reconstruct by using the scientific tools of modern historical research." See John Meier, *A Marginal Jew*, 2:4.

89. Meier, "The Bible as a Source for Theology," 6.

90. Analogous questions have been raised about Elizondo's treatment of Our Lady of Guadalupe (the third element of his "sacred triad"). See D. A. Brading, *Mexican Phoenix: Our Lady of Guadalupe: Image and Tradition across Five Centuries* (Cambridge: Cambridge University Press, 2001), 347–48.

91. Meier, "The Bible as a Source for Theology," 6.

Chapter 9. Christ in Mujerista Theology (Ada María Isasi-Díaz)

1. The *Kyrie* is part of the section of the Mass that deals with confession and forgiveness.

2. Carlos Mejía Godoy y el Taller de Sonido Popular, "Kirye," in *Misa Campesina*.

3. The words of the song are as follows: "Christ, Christ Jesus, identify yourself with us. Lord, Lord, my God, identify yourself with us. Christ, Christ Jesus, be in solidarity with us, not with the oppressive class that squelches and devours the community, but with the oppressed, with my people who thirst for peace."

4. Tom Driver, *Christ in a Changing World* (New York: Crossroad, 1981), 21–24.

5. Lisa Isherwood, *Liberating Christ* (Cleveland: Pilgrim Press, 1999), 133.

6. Ibid.

7. Ibid.

8. Ibid.

9. Gustavo Gutiérrez, *A Theology of Liberation,* 2nd ed. (Maryknoll, N.Y.: Orbis Books, 1988), 99.

10. Ibid., 100–101.

11. Ibid., 101.

12. Jon Sobrino, "Systematic Christology: Jesus Christ, the Absolute Mediator," in *Mysterium Liberationis — Fundamental Concepts of Liberation Theology,* ed. Ignacio Ellacuría, S.J., and Jon Sobrino, S.J. (Maryknoll, N.Y.: Orbis Books, 1993), 441.

13. Ibid., 442.

14. Antonio Gramsci, *Prison Notebooks,* ed. and trans. Quintin Hoare and Geoffrey Nowell Smith (New York: International Publishers, 1975), 9.

15. I am always apprehensive when any list is drawn, for lists are almost always read as if the elements in them could be isolated one from the other. I want to insist on the fact that the struggle for liberation is a holistic struggle, that we cannot be liberated socially, for example, without being liberated personally — within ourselves (psychologically) as well as socially (in our personal relationships). I want to insist especially on the fact that "spiritually" is not a category set apart — that spiritual is intrinsic to the category marked "personally." Here by spiritual I mean simply that the struggle for liberation also has to do with how we relate to God, a God that lives and moves and is among us, in us, a God that is in the social, in the political as well as in the personal.

16. Roberto R. Álvarez, Jr., "The Family," in *The Hispanic American Almanac,* ed. Nicolas Kanellas (Washington, D.C.: Gale Research, 1993), 155. The claims Latinas make regarding family are in no way unique but that they are not unique does not mean that they are not specifically ours.

17. Roberto Goizueta, "*Nosotros:* Toward a U.S. Hispanic Anthropology," *Listening – Journal of Religion and Culture* 27, no. 1 (Winter 1992): 57.

18. "Soap opera" is the name given in the United States to theatrical plays televised Monday through Friday for several months. Women are the target audience for these *novelas* — novels — as they are called in Spanish. It is important to notice that because the target audience of the *novelas* in Spanish television are working-class Latinas — the most numerous group in the Latino population — Spanish *novelas* play at night instead of in the afternoon, when American soap-operas, geared to middle-class women who work in their homes, can watch.

19. I hope the "religious" tone of the title of the *novela* and of the name of the mother — Esperanza means hope — are not lost on the reader.

20. John 15:13, RSV.

21. 2 Corinthians 5:18–19, RSV.

22. John 13:1, 35, RSV.

23. Sobrino, "Systematic Christology," 448.

24. What I call "responsible relativism" is an adaptation of the ideas of feminist philosopher Lorraine Code. She does not use this phrase, but the treatment of this term presented here is influenced by Code's work. See Lorraine Code, *Rhetorical Spaces — Essays on Gendered Locations* (New York: Routledge, 1995), 185–207.

25. Jon Sobrino, "Central Position of the Reign of God in Liberation Theology," in *Mysterium Liberationis*, 379.

26. See Sobrino, "Systematic Christology," 461, n. 10.

27. Ada María Isasi-Díaz and Yolanda Tarango, *Hispanic Women — Prophetic Voice in the Church*, 2nd ed. (Minneapolis: Fortress Press, 1992), 80–91.

28. Ibid., 79. See Dorothy Emmet, *The Moral Prism* (New York: St. Martin's Press, 1979), 11.

29. Mary Grey, *Redeeming the Dream* (London: SPCK, 1989), 87.

30. Ibid., 97.

31. Ibid., 375. "Then the poor can be theologized, posited as a *locus theologicus,* recognized as constituting a world in which the signs of the times occur. Now, one can even accept Isaiah's scandalous thesis: in the poor, in the crucified Servant, there is salvation and there is light."

Chapter 10. The Cross of Christ and Discipleship (M. Shawn Copeland)

1. Ched Myers, "Mark's Gospel: Invitation to Discipleship," in *The New Testament: Introducing the Way of Discipleship,* ed. Wes Howard-Brook and Sharon H. Ringe (Maryknoll, N.Y.: Orbis Books, 2002), 49. For some examples of such scholarly interpretation, see Howard C. Kee, *Community for a New Age: Studies in Mark's Gospel* (Philadelphia: Fortress Press, 1977); Ched Myers et al., *"Say to This Mountain": Mark's Story of Discipleship* (Maryknoll, N.Y.: Orbis Books, 1996); and Brian Blount, *Go Preach! Mark's Kingdom Message and the Black Church* (Maryknoll, N.Y.: Orbis Books, 1998).

2. For some examples, see Barbara E. Reid, *Choosing the Better Part? Women in the Gospel of Luke* (Collegeville, Minn.: Liturgical Press, 1996); and Turid Karlsen

Seim, *The Double Message: Patterns of Gender in Luke-Acts* (Nashville: Abingdon Press, 1994).

3. Clarice J. Martin, "The Acts of the Apostles," in *Searching the Scriptures: A Feminist Commentary,* vol. 2, ed. Elisabeth Schüssler Fiorenza (New York: Crossroad, 1994), 770.

4. Turid Karlsen Seim, "The Gospel of Luke," in *Searching the Scriptures: A Feminist Commentary,* vol. 2, ed. Schüssler Fiorenza, 761.

5. Ibid.

6. Sharon H. Ringe, "Luke's Gospel: 'Good News to the Poor' for the Non-Poor," in *The New Testament,* ed. Howard-Brook and Ringe, 65.

7. N. T. Wright, *Jesus and the Victory of God,* Christian Origins and the Question of God, vol. 2 (Minneapolis: Fortress Press, 1996), 176.

8. Ibid., 175.

9. Martin Hengel, *Crucifixion in the Ancient World and the Folly of the Message of the Cross,* trans. John Bowden (Philadelphia: Fortress Press, 1977).

10. Wright, *Jesus and the Victory of God,* vol. 2, 482.

11. For more on this point, see Hengel, who cites Pliny the Younger's letter to the Emperor Trajan in which he argues that the belief of Christians in a crucified God was a "pernicious and extravagant superstition" (*Epistulae* 10.96.4–8), *Crucifixion in the Ancient World,* 2.

12. Augustine, *City of God,* ed. David Knowles, trans. Henry Bettenson (New York: Penguin Books, 1972), Book 19, Ch. 23, 884–85.

13. Justin writes, "They charge us with madness, saying that we give the second place after the unchanging and existing God and begetter of all things to a crucified man" (13.4, "First Apology," in *Early Christian Fathers,* ed. and trans. Cyril C. Richardson [New York: Macmillan, 1970], 249).

14. Hengel, *Crucifixion in the Ancient World,* 1.

15. Tacitus, *Annals,* 15.44.4, cited in Hengel, *Crucifixion in the Ancient World,* 26.

16. Hengel, *Crucifixion in the Ancient World,* 22–32.

17. In a vision, God tells Catherine of Siena, "I am infinite Good and I therefore require of you infinite desire" (104: 197, in *Catherine of Siena: The Dialogue,* trans. Suzanne Noffke [New York: Paulist Press, 1980]). This is a familiar image for Catherine and appears in her correspondence; see Letter T74/G119, to Fratre Niccolào da Montalcino of the Order of Preachers in Montepulciano, February to April 1376, in *The Letters of Catherine of Siena,* vol. 1, trans. with introduction and notes by Suzanne Noffke (Tempe: Arizona Center of Medieval and Renaissance Studies, 2000), 313–14.

18. For another discussion of this metaphor, see Catherine M. Meade, *My Nature Is Fire: Saint Catherine of Siena* (New York: Alba House, 1991), esp. 107–28.

19. *Catherine of Siena,* 26:65.

20. Ibid., 64.

21. *The Letters of Catherine of Siena,* vol. 1, Letter T109/G41/DT51, to Bérenger, Abbot of Lézat, Apostolic Nuncio to Tuscany, January to February 1376, 266.

22. *I, Catherine of Siena: Selected Writings of St. Catherine of Siena,* trans. Kenelm Foster and Mary John Ronayne (London: William Collins, 1980), Letter 31, 146.

23. Ibid.

24. *Catherine of Siena,* 13: 49.

25. Orally transmitted for more than two centuries, the Negro or African American spirituals have a long and complicated history. These songs arose from the spiritual striving of an enslaved community, rather than from any authorial endeavor of a single individual. I quote here one of the most familiar variants of the spiritual, "We Are Climbing Jacob's Ladder." For readers looking for textual references, this spiritual can be found in *Lead Me, Guide Me: The African American Catholic Hymnal* (Chicago: GIA Publications, 1987), no. 54.

26. Charles H. Long, *Significations: Signs, Symbols, and Images in the Interpretation of Religion* (Philadelphia: Fortress Press, 1986), 7.

27. Josiah Henson, *An Autobiography of the Reverend Josiah Henson,* in *Four Fugitive Slave Narratives,* ed. Robin W. Winks et al. (Reading, Mass.: Addison-Wesley, 1968), 24.

28. Ibid., 25.

29. Marianne Sawicki, *Seeking the Lord: Resurrection and Early Christian Practices* (Minneapolis: Fortress Press, 1994), 90.

30. Ibid., 90–91.

Chapter II. Christology, Ethics, and Spirituality (Lisa Sowle Cahill)

1. See William P. Loewe, "Jesus Christ," in *The New Dictionary of Theology,* ed. Joseph A. Komonchak, Mary Collins, and Dermot A. Lane (Wilmington, Del.: Michael Glazier, 1987) 533–43.

2. James M. Gustafson, *Christ and the Moral Life* (New York: Harper & Row, 1968), 236.

3. Roger Haight, S.J., *Jesus, Symbol of God* (Maryknoll N.Y.: Orbis Books, 1999).

4. Ibid., 388.

5. Gustavo Gutiérrez, *A Theology of Liberation: History, Politics and Salvation,* Revised Edition with a New Introduction (Maryknoll, N.Y.: Orbis Books, 1988), 85.

6. Elisabeth Schüssler Fiorenza, "The Bible, the Global Context, and the Discipleship of Equals," in *Reconstructing Christian Theology,* ed. Rebecca S. Chopp and Mark Lewis Taylor (Minneapolis: Fortress Press, 1994), 85.

7. Karl Rahner, "The Two Basic Types of Christology," *Theological Investigations,* vol. 13 (New York: Seabury, 1975).

8. Ibid., 215–17.

9. Haight, *Jesus, Symbol of God,* 25–26.

10. Leonardo Boff, *Passion of Christ, Passion of the World* (Maryknoll, N.Y.: Orbis Books, 1987), 115.

11. Mary Solberg, *Compelling Knowledge: A Feminist Proposal for an Epistemology of the Cross* (Albany: State University of New York Press, 1997), 164.

12. Jacquelyn Grant, *White Women's Christ and Black Women's Jesus: Feminist Christology and Womanist Response* (Atlanta: Scholars Press, 1989), 212.

13. M. Shawn Copeland, " 'Wading through Many Sorrows': Toward a Theology of Suffering in Womanist Perspective," in *Feminist Ethics and the Catholic Moral*

Tradition, ed. Charles E. Curran, Margaret A. Farley, and Richard A. McCormick, S.J. (New York: Paulist Press, 1996), 155.

14. See, for example, the works of John Dominic Crossan, E. P. Sanders, Robert Funk, Burton Mack, and Marcus Borg. For a rousing (though perhaps overstated) counterargument, see Luke Timothy Johnson, *The Real Jesus: The Misguided Quest for the Historical Jesus and the Truth of the Traditional Gospels* (New York: HarperCollins, 1996).

15. Gerald O'Collins, S.J., *Christology: A Biblical, Historical, and Systematic Study of Jesus* (Oxford and New York: Oxford University Press, 1995), 111.

16. Sean Freyne, "The Quest for the Historical Jesus: Some Historical Reflections," in *Who Do You Say That I Am? Concilium* 1997/1, ed. Werner Jeanrond and Christoph Theobald (Maryknoll, N.Y.: Orbis Books, 1997), 47.

17. Gerald O'Collins, "Jesus," *Church* 13 (1997): 9.

18. Grant, *Christ and Jesus,* 216.

19. Johnson, *The Real Jesus,* 135.

20. Elizabeth Johnson, *She Who Is: The Mystery of God in Feminist Theological Discourse* (New York: Crossroad, 1994), 271.

21. Grant, *Christ and Jesus,* 212.

22. Johnson, *She Who Is,* 268–69.

23. Haight, *Jesus, Symbol of God,* 283.

24. Johnson, *She Who Is,* 198.

25. Catherine Mowry LaCugna, *God for Us: The Trinity and the Christian Life* (San Francisco: HarperCollins, 1991). LaCugna accents the strong relation between the triune nature of God and God's relation to us, and, for feminist theology, uses the model of equal, personal communion as a model for the church. For an argument that the importance of maintaining the unity of God can be undermined by accentuating the communion of three distinct persons, see Sarah Coakley, *Powers and Submissions: Spirituality, Philosophy and Gender* (Oxford, U.K.: Blackwell, 2002), 109–30.

26. Johnson, *She Who Is,* 227–28.

27. Ibid., 387.

28. See Raymond E. Brown, *An Introduction to New Testament Christology* (New York/Mahwah: Paulist Press, 1994); Mark Allan Powell and David R. Bauer, eds., *Who Do You Say That I Am? Essays on Christology* (Louisville: Westminster John Knox Press, 1999); Elizabeth A. Johnson, *Consider Jesus: Waves of Renewal in Christology* (New York: Crossroad, 1990); O'Collins, *Christology;* and Haight, *Jesus, Symbol of God.*

29. Haight, *Jesus, Symbol of God,* 447–54.

30. Consult the works in n. 28 above, and Ralph P. Martin and Brian J. Dodd, eds., *Where Christology Began: Essays on Philippians 2* (Louisville: Westminster John Knox Press, 1999).

31. R. Alan Culpepper, "The Christology of the Johannine Writings," in *Who Do You Say...?* ed. Powell and Bauer, 72.

32. Brown, *An Introduction,* 210.

33. Ibid., 72–73; Brown, *An Introduction,* 205–10; and Johnson, *She Who Is,* 86–100.

34. Haight, *Jesus, Symbol of God,* 280.

35. Ibid., 287.

36. Ibid., 291.

37. Elisabeth Schüssler Fiorenza, *Jesus: Miriam's Child, Sophia's Prophet: Critical Issues in Feminist Christology* (New York: Continuum, 1994).

38. Johnson, *She Who Is,* 152–53.

39. Johnson, "Redeeming the Name of Christ," 128.

40. Grant, *Christ and Jesus,* 213–14. Grant cites Harold A. Carter, *The Prayer Tradition of Black People* (Valley Forge, Pa.: Judson Press, 1976), 49.

41. See Tatha Wiley, *Original Sin: Origins, Developments, Contemporary Meanings* (New York/Mahwah: Paulist Press, 2002), especially 148–208, for a discussion of the meaning of sin's universality in the light of liberation and feminist theologies.

42. Ibid., 208.

43. Serene Jones: *Feminist Theory and Christian Theology: Cartographies of Grace* (Minneapolis: Fortress Press, 2000), 96.

44. Ibid., 97.

45. Ibid., 114.

46. Ibid., 99.

47. Cynthia S. W. Crysdale. *Embracing Travail: Retrieving the Cross Today* (New York: Continuum, 2001), 152, 154.

48. S. Mark Heim, "Christ Crucified," *Christian Century* (March 7, 2001): 13.

49. Ibid., 17.

50. Edward Collins Vacek, S.J., *Love Human and Divine; The Heart of Christian Ethics* (Washington, D.C.: Georgetown University Press, 1994).

51. Haight, *Jesus, Symbol of God,* 389.

52. William C. Spohn, *Go and Do Likewise: Jesus and Ethics* (New York: Continuum, 1999).

53. Ibid., 184.

54. Ibid., 55.

55. Ibid., 165–66.

56. Bruce T. Morrill, S.J., "Anamnetic Action: The Ethics of Remembering," *Doxology* 17 (2000): 5.

57. Ibid., 6.

58. Bruce T. Morrill, S.J., "Practicing Political Holiness," *Doxology* 18 (2001): 91.

59. Bruce T. Morrill, S.J., *Anamnesis as Dangerous Memory: Political and Liturgical Theology in Dialogue* (Collegeville, Minn.: Liturgical Press, 2000), 60.

60. Ibid., 106.

61. Ibid., 89.

62. For a discussion of this possibility, see Anne M. Clifford, C.S.J., "Foundations for a Catholic Ecological Theology of God," in *"And God Saw That It Was Good": Catholic Theology and the Environment,* ed. Drew Christiansen, S.J., and Walter Grazer (Washington, D.C.: United States Catholic Conference, 1996), 19–46.

Glossary

a priori. Prior to experience; a term, statement, or argument that does not stem from or rely on empirical data.

Adversus Judaeos tradition. Polemical tracts "against the Jews" by early Christian writers blaming Jews for the death of Christ and describing Judaism as inferior to Christianity and invalid as a religion. The supersessionist theology portrayed Christianity superseding or replacing Judaism in God's favor and covenant relation with humankind. Christian religious anti-Judaism has been mediated by biblical interpretation, preaching, and theologies of Christ and the church.

Alexandrian school. The patristic Christian church in Alexandria was noted for its christological emphasis of the divinity of Christ and its use of allegorical methods in biblical exegesis. The Alexandrian school was Platonic in philosophical method and more identified with the mystical tradition than the Christian school in Antioch to which it is often compared

altruism. Contrasted with self-centeredness or egoism, altruism is selfless concern for the well-being of others and the ethical view that one ought to act out of regard for the interests of others.

anathema. In Greek, "that which is accursed" and denoting the exclusion of heretics from the Church. The word appears in Paul (Gal. 1:9) and in official church decrees on disputes about faith. Conciliar creeds, formulated to serve as standards of faith, often end with anathemas.

anthropomorphism. Meaning "human form." With respect to God, giving finite human attributes, characteristics or form — gender, motives, emotions — to that which is not finite but infinite, not an object in the world among other objects but transcendent to them.

Antiochene school. The Jesus followers were first called Christians in Antioch, Syria (Acts 11:26). The Antiochene church was known for its Christology emphasizing the humanity of Christ and the use of historical methods in biblical exegesis. Its theological perspective was influenced by Aristotle.

apocatastasis. Also known as *universalism,* the Greek term refers to the final and complete salvation of all beings. All moral creatures will share God's grace of salvation. In the work of Origen (d. 254 C.E.), it expresses the conviction that God's wrath is not the final expression of the divine relation to humankind. The idea was opposed theologically by the Second Council of Constantinople (543 C.E.) as incompatible with the eternity of hell.

apologetics. Justification of Christian faith on rational grounds to nonbelievers or the defense of orthodox teaching against dissenters. The earliest Christian theologians were *Apologists* and their writings *Apologies.* The first Christologies were developed in this period. As proofs for the existence of God, this area is called *natural theology.*

apostolic era. The period between the resurrection of Jesus Christ and the death of the last Apostle. Since the late seventeenth century, writers immediately after the New Testament have been referred to as the apostolic fathers.

Aristotle (d. 322 B.C.E.). Among Greek philosophers, Plato and Aristotle were of most significance to Christian theologians. Aristotle offered a broad range of writings and an empirical method of value in theological reflection. Thomas Aquinas (d. 1274 C.E.) appropriated such ideas as Aristotle's fourfold notion of causality and metaphysics of potency and act to construct an overarching synthesis of the whole of Christian beliefs in his *Summa Theologiae.*

Arius. A respected Alexandrian priest and popular preacher, Arius (d. 336 C.E.) was concerned first for the oneness and transcendence of God. In regard to the preexistence of Christ, Arius held that only the Father was uncreated: "There was once (a time), when he (the Son) was not." The Son is the supreme of God's creatures, but not God (*ho theos*). The Council of Nicea (325 C.E.) rejected subordinationism, declaring that the Son of God was "true God from true God." The bishops' theological concern was with redemption. How could the Son be redeemer if the Son was not God? Arius went into exile rather than sign the Nicene Creed.

atonement. Literally "at-one-ment," the term signifies reconciliation of two parties. Because God is holy, sin estranges humankind from God, thus making reconciliation necessary. A soteriological rather than christological concept, atonement has to do with the "work" of Jesus Christ in the reconciliation — salvation — of human beings with God, particularly the salvific effect of his death. Patristic and medieval theories interpretations of how he accomplishes salvation are diverse, e.g.: Christ's death was a ransom paid to the Devil, who held humankind in his power because of Adam's sin; through the uniting of human with divine nature in the incarnation, Christ restored the image of God in humanity lost through sin; Christ's death satisfied the honor of God offended by humankind in sin; Christ's life and death are the means through which humankind is moved to love God. The twentieth-century theologian Karl Rahner, S.J., emphasizes Jesus himself as the salvific event rather than his performance of a redemptive act.

B.C.E./C.E. "Before the Common Era" and "The Common Era," respectively. The "Gregorian Calendar" instituted in 1582 by Pope Gregory XIII (d. 1585) designated history in Christian terms: B.C. ("Before Christ") and A.D. (*Anno Domini*, "After the Lord"). The newer B.C.E./C.E. designation is less Christian-centered.

basileia tou theou. Translated in English as *rule, reign, kingdom,* or *empire* of God, *basileia* is a Jewish eschatological symbol that expresses hope that God's will for the good will soon establish itself in the world. It denotes both a present and future reality. Biblical scholars concur in the centrality of the symbol in the preaching and life of Jesus but differ in their interpretations of its specific meaning for him.

Bible. From the Greek *biblia* meaning scrolls or books. The Christian Bible includes the Hebrew scriptures, called the *Tanak* by Jews, and New Testament writings. Protestants and Catholics agree on the twenty-seven New Testament writings but differ on their inclusion of some Hebrew writings.

biblical criticism. The scholarly study of the Bible including determination of a manuscript, authorship, date of origin, composition, sources, and its meaning for the original author and audience. Met with religious opposition, Protestant traditions accommodated modern biblical scholarship earlier than did the Catholic church, although Protestant fundamentalism remains opposed. Pope Pius XII's 1943 encyclical *Divino afflante spiritu* opened the way for Catholic biblical scholars to utilize critical methods. Since World War II, scholarly inquiry has expanded to include new methods such as redaction criticism, new literary criticism, feminist biblical interpretation, ideology critique, and social world analysis.

Black theology. A liberation theology emerging in North America in the 1960s shaped by the experience of African American women and men historically victimized by slavery and by the continued effects of racism. The social context of black theology is the experience of an exploited community. It critiques the distortion of the gospel created by white interests and the racism embedded in white churches. As a political theology, it articulates how the gospel speaks to the struggles of African Americans today and calls for justice.

canonical/noncanonical. The word *canon* derives from the Greek meaning "measuring rod" or "rule." In the Christian tradition, it refers to writings containing the "rule of faith" (correspondence to Christian creeds) and considered inspired and authoritative for the community. The process of selection of writings extended over a long period of time, coming to closure for the Hebrew Bible and Jews in the second century C.E. and for the New Testament and Christians in the fourth century C.E.

Cappadocian theologians. Three fourth-century C.E. theologians — brothers Basil and Gregory of Nyssa, and the latter's friend, Gregory Nazianzus — from the area of Cappadocia. Called a "school," the Cappadocians' influence is credited with the rejection of Arianism at the Council of Constantinople (381 C.E.). In their theology of revelation they identified two means of access to God: through visible creation and through the teaching of faith.

Chalcedon. An ecumenical church council held in 451 C.E., Chalcedon formally defined the "doctrine of two natures," the *hypostatic union.* Fully human, the one Jesus is simultaneously the divine Word and Son of God. Chalcedon sought a standard by which to judge the orthodoxy of priests. The subsequent creed, commonly referred to as the Nicene-Constantinople Creed, was similar to the Nicene Creed but enlarged, especially with regard to the Holy Spirit. The exact origin of the creed attributed to the Council of Constantinople, 381 C.E., remains a further historical question.

Chalcedonian Creed. The Council of Chalcedon (451 C.E.) accepted what is now referred to as the "Nicene-Constantinopolitan Creed." In the Catholic liturgy it is the "Profession of Faith" recited on Sundays and major feasts.

> *We believe in one God, the Father, almighty, maker of heaven and earth, of all things visible, and invisible;*
>
> *And in one Lord Jesus Christ, the only-begotten Son of God, begotten from the Father, only-begotten, that is, from the substance of the Father, God from God before all ages, light from light, true God from true God, begotten not made, of one substance with the Father, through Whom all things came into existence, Who because of us men and because of our salvation came down from heaven, and was incarnate from the Holy Spirit and the Virgin Mary and became man, was crucified for us under Pontius Pilate, and suffered and was buried, and rose again on the third day according to the Scriptures, and ascended to heaven, and sits on the right hand of the Father, and will come again*

with glory to judge the living and the dead, of Whose kingdom there will be no end;

And in the Holy Spirit, the Lord and life-giver, Who proceeds from the Father, Who with the Father and the Son is together worshipped and together glorified, Who spoke through the prophets; in one holy Catholic and apostolic Church. We confess one baptism to the remission of sins; we look forward to the resurrection of the dead and the life of the world to come. Amen. (J. N. D. Kelly, *Early Christian Creeds*, 297–98.)

Christ. The English translation of the Greek *Christos*. In Hebrew, *messiah*. It means God's "anointed one."

christocentric. An expression of the centrality of Christ in the relation between God and the world and in Christian faith and life.

christological heresies. Christologies considered inadequate or incomplete expressions of the Christian understanding of Jesus Christ in the judgments issued by church councils, diminishing or overemphasizing Jesus' human nature and/or his divine nature. Among them are: *Adoptionism* (Jesus was essentially human and elevated to divine sonship at some point in his life); *Apollinarianism* (the center of the human personality of Jesus was replaced by the divine Logos); *Arianism* (because only God the Father may be absolute and unbegotten, the "only begotten Son" must be subordinate in some way to the Father); *Docetism* (Jesus Christ was a purely divine being who only had the "appearance" of being human); *Ebionitism* (Jesus Christ is a purely human figure, although endowed with particular charismatic gifts which distinguished him from other humans); *Monarchians* (there is no real distinction between the Father and Son, they are different modalities of the one divine self-revelation); Monarchians divide into two groups, (1) the *Adoptionists*, or *Dynamic Monarchians*, and (2) the *Patripassians*, or *Modalistic Monarchians*; *Monenergism* (companion to Monothelitism, this Christology held that Jesus' two natures were manifested in one divine action); *Monothelitism* (Jesus' two natures were manifested in one divine will), and; *Monophysitism* (the human and divine come together in Christ in one divine nature).

Christology. Study of the person and status of Jesus Christ, particularly the relation of human and divine natures and the relation of the preexistent Christ or Son to the Father in God. It deals with a range of questions regarding Jesus' identity and his significance for humankind. New questions in Christology ask about Jesus' relation to economic, political, and social issues of human history and his distinctiveness as savior if it is granted that other religions mediate salvation to their adherents.

church. The Greek *ekklesia* meaning "those who are called out." In the Greek polis, *ekklesia* referred to an assembly of free citizens. Israel appropriated the term to refer to the people of God. In the first decades after the resurrection of Jesus, Christians took the word as a designation for their Jesus communities.

church fathers. In Latin, *Pater* means "father." *Patres* denotes Christian theologians of the early church whose writings carry authority for the Christian tradition. The patristic period and writings of theologians (many of whom are bishops) are essential for understanding the development of Christian theology and the church as an institution. In the history of theology, the Western church ended the patristic period with Isidore of Seville (d. 636 C.E.) and the Eastern church with John of Damascus (d. ca. 749 C.E.).

Constantinople. Following the Council of Nicea (325 C.E.) that the "Son is one in being with the Father" (*homooúsios,* consubstantiality), the first Council of Constantinople (381 C.E.) reaffirmed this understanding and, by the same term (*homooúsios*), defined the divinity of the Holy Spirit. The third Council of Constantinople (680 C.E.) condemned the Christology called *Monothelitism,* which understood Jesus Christ to have two natures (human and divine) but only one will (divine).

cosmological. *Cosmos* denotes an orderly, harmonious universe. *Cosmology* denotes either the metaphysical study of the nature of the universe or the astrophysical study of the history, structure, and constituent dynamics of the universe. The adjective refers to a theory about the universe.

creed. A formal definition or summary of the Christian faith, held in common by all Christians. Among important creeds are the Apostles' Creed and the Nicene creed.

demythologization. An approach to theology especially associated with the German theologian Rudolf Bultmann (1884–1976) and his followers, which depicts the premodern New Testament worldview as "mythological." In order for it to be understood in the modern situation, it is necessary that the mythological elements be eliminated.

disciple. From the Greek word meaning "learner," disciple refers to the follower of Jesus

dogma. A word meaning teaching, opinion, decree, or principle. Originally used for Jesus' teaching or that of the apostles, it came to mean a doctrine or belief considered binding on Christians because it expressed a truth of revelation. Vincent of Lérins in the fifth century C.E. used the word to mean "what has been believed everywhere, always, and by all" (*dogma catholicum*). As judgments of faith, dogmas emerge from concrete historical situations in which differences in understanding must be resolved.

ecclesiology. Theological reflection on the origin, nature, structure, and tasks of the church. The New Testament and patristic tradition offer a broad set of images for the church and a discussion of particular questions. The first systematic treatise was that of John of Ragus, ca. 1450 C.E.

Enlightenment. The term denotes European philosophical movements and ideas of the seventeenth and eighteenth century C.E., among which was the emancipation of reason from religious authority; the appropriation of the definition of truth in modern science as the product of inquiry, experimentation, and verified hypothesis; and the exercise of individual freedom. Socially and politically, the Enlightenment value of the dignity of each human being was expressed in democratic movements.

eschatology. The theological consideration of "last things" (death, resurrection, hell, eternal life) and the consummation of God's purposes in creation. In the Hebrew Bible and New Testament, God's purpose includes establishment of God's reign in the world through the concern of human beings for the weak, poor, and marginalized (see Matt. 25:31–46). This is the meaning of the Jewish eschatological symbol *basileia tou theou* central to the preaching of Jesus. Because of his proclamation of the *basileia*, Jesus is described as an "eschatological prophet."

Essenes. A major Jewish sect of first-century C.E. Judaism commonly identified with the ascetical community at Qumran, which produced the Dead Sea Scrolls.

exegesis. The literary analysis of a text. *Exegesis,* as the act and process of interpreting a writing, is distinguished from *hermeneutics,* the theoretical formulation of the principles of interpretation.

existential. Derived from Søren Kierkegaard (d. 1855), existentialism is a way of thinking rather than a philosophy per se. Central is the individual, freedom, and taking responsibility for one's life. Dynamic categories of analysis of becoming and potentiality for subjects as well as history replace static concepts of history and human nature as given. History is a dynamic process, its future open and undetermined. Individually and collectively, subjects make that future. Emphasizing human potentiality, existential categories of authenticity and unauthenticity evaluate the realization of that potentiality.

feminism. Feminism critiques and corrects sexism. It starts with what patriarchal anthropologies deny — that women are fully human. Feminist theologians reject the gender dualism of patriarchal culture and religion with its definition of female nature as inferior and evil, the absolutizing of male images for divine reality, and the assumption that patriarchal structures are themselves part of revelation, insisting rather on the equality of women and men. Unjust social, political, and economic relations and structures are judged sinful.

fundamentalism. A nineteenth- and early twentieth-century religious movement within evangelical Protestantism characterized by its rejection of the central features of modernity — modern science (especially Darwinism), philosophy, history, critical biblical scholarship, and liberal theology. It emphasizes biblical inerrancy, the divinity of Christ, and his substitutionary atonement.

Gnosticism. Religious movements that correlate salvation, denigration of the material, and a special secret knowledge (Greek, *gnosis*) revealed to an elite few (*gnostics*) through a spiritual savior. Many early Christian groups embodied gnostic views. Theologians such as Irenaeus (d. ca. 200) argued against this narrow view of salvation, affirming instead that knowledge of the work of Christ is available to everyone.

hegemony. From the Greek *hēgemōn*, meaning "leader," the term refers to the dominance or control of one nation or group over another.

Hellenistic. Pertaining to Greek ideas. The Hellenistic Age (Greek *Hellas*, "Greece") extends from the conquests of Alexander the Great in the fourth century B.C.E. to the Roman empire of the first century C.E. With Alexander, Greek became the language of the empire and Greek culture the normative way of life.

heresy. A belief held by a church member that rejects a teaching central to the faith of the community or advocates one contrary to that faith. It is distinguished from *apostasy* (the complete denial of the community's faith) and *schism* (a movement that divides the community). The early centuries of Christianity are marked by christological heresies, positions that contradicted the church's belief that Jesus was both human and divine.

hermeneutics. From the Greek *hermeneuein* meaning to interpret or explain. Hermeneutical theory formulates the principles underlying the interpretation of texts. It draws out the features of understanding involved in interpretation, for example, understanding is historically conditioned, situated in particular contexts, and subject to distortion by interests. A central hermeneutical question is how we can understand ancient texts whose cultural life and worldview so different from our own. Contemporary theorists acknowledge that the complexity of texts requires a pluralism of interpretations.

historical Jesus. Modern biblical scholars distinguish between the historical event of Jesus and the postresurrection New Testament portrayal of him. Debates continue about the adequacy of the terms *historical Jesus* and *Christ of faith* to express this contrast, fearing that some take the historical Jesus as the "real" Jesus and the Christ of faith a projection. Some use *historical Jesus* for the Jesus reconstructed by scholars. Others distinguish between the "pre-Easter" and "post-Easter" Jesus.

historicity. Acknowledgment that human existence is embedded in particular places and time. Human being is not given as a static essence but becoming, affected and shaped by historical contexts, race, gender, relationships, social institutions and other features of the concrete situation.

Holocaust. The Nazi extermination of eleven million people during World War II of which six million were Jews, the Nazi's "final solution" (*Endlösung*). The word *holocaust* comes from the word used in the *Septuagint* (Greek translation of the Hebrew Bible) for burnt offering, a sacrifice completely consumed by fire. Because sacrifice to God was not Hitler's intent, many Jews believe a more accurate term is *Shoah* meaning "destruction."

homooúsion. In Greek, *ousia* means "substance" (being, essence, reality). *Homooúsion* means "of one substance" or "of the same substance." In the christological and trinitarian debates of the patristic church, it signified the ontological equality of the Son and Father, countering views that the Son was "of like substance" (*homoiousion*) with the Father. A nonbiblical term new to the bishops of the Council of Nicea (325 C.E.), *homooúsion* was adopted with hesitation. For Athanasius (d. 373 C.E.), who promoted it, the term established a rule for speaking properly about God. What is said of the Father must be said of the Son (e.g., eternity) except what is proper to being Father (e.g., unbegotten).

hypóstasis. From the Greek, literally, "substance," commonly used to distinguish "objective reality" from illusion. The Alexandrian theologian Origen used it to connote *ousia,* "being" or "substantial reality." It came to mean "individual reality." In the patristic christological debates, theologians used it in the sense of "person" (*prósopon*). Over the centuries of these debates, the word changed in meaning. The Council of Nicea (325 C.E.) spoke of one substance or *hypóstasis* in God. The Council of Constantinople (381 C.E.) referred to three hypostases: Father, Son, and Spirit. Used in a heuristic fashion, *hypóstasis* denotes "what there are three of" in the divine godhead. In

the late fourth century C.E., the Cappodocian fathers settled what was to become the rule of language: God is one divine being (*ousia,* one substance,)
but three persons (hypostases). This became the church's basic trinitarian
formulation. The Council of Chalcedon (451 C.E.) used *hypóstasis* to affirm
the divinity of Jesus Christ. The divine and human natures in Jesus Christ
are unified in one divine *hypóstasis,* the *Logos.*

hypostatic union. The union of divine and human natures in one person
(Greek, *hypóstasis, prósopon*). The Council of Chalcedon (451 C.E.) moved
beyond the language of the Council of Nicea (325 C.E.) with the term
hypóstasis. The idea was intended as a theological reconciliation between
the emphasis of the Alexandrian church (the divinity of Christ) and the Antiochene church (the humanity of Christ). Chalcedon's acceptance of this term
became the starting-point for Christology, prevailing from the fifth century
to the present day. The Son is truly God, consubstantial with the Father, and
truly human, consubstantial with humankind.

idealism. The philosophical position that the real is an idea in the mind.

ideology. A core element of economic analysis derived from Karl Marx, ideology denotes the distortion of truth for the sake of the collective interests of
those with power. Economic structures of exploitation such as slavery are legitimized as "natural" or the "order of creation." Language is an instrument
of power. Religious doctrines can sanctify the structures of domination that
constitute the present historical order. Theologians have integrated Marx's
systematic ideology critique into theological method. From within faith,
they engage the question how religious doctrines, texts, symbols, and values
are ideological. The gospel and the inherited tradition can be distorted by
colonial interests, male privilege, and other forms of domination.

imago dei. Used now as a technical term to express a fundamental aspect
of a Christian anthropology, *imago dei* comes from Genesis 1:26. Human
beings are made "in the image of God." Because of sin, *imago dei* signals
not only what human beings are to be but also what they are not.

immanence. Immanence and transcendence are two ways of describing God's
relation to the created order. God is present to creation (immanence) yet not
an empirical object within it (transcendence).

incarnation. The trinitarian God assumed human reality in the person of the
Word, who is the Father's eternal self-expression. This formulation reflects
the controversies of the fourth and fifth centuries C.E. and the ecumenical
councils that formulated an orthodox position. A primary biblical influence
is the Logos Christology in the Gospel of John: "In the beginning was the
Word, and the Word was with God and the Word was God.... And the

Word became flesh" (1:1, 14). "The Logos became flesh" is equivalent to "God became human."

kenosis. Greek for "emptying." A *kenosis* Christology maintains that the divine Son sets aside certain attributes of divinity in becoming human. The early Christian hymn cited by Paul in Philippians evokes a *kenosis* Christology: Christ Jesus "who, though he was in the form of God, did not regard equality with God as something to be exploited but emptied himself, taking the form of a slave" (2:6–7).

kerygma. In the Hebrew Bible *kerygma* refers to prophetic and priestly proclamation. The New Testament *kerygma* is the proclamation of the crucified and risen Christ as the event of salvation. Jesus announced the message of God's salvation and then became the means of that salvation.

kyriarchy, kyriocentrism. A Greek term, *kyrios* means lord, master, father, or husband. Elisabeth Schüssler Fiorenza replaced *patriarchy* (too often understood simply as gender domination) with *kyriarchy* ("rule of elite males") to express the interstructuring of domination. Schüssler Fiorenza uses *kyriarchy* as an analytical category to locate sexism and misogyny within a political context and a broader range of oppressions.

liberation theology. A theological method developed by Latin American, Black, and feminist theologians in the 1960s, grounded in the biblical image of divine concern for the poor and situated in poor communities engaged in a critical reading of the gospel. Gustavo Gutiérrez calls theological reflection a "second step." The first step is solidarity with society's victims, the act of love. Liberation theology articulates the distortion of the social order by structural sin and the relation of the gospel to the transformation of the existing order.

Logos. A Greek term meaning "word" or "reason." A Hellenistic concept, *Logos* denotes the principle of rationality in the universe. For Jews, the *Logos* was God's presence in history, present at creation and in the prophets. The functional equivalent to *Logos* in the Wisdom literature is *Sophia,* God's creative Wisdom. For the Jewish philosopher Philo, *Logos* was a divine intermediary between God and humankind. In the New Testament, *Logos* is confined to the Johannine writings whose author united the Jewish and Hellenistic meanings. The *Logos* makes the Father known. The concept offered a means of formulating the relation of Christ to God the Father. Taking Christ's preexistence for granted, the idea of Christ as the Father's Word and its expression in creation and redemption avoided tritheism. For Justin Martyr, the "seminal *logos*" was the universal functioning of the *Logos.* Its "seeds," *logoi spermatikoi,* are found in every human mind and are what unite human beings to God and allow them to have knowledge of God. In Christ, the seminal *logos* has is personified.

messiah. Translated *Christos* in Greek, the Hebrew *messiah* means God's "anointed" or "chosen" one. The title derives from the anointing of kings in ancient Israel. It is an early postresurrection christological title for Jesus.

modernity. The term denotes a world shaped by Enlightenment ideas and developments, chief among which are individual autonomy, independence of human knowledge from authority, acceptance of the pluralism of competing views of the world, confidence in historical progress, the spread of a capitalist form of economy, technological innovation, and globalization.

Montanism. A second-century C.E. Christian apocalyptic and ascetical movement (judged heretical) originating with a man Montanus who believed the outpouring of the Holy Spirit would happen very soon. It is described as a "purist" sect for criticism of the moral decline of the church and its rigorous demand that no sins be committed after baptism. It maintained that bishops had no right to forgive those guilty of serious sins such as adultery, murder, and apostasy.

***mujerista* theology.** Feminist, black, womanist, and *mujerista* theologies are examples of liberation theology and have as their starting point an emancipatory faith commitment. The starting place of *mujerista* theology is the lived experience of Latinas, specifically the injustice to which Hispanic women are subject. It is the attempt to articulate and to bring about justice, what Ada María Isasi-Díaz calls Latinas' *proyecto histórico,* "our preferred future." One reason for using this experience as the source of theology, she argues, is the gospel demand to stand in solidarity with those who are victimized.

neoscholasticism. An eighteenth- and nineteenth-century development in Catholic theology and one means through which modern ideas and developments were refuted and pronouncements of the church defended. Leo XIII's encyclical *Aeterni Patris* (1879) articulated the theological task for neoscholasticism, giving the work of Thomas Aquinas special theological status and utilizing it as a counter to modernity. Thomistic theology was made mandatory for Catholic seminaries. The renewal in Thomistic studies with philosophers such as Jacques Maritain (d. 1973), who tried to relate Thomas to modern culture is called *Neo-Thomism.*

Nicea. An ecumenical church council called in 325 C.E. to resolve disputes about Jesus Christ arising from the subordinationist Christology of the priest Arius. Doctrinal unity was achieved through the formulation of an "ecumenical creed," one that would then function as a criterion of orthodoxy for priests and as church law for all churches The resulting statement, the Nicene Creed, countered Arian subordinationism with an affirmation of the equality of divine status of the Son and Father. Central was the concept of *homooúsios* (*homo-ousios*, "of the same being" or "of the same substance"). This consubstantiality means that the Son is *God* as the Father is *God*.

Nicene Creed. The Council of Nicea (325 C.E.) formulated the creed below as its criterion for orthodoxy, aiming in particular at the subordinationist Christology of the Alexandrian priest Arius:

We believe in one God, the Father, almighty, maker of all things visible, and invisible;

And in one Lord Jesus Christ, the Son of God, begotten from the Father, only-begotten, that is, from the substance of the Father, God from God, light from light, true God from true God, begotten not made, of one substance with the Father, through Whom all things came into being, things in heaven and things of earth, Who because of us men and because of our salvation came down and became incarnate, becoming man, suffered and rose again on the third day, ascended to the heavens, will come to judge the living and the dead;

And in the Holy Spirit.

But as for those who say, There was when He was not, and Before being born He was not, and that He came into existence out of nothing, or who assert that the Son of God is of a different hypóstasis or substance, or is subject to alteration or change — these the Catholic and apostolic Church anathematizes. (J. N. D. Kelly, *Early Christian Creeds*, 215–16).

ontological. Ontology, or metaphysics, is the philosophical inquiry into the nature of being. The adjective refers to that relating to being or existence. Anselm of Canterbury's argument for God's existence, derived from the meaning of the term *God*, is called an "ontological argument."

orthodoxy. Commonly understood as "right belief," as opposed to error or heresy, the term literally means "right praise." As an evaluative category, it denotes whether a theological position is consistent with the faith of the church, in particular, church dogmas, beliefs explicitly formulated by the church and held to be normative for believers.

parousia. A Greek term, which literally means "coming" or "arrival," used to refer to the second coming of Christ.

patriarchy. From the Latin word *pater, father,* meaning the "rule of the father." As Rosemary Radford Ruether defines it, patriarchy refers to systems of legal, social, economic, and political relations that validate and enforce the sovereignty of male heads of families over dependent persons in the household. Dependent persons are women and also men — dependent sons, servants, slaves.

patristic period. The first centuries in the history of the church following the writing of the New Testament. Historians vary in ending the period, some end it with the Council of Chalcedon in the fifth century C.E., others extend it to the ninth century C.E.

person. The understanding of divine reality accepted in the Councils of Nicea (325 C.E.) and Chalcedon (451 C.E.) in the Western church affirmed that God is one being or nature (Latin *una substantia,* Greek *ousia*) and three persons (Latin *personae,* Greek *prosopa hypostases*).

Pharisees. The Hebrew and Aramaic root of *pharisee* is thought to be *prs,* meaning "separate" or "interpret." For contemporary scholars it denotes a small social and political group, a Jewish sect that wished to influence fidelity to a way of living mandated by the Torah. Their prominence in the New Testament led Christian biblical scholars to overestimate their political status at the time of Jesus. The polemical portrayal of them in the New Testament reflects tensions between Jesus followers and the Pharisees in the late first century C.E. The few references to them in the many volumes of the Jewish historian Josephus reflects their minor significance in the perspective of the ruling classes.

phenomenological. Phenomenology is a philosophical study of human consciousness, examining the formal structure of the objects of awareness and of awareness itself. The adjective points to the methodological features of a particular inquiry.

Platonism. The term denotes the teachings of Greek philosopher Plato himself (d. 347 B.C.E.) or to philosophical ideas and traditions shaped by him. Plato is known especially for the dialogue form of philosophical reflection in which he communicated the ideas of his teacher Socrates and for his theory of ideas.

pluralism. The term carries several meanings, e.g., the cultural diversity of practices and beliefs; the political pluralism of a social order that does not impose a particular ideology or faith; a theory of religion that holds that all religions ultimately point to the same truth. In general, it refers to a situation in which are a variety of viewpoints and perspectives accounting for the same reality. Theological pluralism has been a feature of the Christian tradition since its beginning.

postcolonial. Colonialism denotes a nation's domination and control of another nation, now defined in its subject status as "colony." Control over a native population extends with the structural imposition of the norms and values of the dominant "superior" culture and the denigration of the colonized "backward" culture. Postcolonial thought addresses this legacy.

postliberalism. A theological movement, especially associated with Yale Divinity School, which criticized the liberal reliance upon human experience and reclaimed the notion of community tradition as a controlling influence in theology. Religious doctrines are "rules" for appropriate ways of living and talking within the community rather than assertions about reality, e.g., the doctrine of the Trinity is not so much a claim about the real nature of God as about what Christians should or should not say about God.

postmodern. Literally the term means what comes after "modern" or "modernity." Some features are the critique of the universalism and rationalism of the Enlightenment, the acknowledgment of contextual and pluralistic modes of thought, and the existence of a diversity of perspectives in all areas. Friedrich Nietzsche's denial of a single meaning for history, truth, or moral right stands at the forefront of postmodernism.

prelapsarian. The understanding of human nature prior to the fall. In the Christian anthropology developed by patristic and medieval theologians, prelapsarian human nature possessed certain capacities that were "over and beyond nature." Human beings were given the gifts of justice, integrity, and immortality. The first is called a *supernatural* gift; the latter two are called *preternatural* gifts. Classical theology described the prelapsarian or pre-fall state of Adam and Eve as one in which they were in a state of sanctifying grace (justice), free from concupiscence (integrity), and not subject to death (immortality). All three were lost through sin, leaving nature to nature. Lost, too, was the original friendship shared with God. The effect of the fall is estrangement from God, a state from which humankind is redeemed through the incarnation.

psilanthropism. In Greek, "merely human." In the early church, it describes a Christology that conceives of Jesus as a human being whom God has favored. This denies Christ's divine nature.

religious exclusivism. The fact of many religions raises a question of how to reconcile the Christian claim to the *unicity* of divine truth and salvation in Christ with the *plurality* of religions. In its christocentric form: What is the distinctiveness of Christ *if* other religions are mediators of divine truth and salvation to their adherents? *Religious pluralism* holds that other religions have a validity of their own. They are a means of revelation and salvation for their adherents. *Religious inclusivism* maintains that other religions are salvific inasmuch as they share in Christian truth. *Religious exclusivism* holds that there can be only one true religion. Belief in Christ is necessary for salvation. The exclusivist position is rooted in scripture: "And there is salvation in no one else, for there is no other name under heaven given among men by which we must be saved" (Acts 4:12).

satisfaction theory. A theory of atonement proposed by Anselm of Canterbury (d. 1109) in his work *Cur Deus homo* (1098). Humankind owes God honor and worship. Sin is a refusal of what is owed to God. Because they are finite, human beings cannot make the infinite satisfaction that their sin requires. Only an infinite reality can do so, thus the reason for a God-man and the incarnation.

Scholasticism. A style of systematic theological reflection originating with the medieval universities and the Schoolmen or Scholastics. Scholasticism was developed by theologians such as Anselm of Canterbury (d. 1109 c.e.) for whom theology was "faith seeking understanding" (*fides quarens intellectum*). Reason was affirmed as capable of coming to some understanding of revealed truths. Theological arguments were logical rather than biblical. The overarching synthesis of faith found in the *Summa Theologiae* of Thomas Aquinas (d. 1274 c.e.) reflects this goal of theology and confidence in reason.

Son of Man. In the Hebrew Bible, the term denotes a human being (see Ps. 8:4). Ezekiel uses it as a reference to the prophet himself. In Daniel, it refers to Israel or to a future ruler of Israel. Though controverted, in the New Testament gospels, the phrase is thought to be Jesus' self-designation or alternatively a corporate designation of humankind (Matt. 8:20).

Sophia. In Wisdom writings of the Hebrew Bible divine wisdom (in Greek, *sophia*) is personified as a woman who mediates between God and humankind. This concept of divine creativity or intelligence merges in the New Testament with the *Logos* of John's Gospel. The linking of Jesus with Sophia is one of the earliest Christologies found in the Synoptic Gospels and Pauline letters. He is Sophia's prophet and messenger. Christ is "the wisdom of God" (1 Cor. 1:30). The Johannine *Logos* Christology and *Sophia* Christology are functionally equivalent.

soteriology. In Greek, *soteria*, redemption. While the "work" and "person" of Christ are ultimately inseparable, soteriology traditionally has been correlated with "Christ's work of redemption" and Christology with his "person."

Stoicism. A Greek philosophical movement whose adherents emphasized self-control, endurance, duty, and service to the family, the state, and the gods. In the Hebrew Bible, writings such as Ecclesiastes reflect the influence of Stoic ideas.

subordinationism. The assertion that the Son or Logos is not of the same substance as the Father but subordinate. For Arius, whose views the Council of Nicea (325 C.E.) condemned, *begotten* meant there was a time when the Son was not, thus the divine attribute of eternity does not apply to the Son.

supersessionism. The theological depiction of Christianity displacing Judaism in God's favor and covenant relation with humankind. Supersessionist theology characterizes Jews as cursed by God for their rejection of Jesus and their role in his death.

Synoptic Gospels. The first three gospels (Matthew, Mark, and Luke) "see together" (Greek, *synopsis*) in the way they present the life, death, and resurrection of Jesus Christ.

Tanak. An acronym for the Hebrew Bible consisting of three consonants that represent the three divisions of the Hebrew Bible: the *Torah* (Law), the *Nevi'um* (Prophets), and *Kethivium* (Writings).

theocentric. Making God the ultimate concern and central interest — of a life, theology, tradition.

theological anthropology. A theory of human nature conceived in a framework of divine creation, human historicity, sinfulness, divine grace, salvation, and ultimate destiny. It is in relation to Jesus Christ that theologians develop an understanding of the meaning and direction of human existence. Christology is thus prior to a Christian theological anthropology. Modern developments in philosophy, psychology and other disciplines have advanced a new set of insights into an existential and empirical anthropology in contrast to the traditional metaphysical concept of the person.

Theotokos. A title given to Mary, "Mother of God." Designating Mary this way caused much debate — many thinking that she should be called Mother of *Christ,* inasmuch as she is mother of Jesus' humanity, not Mother of *God.* The context for doing so, however, is the doctrinal affirmation of the Council of Nicea (325 C.E.) that Jesus is fully human and fully divine. On this basis, the Council of Ephesus (431 C.E.) declared Mary *Theotokos.*

Torah. The first five books of the Hebrew Bible, also called the Pentateuch and the Books of Moses. The Hebrew word, often translated "law" or "teaching," means "way of the covenant" or "way of living." As Deuteronomy expresses so poignantly, Jews believe the Torah God's gift, the means through which they could be faithful to the covenant God had established with Israel.

transcendence. In its verb form, *transcend* means to go beyond, to exceed, or to surpass. In reference to existence, it means to exist "above" or "independent of." Divine transcendence does not mean that God is "up there" but that God is not an object among objects in the empirical world of sense experience. To be an "object" is to be finite. Two terms are united in conjunction with one another. By immanence is meant God is present to the world — in the depths of our being, as theologians such as Paul and Augustine have affirmed. Transcendence means that God's presence is not as an empirical thing. God is at once transcendent and immanent to the world.

transculturation. The culturally sensitive presentation of the biblical message so that it is effectively communicated to people whose culture is different from that of the social worlds of the Hebrew Bible and New Testament.

trinity. The distinctive Christian understanding of the threefold nature of God. The New Testament language of the Father who is revealed through the Son and sends the Holy Spirit. How to affirm the divinity of Jesus Christ and avoid tritheism was a major dilemma for patristic theologians. Their starting point was monotheism: God is one. Theologians drew on the concept of *person* (Greek, *prósopon,* also *hypóstasis*; Latin *persona*) to denote the inner relational nature of God. The Latin *trinitas* and the formula of three *personae* appears in the work of African theologian Tertullian (d. 225 C.E.). "Person" denotes real identity, signifying what is proper to each in the history of salvation and in the godhead. The Council of Nicea (325 C.E.) defined the consubstantiality (*homoousios*) of the Son with the Father. The First Council of Constantinople defined the consubstantiality of the Holy Spirit with the Father and the Son. *Homoousios* means "of one substance" or "of the same substance." It was used in the christological and trinitarian debates to denote the ontological equality in divine status of the Father, Son, and Holy Spirit. By the fifth century C.E., the Cappadocian theologians understood the terms *economic trinity* and *immanent trinity* to refer to as God's self-communication in creation, redemption, and sanctification (economic) and to the divine life itself (immanent).

trinitarian heresies. Theological perspectives rejected by the church as inadequate ways of understanding divine reality. Among them is *Monarchianism* (the three persons of the trinity are different historical manifestations or modes of the one God). *Modalism* and *Sabellianism* are variations of Monarchianism.

Vatican II. An ecumenical council called by Pope John XXIII, meeting four times between 1962 and 1965. The council effected fundamental changes in theology and in the pastoral and liturgical life of the church. Its documents often show a tension between traditional theological ways of thinking and new insights about such issues as revelation, religious pluralism, the social meaning of the gospel, and biblical criticism. Vatican II is considered a watershed event that brought the Roman Catholic church into a new era. With bishops attending from around the world, the council marked the beginning of a shift from a European-centered to a global church.

womanist theology. Coined by the contemporary writer Alice Walker, a "womanist" is feminist of color characterized by strength and love and committed to the wholeness of both women and men. Appropriated by theologians, the term denotes a theology emerging from the experience of black women and their concerns and that allows for a conscious naming of this experience. It intends to shape a distinctive perspective regarding the liberating message of the gospel.

Index

Printed in the United States
133375LV00008B/37-51/P